COMPLETE BOOK OF
ANTIQUES
& COLLECTABLES

MILLER'S

COMPLETE BOOK OF

ANTIQUES
& COLLECTABLES

MILLER'S

Complete Book of Antiques & Collectables

First published in Great Britain in 2002 by Miller's,
a division of Mitchell Beazley,
imprints of Octopus Publishing Group Ltd
2–4 Heron Quays
London E14 4JP

Copyright © Octopus Publishing Group Ltd 2002
Reprinted 2002

Miller's is a registered trademark of Octopus Publishing Group Ltd

Designer Victoria Bevan
Production Angela Couchman
Editorial Assistant Rose Hudson
Indexer Sue Farr

Material in this book has been previously published in
Miller's Antiques & Collectables The Facts At Your Fingertips
Miller's Collecting Furniture The Facts At Your Fingertips
Miller's Collecting Pottery & Porcelain The Facts At Your Fingertips
Miller's Collecting Glass The Facts At Your Fingertips
Miller's Collecting Silver The Facts At Your Fingertips

A CIP catalogue record for this book is available from the British Library
ISBN 1 84000 635 8
Set in Bembo
Printed in Hong Kong

Jacket illustrations clockwise from the top. Front: Trian Minic tinplate fire engine,
c.1952 (OPG/CSK); Late 17th-century Imari vase (SL); Regency chaise longue,
c.1845 (REN); Steiff bear, c.1905 (OPG); Nanking blue-and-white porcelain
plate, 19th century (OPG/ST/John Sandon); "February" Freda Doughty
(OPG/ST/John Sandon); Clarice Cliff "Coral Firs" jam pot, early 1930s
(OPG/TR/B & B Adams). *Back:* Arnold "Mac" motorbike, c.1955
(OPG/CSK); Silver Kiddush cup, c.1920 (OPG/AJP/CSK); Silver "Mr Punch"
character jug, late 19th century (OPG/AJP/CSK); Meissen "Bandmaster",
c.1745 (OPG/ST/John Sandon); Walnut chest-of-drawers, c.1695
(OPG/SL/PP); Victorian balloon-back mahogany chair (OPG/BO/PP); Silver
helmet-shaped milk jug, c.1800–15 (OPG/AJP/CSK); 19th-century Caucasian
rug from the Kazak region (OPG/TR)

CONTENTS

Introduction 8
Periods & Styles 11

**PART 1 Where to
Begin 13**
Auctions 14
Antiques Shops 18
Antiques Fairs &
Markets 22
Car Boot Sales 25
Adverts 27

**PART 2 Bringing it
Home 29**
Valuing & Insuring 30
Security 32
Display 34
Care & Restoration 36

**PART 3 Collector's
Compendium 39**
Furniture 40
Basics 40
Styles 44
Chairs 46
Dining Chairs 48
Country Chairs 50
Chair Styles 52
Upholstered Chairs
& Sofas 54
Open Armchairs 56

Stools 58
Dining Tables I 60
Dining Tables II 62
Medium-sized Tables 64
Small Tables I 66
Small Tables II 68
Card & Games Tables 70
Chests 72
Dressers, Cabinets
& Credenzas 74
Corner Cupboards 76
Display Cabinets 78
Cupboards &
Wardrobes 80
Sideboards & Dining
Accessories 82
Desks & Bureaux 84
Pedestal Desks 86
Pine Kitchen
Furniture I 88
Pine Kitchen
Furniture II 90
Miscellaneous
Furniture 92
Garden Furniture I 94
Garden Furniture II 96
Wicker & Bamboo 98
20th-century
Designers I 100
20th-century
Designers II 102

Pottery & Porcelain 104
Basics 104

**Oriental Pottery &
Porcelain**
Chinese Pottery &
Porcelain 106
Japanese Pottery &
Porcelain 108
Chinese Stonewares 110

British Pottery
Early English Pottery 112
Slipware 114
Salt-glazed Stoneware 116
Whieldon & Other
Coloured Lead-
glazed Wares 118
Creamware &
Pearlware 120
Later English Pottery 122
Majolica 124
Doulton 126
Wedgwood I 128
Devon Potteries 130
Lustre 132
Ironstone 133
Commemorative
Ceramics 134
Goss & Crested China 135
Susie Cooper 136

Poole Pottery 137
Doulton Figures 138
Wedgwood II 140
Carlton 142
Shelley 143
Wade Figures 144
Beswick Figures 145

British Porcelain
Early English
   Porcelain 146
Other English
   Factories 148
19th-century English
   Porcelain 150
Royal Crown Derby 152
Royal Worcester 154
Nantgarw & Swansea 156
Minton 158
Coalport 160
Rockingham 161
Spode 162
Davenport 163
Parian 164
Belleek 165

European Pottery
Continental Pottery 166

European Porcelain
Continental Porcelain
   Figures 168
Continental

Tablewares 170
Berlin & Later German
   Factories 172
Vienna 174
Italy 176
Vincennes & Sèvres 178
Later French Porcelain 180
Other Porcelain Centres –
   Denmark & Low
   Countries 182
Other Porcelain Centres –
   Russia 184

Silver & Metalware 186
Basics 186
Decoration 188
Teapots, Coffee &
   Chocolate Pots 192
Mugs & Jugs 194
Caddies & Casters 196
Salvers & Trays 197
Flatware 198
Candlesticks 199
Dressing-Table Sets 200
Miscellaneous Silver 202
Cigar & Cigarette
   Cases 204
Vesta Cases 206
Other Metals 208

Glass 210
Basics 210
Drinking Glasses &

Decanters 212
Cut & Pressed Glass 214
Coloured Glass 216
Paperweights 217

Clocks 218
Basics 218
Bracket Clocks 220
Longcase Clocks 222
Carriage Clocks 224
Novelty Clocks 225

Rugs & Carpets 226
Basics 226
Persian Rugs 227
Caucasian & Turkish
   Rugs 228
Indian & Chinese
   Rugs 230
European Rugs 231

*Art Nouveau & Art
Deco 232*
Furniture
*C.R. Mackintosh,
Liberty & Co. 232
Emile Gallé, Ludwig
Mies van der Rohe 233*

Glass
*Emile Gallé, Daum Frères,
Tiffany 234
René Lalique 235*

Ceramics
William Moorcroft,
Doulton & Co,
Royal Copenhagen 236
Clarice Cliff 237

Sculpture
Gustav Gurschner,
Ferdinand Preiss,
Demètre Chiparus 238

Posters
Alphonse Mucha, Jules
Chéret, J.M. Cassandre
239

Textiles 240
Embroidery 240
Woven Textiles 242

Dolls & Bears 244
Doll Types 244
Bisque Dolls 246
Teddy Bears 248

Toys 250
Wood, Lead & Die-Cast
  Toys 250
Tinplate, Trains &
Celluloid 252

Rock & Pop 254
The 50s & 60s 254
The 70s 256
The 80s & 90s 257

Arms & Militaria 258
Edged Weapons &
  Firearms 258
Armour 260
Miscellaneous
  Militaria 261

Other Collectables 262
Scientific Instruments 262
Cameras &
  Photographs 264
Film Memorabilia 266
Sporting Collectables 268
Boxes 270
Vintage Fountain Pens 271
Tribal Art 272
Antiquities 273

PART 4 Fact File 275
Where to See 276
Where to Buy 278
Glossary 279
Index 283
Acknowledgments 288

INTRODUCTION

People become interested in antiques and collectables for a variety of reasons. In my own case there was nothing in my background to suggest that I would – my parents had none. Indeed, my mother was of a generation which, for the most part, used to discard everything once it was old. However, as an impoverished student living in a run-down part of Edinburgh during the late 1960s I bought a few cheap, pretty plates from the local junk shops that I passed every day on my way to and from the university. To me they provided a far more attractive and unusual means of decorating the walls of my room than the posters favoured by my flatmates. In much the same way as many other people who inherit or buy the odd item of china or furniture, I then became increasingly intrigued as to when and where the plates had been made. Later still, I also became interested in their value. Were they now worth much more than I paid for them?

While my first foray into the world of antiques did not realize any profit to speak of, this in no way detracted from the great enjoyment my purchases gave me. Indeed, over the subsequent years, almost every collector I have met has bought for pleasure rather than profit; the value of any particular piece usually being a side issue to the joys of researching it, tracking it down, buying it, holding or looking at it, showing it off and even the simple fact of owning it.

Nevertheless, during a period in which buying and selling shares on the stock market has sometimes been a bit like swapping deck chairs on the *Titanic*, antiques and collectables have, for the most part, proved to be a good investment. This is undoubtedly one of the main reasons for the enormous ground swell of interest in the subject over the last decade or so. Moreover, the prospect of finding a long-forgotten object gathering dust in the attic, or buying for a few pounds an insignificant-looking item at a car boot sale that at auction turns out to be worth a small fortune, lends to this fascinating leisure activity all the excitement of a treasure hunt.

People often ask me how they can learn about antiques. Although there is no magic way of becoming an expert overnight, there's no great mystery to it either. Learning about antiques is great fun and the best way of going about it is to do what I did: visit museums and stately homes, read books and attend courses on the subject, look around antiques shops, markets, fairs and auctions and, above all, ask questions.

Museums and stately homes are a great place to start. Invariably they contain some of the finest examples of all manner of antiques and thus help you to get your eye in and learn when a piece looks right. However, don't try and take in too much at once. You'll learn far more quickly if you concentrate on one subject at a time.

There are also lots of books on antiques and collectables available today – many more than when I first became interested. The *Miller's Price Guides* and *Checklists*, for example, are particularly useful! Containing thousands of pictures of antiques they give you a pretty good idea of current prices and help to familiarize you with the language of antiques. Adult education courses run by leading auctioneers, such as Christie's and Sotheby's, or local education departments are also now widely available and offer expert tuition in a particular subject. If you do decide to attend one, don't feel embarrassed about asking questions. I remember attending a weekend course on porcelain run by Geoffrey Godden a few years ago. Right at the end a man suddenly confessed he had been confused by much of what had been said over the two days; he didn't understand the continual references to hard- and soft-paste porcelain, or what the difference was between them – a crucial piece of information that could have easily been explained if only he had asked at the outset.

Many people also feel intimidated about striking up a conversation with a dealer when visiting a shop, antiques fair or market. However, as I have found over the years, this is one of the best ways of acquiring knowledge. Indeed, most dealers are only too happy to discuss a piece and answer a reasonable number of questions. But do be sensitive to the fact that dealers have to make a living. Pick a quiet moment when they're not busy.

Attending auctions, which are held once a week or fortnight in most parts of the country, gives you the opportunity to view an enormous range of antiques and also introduces you to the real nitty-gritty of buying and selling. Go to the sale previews, buy a catalogue and, if you are particularly interested in a piece, ask to see someone from the auction house and discuss factors such as its history, any damage and the estimated price. Also go along to the sale itself, even if you have no intention of buying, and write down on the catalogue the prices pieces fetch as they go under the hammer. By doing this you will be able to compare estimates with realized prices, and gradually build up a feel for how the market is doing in particular areas.

By the time you have done all or most of the above you will have acquired a considerable amount of knowledge about the antiques you have become interested in. However, do bear in mind that we are not talking about an exact science here. For every rule there is an exception. For example, I once wrote an article confidently stating that all 18th-century sideboards had six legs. When this appeared in print it was accompanied by a number of illustrations, one of which showed a totally authentic piece with four legs! I have also heard three eminent experts in their field disagree vehemently over the authenticity of a piece

of oak furniture. This is not an unusual occurrence and is very much part of the joy of antiques.

On a slightly more serious note, I've also seen so-called "antique" furniture made up by modern craftsmen using old wood and traditional techniques. Some pieces are so well done it's virtually impossible to distinguish between the fake and an original. As someone pointed out to me: there are more English oak refectory tables distributed around the world than there were houses in 16th-century England of a sufficient size to even get them in the front door. So do be careful, especially if you are thinking of paying a considerable amount of money for something. Most antiques dealers are both honest and honourable, but as is the case in most spheres of business, there are exceptions.

The questions I am most often asked are: how much is something worth, or how much should I pay for it? Well, price is almost always determined by a combination of four factors: condition, age, rarity and desirability. Condition can be vital. After a pristine Steiff teddy bear went for £55,000 at Sotheby's a few years ago, Bond Street was inundated with gentlemen in pinstripe suits clutching their play-worn childhood companions. There was then considerable disappointment when they were informed that they were, at best, only worth £50–£100. Age is also obviously always important, as the older something is the greater the likelihood few examples will have survived. However, the rarity of a piece does not guarantee desirability, and it is the latter that is the most important factor in determining the price something will fetch. For example, Roman glass is certainly old, can be found in good condition and some pieces are quite rare. However, if it is not considered desirable it will sell for a very low price at auction. In other words, the old adage that a piece is only worth what two people are prepared to pay for it usually holds good.

Assessing the value of an antique or a collectable is more difficult in some areas than others. For example, a good-quality 19th-century mahogany dining table with chairs by a well-known maker can be said to have an intrinsic value. Precedent says they will at least have held their value 10 years on. Much the same can be said for pieces of 18th-century porcelain or silverware. However, it is far more difficult to predict whether a 1950s Japanese plastic robot, a smashed-up Fender guitar once played by Jimi Hendrix (about ten years ago one fetched £35,000 at auction) or a Jean Paul Gaultier dress designed for Madonna will be worth in 30 years' time the sort of sums of money the present generation are prepared to pay for them. Of course, trying to predict these things is very much part of the fun of collecting – provided, that is, you stick to the following rules: always buy the best piece you can afford, especially in terms of condition and rarity. Never buy anything you don't like or you can't live with – you may have to live with it for a long time before you can get your money back. In fact, as long as you know what you're buying and the price you pay is appropriate at the time, you probably won't go far wrong.

JUDITH MILLER

The values given in this book for featured objects reflect the sort of prices you might expect to pay for similar pieces at an auction house or dealer. As there are so many variable factors involved in the pricing of antiques, the values should be used only as a general guide.

PERIODS & STYLES

DATES	BRITISH MONARCH	UK PERIOD	FRENCH PERIOD	GERMAN PERIOD	US PERIOD	STYLE
1558–1603	Elizabeth I	Elizabethan	Renaissance	Renaissance (to c.1650)		Gothic
1603–1625	James I	Jacobean				
1625–1649	Charles I	Carolean	Louis XIII (1610–1643)		Early Colonial	Baroque (c.1620–1700)
1649–1660	Commonwealth	Cromwellian	Louis XIV (1643–1715)	Renaissance/ Baroque (c.1650–1700)		
1660–1685	Charles II	Restoration				
1685–1689	James II	Restoration				
1689–1694	William & Mary				William & Mary	
1694–1702	William III	William III			Dutch Colonial	Rococo (c.1695–1760)
1702–1714	Anne	Queen Anne		Baroque (c.1700–1730)	Queen Anne	
1714–1727	George I	Early Georgian	Régence	(1715–1723)	Chippendale	
1727–1760	George II	Early Georgian	Louis XV (1723–1774)	Rococo		
1760–1811	George III	Late Georgian	Louis XVI (1774–1793)	Neo-classicism (c.1760–1800)		Neo-classical (c.1755–1805)
			Directoire (1793–1799)		Early Federal (1790–1810)	
			Empire (1799–1815)	Empire (c.1800–1815)	American Directoire (1798–1804)	Empire (c.1799–1815)
					American Empire (1804–1815)	
1812–1820	George III	Regency	Restauration (1815–1830)	Biedermeier (c.1815–1848)	Later Federal (1810–1830)	Regency (c.1812–1930)
1820–1830	George IV	Regency				
1830–1837	William IV	William IV	Louis Philippe (1830–1848)	Revivale (c.1830–1880)		Eclectic (c.1830–1880)
1837–1901	Victoria	Victorian	2nd Empire (1848–1870)		Victorian	
			3rd Republic (1871–1940)	Jugendstil (c.1880–1920)	Art Nouveau (c.1900–1920)	Arts & Crafts (1800–1900)
1901–1910	Edward VII	Edwardian				Art Nouveau (c.1900–1920)

PART 1

WHERE

TO BEGIN

ABOVE ROYAL DOULTON BUNNYKINS DICOVERED AT A CAR
BOOT SALE AND LATER SOLD FOR NEARLY £4,000.

LEFT PORTOBELLO ROAD MARKET, LONDON

AUCTIONS

Auctions are one of the most exciting ways in which to buy antiques. Here you will find almost every type of collectable; from objects worth millions, to boxes of bric-a-brac costing just a few pounds. But buying at auction is quite different from buying in a shop or market, and can seem a bit bewildering to anyone who has never visited a saleroom or bought items in this way before. Auctions are not limited to the big city salerooms. The London branches of famous firms such as Sotheby's, Christie's, Phillips and Bonhams may account for the vast majority of more expensive antiques sold at auction in this country, but they also have provincial branches and there is a network of local auctioneers throughout the country where you can often buy less expensive antiques and bric-a-brac, provided you are willing to sift through the varied goods on offer to find whatever it is you are looking for.

Most would-be collectors who overcome their initial misgivings and visit an auction for the first time find themselves hooked on

> **BUYING AT AUCTION**
> - **BUY THE CATALOGUE**
> - **VIEW THE SALE VERY THOROUGHLY**
> - **DECIDE ON YOUR PRICE LIMIT AND STICK TO IT**

the exciting atmosphere of the saleroom. The large turnover of goods means that there is always a possibility of uncovering an undiscovered treasure – or "sleeper" as it is known in the trade – and provided certain basic guidelines are followed, auctions are still one of the best places to buy objects of good quality at a reasonable price.

Going to auctions regularly can also be an excellent way to learn about the area you are interested in before beginning to collect. If you attend saleroom previews regularly and read the auction catalogues carefully, you will soon acquire a sound knowledge and a feel for prices which will stand you in good stead when you begin to spend money on your collection.

BUYING AT AUCTION
CATALOGUES

Before every sale is held, the saleroom will identify the goods to be sold in a catalogue. Whether it's a typed sheet or a glossy illustrated publication, it will list and number the objects in the order in which they will be sold. The numbers in the catalogue, known as "lot" numbers, correspond to those attached to each object or "lot".

Next to each catalogue entry there may be a suggested price range, for example £50–80. These figures show the price the auction house valuer expects the object to fetch, and are known as the "estimate". If there are no estimates printed in the catalogue they may be pinned up in the saleroom; if not, ask the auctioneer. Estimates should only ever be taken as a rough guide; they are never a guarantee of the price for which something will be sold. Ultimately any work of art, no matter how

Some lots contain more than one item; all these albums were sold together in a stamp sale.

rare or valuable, is only worth at auction what two or more people are willing to bid for it, and it is this element of uncertainty that gives auctions their special appeal.

VIEWING THE SALE

About two or three days before the day of the sale, all the objects to be sold will be put on display, so that buyers can examine them; this is known as the "view" or "sale preview". If you are hoping to buy at the sale it is important to attend one of these preview days because on the morning of the sale, when the porters are getting everything ready for sell-ing, it may be impossible to view properly.

At the preview you will notice that every object has been marked with its lot number which corresponds to the number in your catalogue. Objects are rarely displayed in numerical order, so if something sounded fascinating in the catalogue and you can't find it at the view, ask one of the saleroom staff to help you. That way you won't miss anything which has been badly displayed.

When at larger auction houses, pay careful attention to the exact wording of each catalogue entry. Read the explanations at the beginning of the catalogue, which tell you the significance of words such as "attributed to", "style of" and "after". This catalogue terminology is like a code which tells you the valuer's opinion of the date and authenticity of a piece and will have an important bearing on its value.

Above Each lot should be clearly marked with a number.
Right Viewing before the auction takes place.

Ask to speak to the expert in charge of the sale if you would like more information about a particular piece.

Always examine very, very thoroughly any object on which you intend to make a bid, and make up your own mind as to its authenticity. Pay particular attention to the condition of the piece and take into account the potential cost of restoration, which may be quite considerable, before deciding on your bidding limit. Also bear in mind that an auctioneer's commission (usually around 10–15% added on to the hammer price – the price at which the object is sold in the saleroom) and VAT on the commission, will usually be added to the hammer price.

BIDDING

If after viewing the sale, you decide you might want to bid, find out if you need to

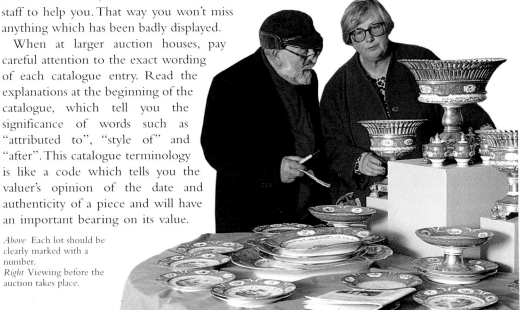

An auction of silver in progress.

(usually about 100) to work out roughly when your lot will be sold; but always remember to allow yourself a bit of extra time so you don't arrive too late.

If you can't get to the sale you can usually leave a bid with the commissions clerk, who will bid on your behalf.

When the sale begins, the auctioneer will call out each lot number to be sold and will start the bidding at a figure which is usually slightly below the lower estimate. As the people present signal to him by waving or nodding he will call out their bids in regular sums, called increments. Depending on the value of the piece, the bidding could rise in £5s, £10s, £20s, £100s, £1,000s, or more, the increments increasing as the price rises. The auctioneer will indicate that the bidding is finished by banging a small hammer, called a gavel, on the rostrum, and recording the sale and the name or number of the successful bidder. People who have never been to an auction before often worry that an ill-timed cough or sneeze could be mistaken as a bid and land them with a masterpiece; ask anyone with experience of auctions and they will tell you that this is unheard of.

When you are bidding for the first time remember to make your bids clearly and quickly. In a packed saleroom it can be quite difficult to attract the auctioneer's attention, so don't be faint-hearted: wave your catalogue or bidding card and call out if need be. However, if the bidding is rising rapidly and the auctioneer seems to be ignoring you, don't worry; an auctioneer will usually only take bids from two people at a time; when one drops out he will look around the room for someone else to join in. If you are still within your limit that is your moment!

SELLING AT AUCTION

Taking a prized possession for sale at auction can seem every bit as daunting as

register first. Some salerooms will want you to fill in a form with your name, address and phone number before the sale; some issue you with a number to hold up should your bid be successful; in others you simply call out your name and fill in a form at the time.

If you are not paying in cash, ask before the sale whether a cheque or credit card will be acceptable as a method of payment. If you intend to spend a large sum of money you may have to supply bank references.

Some sales last for several hours; if the lots which interest you are towards the end of the sale and you don't want to sit through the whole auction, find out how many lots the auctioneer expects to sell per hour buying, especially if you don't know the object's history or what it might be worth. You are, after all, taking along something you hope may be valuable, and quite possibly have treasured for a very long time. But although many would-be vendors are put off by the thought of rejection, auction houses actually offer a very useful way of finding out more about your property and their advice is nearly always absolutely free.

WHAT IT'S WORTH

When you are visiting one of the larger auction houses you will probably have to queue up and show your property to a receptionist who will decide which expert should be called to value it for you.

Before the auction-house expert examines your property he (or she) will probably ask you for anything you can tell him about the object. The history of an object, known as its "provenance", can help enormously in its correct identification and valuation. Even details which might seem insignificant to you can help a valuer, so if you know your table once belonged to Aunt Ethel who lived in Devon and bought it from a local Duchess, then don't forget to say so.

After careful examination the valuer will probably tell you what he can about your object. This may be where, when and by whom it was made, as well as what he thinks it might fetch at auction.

Should you decide to sell, the valuer should also advise you whether a "reserve" price is necessary. A reserve is the minimum price for which the auctioneer may sell your property, and can act as an important safeguard if the sale turns out to be very

> ### SELLING AT AUCTION
> - TRY TO GET MORE THAN ONE VALUER'S OPINION
> - PHONE TO MAKE AN APPOINTMENT IF NECESSARY
> - AGREE ALL CHARGES BEFORE LEAVING YOUR PROPERTY FOR SALE
> - FIND OUT HOW SOON YOUR PROPERTY WILL APPEAR AT AUCTION

poorly attended. You should also remember to ask the valuer how quickly your property will be sold. If the property is of exceptional quality you may be advised to wait for a particular sale which will feature other high-quality objects and attract better prices. Certain specialist sales are only held once or twice a year, and it may be that you could sell your property more quickly elsewhere.

THE COST OF SELLING

An auction house does not buy your property from you, instead it sells on your behalf. For this service you will be charged a commission (usually about 10–15% deducted from the hammer price), VAT on the commission and costs, such as an insurance charge and a handling charge. If your item is illustrated in the catalogue you may also be charged a fee to cover the photographic costs. Finally, in the unlikely event that your property remains unsold there may be other charges, albeit reduced.

An auction-house expert giving an over-the-counter valuation.

ANTIQUES SHOPS

Antiques shops are among the easiest of places in which to begin learning about and buying antiques. They are less frantic than auction rooms, you can buy when you feel like it, and you don't have to compete with anyone else for the object of your choice.

There is an enormous variety of antiques shops, from the smart London West End galleries to small country and local dealers. Obviously the dealer you choose will be determined to some extent by personal taste and how much money you have to spend. But as in any trade there are disreputable dealers as well as honest ones, and, particularly if you are an inexperienced buyer, it is always very important to pick a dealer who is both knowledgeable and trustworthy.

One of the best ways to find a reputable dealer is through trade associations like the BADA and LAPADA (see p279). You can phone these organizations and ask for lists of local member dealers to be sent to you, free of charge. If, on the other hand, you are wandering down your high street and about to enter a tantalizing shop, remember to look in the window or on the door first; a trade association sign is a good indication that the dealer has stock of good quality and also knows his subject.

In Britain the two major trade associations are the LAPADA and BADA (the equivalent American bodies are the AADLA and NAADA). Those dealers who wish to become members of these bodies have to undergo a very rigorous selection procedure. This assesses both the quality of their stock and knowledge. Once members they are bound to keep to a strict code of practice which offers you, as a buyer, reassuring protection, especially if you are about to purchase something costly for the first time. Member dealers are bound to tell you as much about the piece as they can; and this includes pointing out any restoration the piece may have had. If after buying something from a member dealer, you discover it is not genuine, the organization will themselves organize a panel of independent experts to investigate your claim and make sure, if it is upheld, that you get a full and speedy refund. Remember that even the best-intentioned dealers can make the odd genuine mistake. But a good dealer will want you to come back so it's not in their interests to "do" you.

The ideal antiques shop should not only be reputable, it should also have a welcoming atmosphere in which you do not feel intimidated or pressurized to buy. It is worth

> **BUYING FROM ANTIQUES SHOPS**
> - PICK A REPUTABLE DEALER
> - TAKE YOUR TIME WHEN DECIDING WHAT TO BUY
> - GET A DETAILED RECEIPT

Below The Lanes, Brighton, Sussex.
Right A general antiques shop, Brighton

similar pieces at other shops or auction houses, to make sure the price is a fair one. It is almost expected to ask the dealer whether the price he first mentions is his "best" one. Don't feel embarrassed to do this, most are quite happy to haggle and will come down a little – one well-known London dealer even takes buyers to task if they don't ask for a discount!

Before you make your final decision, ask the dealer as many questions as possible about the piece. Find out how old it is, whether it's marked, what it's made from, who made it, where, and whether it has been restored.

If you decide to buy the piece, make sure you are given a full written receipt, which states the dealer's name, address and telephone number, together with the date the piece was made, a full description of it, the price you have paid, and the date of the purchase. It is very important to keep this receipt in a safe place. You will need it for insurance or in the unlikely event that the piece turns out not to be genuine.

returning to a dealer you trust because as you build up a rapport he will probably be able to help you in a variety of other ways. He might let you take things home "on approval". He may operate a "buy back" scheme, which means he will let you sell back to him the objects your bought from him for the price you paid for them (a useful way of upgrading your collection). He may also look out for special things to add to your collection, and give advice and condition reports on objects you have seen at auction. Above all, a friendly dealer is one of the best ways of learning, from the inside, about your chosen subject and the fascinating world of antiques.

BUYING FROM ANTIQUES SHOPS

Unlike buying at auction, there is no pressure to buy at a particular moment from a dealer, and this gives you plenty of time to decide whether you really want the object.

Before buying any antique do try to price

JUNK SHOPS

The contents of many junk shops come from house clearance sales and deceased properties where the entire contents were bought for a fixed sum. Thus you will probably find an enormous variety of different types of objects all for sale, usually for relatively inexpensive prices. Most of the items for sale in a junk shop will not be "antiques", but they are a good place to look for early 20th-century furniture and decorative items. Buying from a junk shop is rather different from buying from an antiques shop, because you must decide for yourself on the age, value and authenticity of a piece. Nonetheless, if you have a keen eye, they can be a fruitful source of inexpensive collectables and a trawl through dusty boxes may reveal an unexpected bargain. As always, be ready to haggle and remember to ask for a receipt.

SELLING TO AN ANTIQUES SHOP

Contrary to popular belief it is not always best to sell at auction. Selling to an antiques shop has numerous advantages. Once you have reached an agreement with a dealer in an antiques shop, you will probably be paid as soon as you hand over your property, and there will probably be no hidden deductions for commission, insurance etc. (see p30). Selling to a dealer saves waiting for the sale which may be several weeks away and waiting for payment after the sale (usually at least two weeks).

Before selling to a dealer, however, you do need to be sure of the value of your property. The public nature of auction sales means that objects of value should always realize their potential value, even if the auction–house valuer has underestimated them. In selling to a dealer

Opposite An antiques emporium, Portobello Road, London.
Below A variety of decorative 19th- and 20th-century ceramics for sale.

you have no such safeguard; you get the price you agree, no more and no less.

Do a little research before offering your property for sale and find out which dealers specialize in the type of object you are offering. You are far more likely to be quoted a fair price for a Victorian chair if you take it to a dealer in 19th-century furniture, than if you show it to an 18th-century specialist.

If your property is too large or difficult to take to the dealer's shop, many are very happy to visit you in your home, although do make sure you pick a reputable one (see p18) before inviting him in.

There is an old adage about dealers with more than a little truth in it: if there were four dealers and one Chippendale chair on an island, all the dealers would make a living! Don't be surprised if you are offered a wide range of prices for your property as you do the rounds with it. A dealer's offer will, to some extent, be dependent on what he thinks he can sell it on for, and remember he has to make a profit or he would not be in business.

> **SELLING TO ANTIQUES SHOPS**
> - FIND OUT WHICH SHOPS SPECIALIZE IN YOUR TYPE OF PROPERTY
> - TRY TO GET MORE THAN ONE OFFER BEFORE SELLING
> - NEVER SELL TO ANYONE WHO TURNS UP UNINVITED AT YOUR HOME

KNOCKERS

Never open your door to any "dealer" who calls uninvited, or who puts a note through your door telling you that they will pay cash for valuables and will return a day or two later. Many of these so called "knockers" are of very dubious integrity and their aim is to trick owners, particularly the elderly and vulnerable, into selling their property for much less than its true value. There is also the added risk of allowing into your home an unknown person, who may well be using the visit as an opportunity to plan to return later without an invitation.

ANTIQUES FAIRS & MARKETS

Visiting antiques markets and fairs is a fairly effortless way of seeing a large number of dealers together and gives you a useful opportunity to compare their stock, and its quality and price. You can find out where and when they are held from local papers and antiques magazines. There are several different types of antiques markets and fairs:

- Large "vetted" fairs – where dealers from all over the country take stands and every exhibit is checked to make sure it is genuine.
- Fairs where the objects are not checked and anyone can take a stand.
- Permanent markets where specialist dealers congregate with shops and stalls every day, or several days a week.
- Weekly street markets where small traders sell goods from the early hours of the morning to other dealers, as well as the general public.

VETTED FAIRS

At a large antiques fair you will probably have to pay an admission charge; for this you may be given a catalogue to the fair which lists the various dealers exhibiting and their specialities; if not, such catalogues will usually be available to buy. Many of the larger fairs which are held on a regular basis protect buyers by "vetting" all the exhibitors and their stock. This means that before the fair opens, a panel of experts on each subject will examine items for sale on each stand to make sure they are authentic. At the best fairs, the vetting is an extremely rigorous procedure and even the most eminent dealers have been known to quake with anticipation at the arrival of the panel on their stand!

Most larger fairs operate a "dateline", which means that only objects made before a certain date may be exhibited at the fair. The datelines will usually be mentioned in the catalogue, but they may vary for different

The British International Antiques Fair at the National Exhibition Centre, Birmingham.

types of collectable. For example, pre-1900 for furniture, but pre-1930 for ceramics and pictures.

Large fairs usually feature a wide variety of different types of collectables, so you will find furniture, silver, ceramics, jewellery, textiles and much more besides, under one roof. There are also annual specialist fairs which focus on one particular collecting area: silver, ceramics and even dolls all have their specialist fairs. If you are a keen collector such events can offer a golden opportunity to meet leading authorities in their field, who may come from other distant parts of the country and otherwise be difficult to visit.

If you find yourself bemused by the bustle of the fair, don't be afraid to ask for a dealer's card, and arrange to visit them at their premises after the event. Dealers view fairs as a place to meet new collectors and forge new contacts, as well as make sales.

OTHER FAIRS

There is a world of difference between the large vetted fairs, and the plethora of smaller "antiques" fairs which are held up and down the country in church halls, schools and other similar venues. There you may still be charged an entrance fee, but there will probably be no catalogue, and no dateline or vetting, of the goods on offer. Many of the objects for sale may be better described as second-hand rather than antique, but nevertheless, provided you realize that you must satisfy yourself of the authenticity of anything you buy, such events can prove entertaining for a browse, and are sometimes a good place to buy inexpensive bric-a-brac and decorative items – and you may even find a bargain.

MARKETS

Throughout the various antiques centres in Britain there are many permanent antiques markets where several traders have stalls under one roof, or in a particular street

Portobello Road, London.

(see p278). In London there are a variety of different types of market, many of which (Portobello Road, for example), have become famous tourist attractions, as well as being busy antiques markets.

Highly reputable specialist dealers, many of them members of trade associations, often choose to operate from large permanent antiques markets. Visiting such markets can be a good way of discovering dealers who specialize in particularly unusual types of collectables, and the goods on offer will usually be fairly priced. Since, unlike a non-specialist who may be inclined to over-value an object with which he is not particularly familiar, a specialist will know precisely what it is worth and will be competitive with other local traders.

Throughout the country, and especially in London, there are also weekly markets where you can buy antiques. One of the largest and most fascinating is held in

Bermondsey in the East End of London from 5am every Friday morning. Here traders buy and sell to one another, as well as to private collectors, and provided you are confident enough in your particular field of interest, such street markets can be wonderful sources of bargains and great fun, but you usually need to get there early to find the best buys.

SELLING AT FAIRS AND MARKETS

If you have a considerable quantity of suitable goods to sell you might want to take a stand in a local antiques fair. You can find out how to set about this from the fair organizers. Hiring a stand will probably involve a deposit or payment up front and there may be a waiting list if competition for spaces is fierce. If you only have a few pieces, you could try selling them direct to a

Bustling London market stalls at Bermondsey (above left) and Portobello Road (top and right).

BUYING FROM
FAIRS AND MARKETS

Whatever type of fair or market you attend, if you decide to buy, always make sure you get a written receipt, with the dealer's name and address and a description of your purchase on it (see p18).

market trader. To sell in this way, pick a stand where they sell objects similar to yours. Go early and, when the market is quiet, approach the trader. If you don't manage to sell at the first stand, make sure you pack your treasures carefully before you go on to the next stall.

CAR BOOT SALES

A few years ago, a buyer at a car boot sale spotted some appealing pottery rabbits and bought them for a few pounds (see illustration on p13). The new owner then took her bunnies along to an auction house for an expert opinion. They were immediately identified as being rare early examples of Royal Doulton's Bunnykins series and sold soon after for nearly £4,000. Such stories are not everyday occurrences, but the mere fact that they happen at all has helped ensure the growing appeal of the car boot sale.

Car boot sales are held in a wide variety of venues, usually fields, school playgrounds or car parks. They may be advertised in the classified columns of certain magazines, local papers, or simply by notices pinned up in your area. Some are regular events, held every Sunday, others are "one-offs", or held only occasionally.

The boot sale is a good way of emptying the contents of your loft or garage, and raising some cash for your collection. For a small admission charge anyone can fill their car with their unwanted property and sell it for whatever they can. You can buy and sell almost anything at a boot sale – old furniture, second-hand clothes, books, electrical equipment and much more besides. If you are a collector of modest means, car boot sales provide an excellent opportunity to buy relatively inexpensive collectables, but you have to be determined enough to sift through the endless piles of uninteresting objects to find the tantalizing but elusive treasures.

BUYING AT A BOOT SALE

If you are about to visit a car boot sale for the first time there are a few simple guidelines which could help make your day more successful.

Firstly, remember to arrive early – very early. This way you will be able to get the pick of the items on offer and will be more

Vintage cameras at a car boot sale.

likely to spot any bargains before they can be snapped up by someone else. If it's wintertime, make sure you take a torch with you; you'll need it to see what's on offer in the poor light. You should also remember to take plenty of cash, preferably in coins and small notes. You can't expect people at a boot sale to welcome cheques, nor to have unlimited amounts of change available. Keep your cash in a purse belt or something similar, not only for the sake of security, but also because this will leave your hands free to examine the goodies!

If you do see something which takes your fancy, ask its price, but feel free to haggle over it. Bear in mind that there are no fixed prices at a boot sale; the objects on offer are only worth what someone is willing to pay for them.

SELLING AT A BOOT SALE

Careful planning and preparation are the key to successful selling at a boot sale. Work out what you are taking, and whether it will all fit in your car. Remember to allow extra space for a table, to display your property (a wall-papering table or picnic table would be ideal) and a collapsible chair to sit on. When you pack the car, try to pack the table on top, so that you don't have to unload everything on to the ground before being able to get the table out.

If you want to price things, do so clearly with sticky labels or tickets. Put on the price you would ideally like to receive, but be prepared to come down a little from this figure if need be. Remember to pack anything fragile with plenty of wrapping: newspaper and cardboard boxes are best for china and glass, etc. Old blankets are useful for wrapping round pictures and prints.

Wear suitable clothes: rainwear and boots are often a good idea if the sale is in a muddy field. Take some sandwiches and a thermos of tea or coffee so you are well prepared for your day. Allow plenty of time for the journey, and try to arrive early so you can get a good position where the maximum number of buyers will spot your goods early on, before they have spent all their money somewhere else. Don't be surprised if dealers start to rummage in your boot while you're unpacking – it can be disconcerting but it's also a good way to "break the ice"! Try and take plenty of spare change with you (keep it safe in a purse belt), and avoid accepting cheques whenever possible.

Finally, before the sale is over, try and arrange for a friend to come and help you. That will give you a chance to take a break and look at what everyone else has to offer, and maybe spend some of your earnings at the same time.

Bargain-hunting at a boot sale.

ADVERTS

Private advertisements are an alternative way of buying and selling antiques. You may find advertisements for antiques in a wide variety of publications, from national newspapers to specialist magazines.

One of the main worries with buying and selling through adverts is the danger to your personal safety, and the security of your property. However, provided you take the necessary precautions to minimize risks, this can be an effective way of buying and selling antiques.

BUYING FROM ADVERTS

If you're responding to an advertisement in a newspaper or magazine, try and find out as much as possible about the piece before you go and see it. Ask how big it is, what sort of condition it is in and the price.

If after all this you are still interested in the piece, make an appointment to go and see it. Find out the vendor's name as well as the address, and the home phone number if this is not the one in the advertisement. Try to go with someone else; if you must go alone, tell someone where you are going, including the name, address and phone number of the person, and when you expect to be back.

When you see the piece, remember to examine it very thoroughly for damage and restoration before making up your own mind as to its age and authenticity. If you decide to buy it, or if you have to leave a deposit, remember to ask for a written receipt, which includes the name and address of the person you are buying from and the date.

SELLING THROUGH ADVERTS

Adverts can be a good way of selling your property if you don't want to sell through a dealer or at an auction, but first you must decide where to place your advert and how much your property is worth.

Your choice of publication will probably be dictated by both your budget and the value and type of your property. Look for a publication which has a large number of objects of a similar sort to yours. If the object you are selling might be of interest to a particular type of collector, look at the specialist collectors' magazines, as these are usually relatively inexpensive to advertise in and will reach a wider audience of potential buyers than a more general publication. If, for example, you are selling an old doll, you might well be more successful if you advertise in a doll collectors' magazine, rather than in your local paper. Once you have narrowed down the field of possible publications, you could even try phoning the numbers in one or two similar advertisements to see what sort of response they have had.

Before you place the advertisement, find out what your property is worth. Show the object to a few reputable dealers, or take it to an auction house to get a good idea of what you could reasonably ask for it.

Word the advertisement clearly and succinctly; try to mention the age of the piece if you know it. You can either give a box number or your phone number for interested buyers to respond to, but don't mention your name and address because this might encourage If you have given a telephone number, try to be in to take calls when the publication first appears, and be prepared to give callers a full description over the phone (writing this out beforehand will make your life easier). It is quite a good idea to take a deposit from anyone who says they want to buy the object but will come back at a later date to pay and collect it. That way you will ensure you do get paid and will not lose out on other potential buyers who may respond to your advertisement. Try to avoid cheques; cash or a banker's order are much safer.

PART 2

BRINGING IT HOME

ABOVE UNWRAPPING A 19TH-CENTURY
CARRIAGE CLOCK.

LEFT PORCELAIN DISPLAYED IN PURPOSE–BUILT
CABINETS

VALUING & INSURING

No keen collector enjoys contemplating the thought of losing a prized possession, but unfortunately, an unpleasant aspect of collecting antiques today is the growing risk of burglary. One result of the increasing number of art and antiques thefts is that the majority of insurance companies now demand a full, professionally written, valuation to cover objects worth more than a certain amount.

If you are beginning to buy antiques you will certainly know what each piece is worth, and whether you need a valuation. But supposing you bought them a decade or more ago, or have been given or inherited them, do you really know what they're worth, and for what sums they should be insured? In recent years, many types of antiques and collectables have risen dramatically in value. Numerous, once modestly valued items are now worth substantial sums, so if you are unsure about the value of your collection, and whether you need a valuation, it is always a good idea to take professional advice. Remember, although a valuation will involve some expense, if you don't have your possessions valued you could find that in the event of burglary or accident you are inadequately insured and as a result are unable to replace your property.

VALULATIONS

There are various ways of having your antiques valued. If you know a friendly local dealer, and only have a few items, they may be able to provide you with a valuation, although you should check with your insurance company that this will be acceptable. If you have a fairly extensive collection, your insurance company may prefer a valuation from a specialist valuer, or one of the larger auction houses, all of whom have large valuation departments.

One of the main advantages in using an auction house is that although most of the valuing will be done by "generalists" (valuers with experience in assessing many different types of antiques), if there is

Opposite A Japanese cloisonné vase c.1910, discovered by one of Bonham's insurance valuers. Its owner thought it was worth around £2,000. The vase was identified as the work of one of Japan's most prominent cloisonné craftsmen, Kyoto Namikawa, and later sold for over £60,000.

Below Valuation documents are required by increasing numbers of insurance companies.

anything unusual in your collection, or anything they are unsure of, they can call upon specialist experts for advice. Every year an amazing number of valuable treasures are brought to light when auction-house valuers visit collectors' homes. Among the most amazing finds of recent years are a priceless Ming bowl being used as a dog's water bowl, and a medieval bronze employed as a door stop! Both of these were later sold for several thousand pounds.

THE COST OF VALUING

Before you decide who to call in to value your property, do shop around and look for the best deal. Prices for valuations vary, and can be calculated in various ways, either as a percentage of the total value of your property (usually between ½% and 1½%), on a daily rate, or as an agreed flat rate. As a general guide, a valuer will be able to assess between 100–300 pieces per day. To some extent the fee you are quoted for your valuation will depend upon how much the auction house wishes to secure you as a client. To an auction house, a valuation is recognized as being an important way of establishing loyalty with their firm. So the chances are that if you have an unusually extensive collection of, say, Dinkies, the auction house will be keen to lure you to their firm, and may be prepared to negotiate. You should always make sure you agree the final figure before the valuation takes place, not afterwards. Some auction houses offer an added bonus by reducing their commission rates, should you decide to sell any of the items they have valued within a reasonably short period of time.

Whoever carries out your valuation, you should make sure it includes a full description of every item, together with its dimensions and a value for insurance purposes. The value placed upon each object will to some extent depend on where you would go to replace your property; would you go shopping in Bond Street, or at your local auction house? The price an insurance valuer puts on your property will probably be at least 20% higher than what you could expect to get should you decide to sell. If you feel that this will make your insurance premiums too high, you can opt for "market valuations" – in other words auction prices – instead. But bear in mind if the valuation is too low you could find yourself unable to replace lost items satisfactorily.

INSURING

The person you choose to value your antiques may be able to advise you on a suitable insurer. One way of reducing premiums is to shop around. If your collection is moderately large and valuable you will probably find it is less expensive to insure through a broker specializing in art and antiques, rather than through a large composite insurer. Whereas a large insurer will usually lump together your antiques as part of the general household policy, a specialist broker will assess the risk of different categories of antique individually, which will tend to reduce the premiums. The cost of insuring the different categories will vary, with large items like furniture often less expensive than particularly fragile pieces or small items like boxes, dolls, teddy bears and dressing-table silverware which are easily portable and so incur a higher risk of theft.

SECURITY

There are two important ways in which you can protect your collection. Firstly, you should try to deter potential thieves from entering your home by making it as secure as possible. If you are unsure about how to go about this, you can contact the crime prevention officer through the local police station. He will be able to advise you on ways of safeguarding your belongings and should be able to recommend a reputable security firm in your area who can install additional locks or alarms or whatever other equipment may be necessary.

But what if disaster should strike, and you do find yourself the victim of crime? You can assist the recovery of the stolen property by marking your belongings with a security pen (available through the crime prevention officer), which only shows up under an ultraviolet light. However, many collectors prefer not to mark their antiques in this way, because the pen is indelible, and should you want to sell the item at a later date it could deter prospective buyers. By far the best way of helping the police to retrieve your possessions is by supplying them with as much information about your stolen property as possible. An inventory, or list of your collection, will be invaluable for this (see p33), but it is also vitally important to have a clear photograph of each object in your collection.

Photographs of any stolen antiques can be logged via your local police officer with the Art and Antiques Squad at Scotland Yard. This police department has a national database, which contains descriptions and photographic images of works of art

stolen throughout the country. When stolen property is recovered, the Art and Antiques Squad can identify the rightful owner – provided the object has been logged on their computer system. But you do need a photograph to stand a good chance of success. It's salutary to remember that the vast majority of stolen antiques and collectables the police recover are never claimed. In such cases not only does the culprit evade prosecution, but the property in question is returned to him! By keeping photographs of the items in your collection, you will help to redress this balance, and increase the chances of recovering stolen items should you fall victim to crime.

> **THE ART & ANTIQUES POLICE SQUAD'S TIPS**
> - PHOTOGRAPH ITEMS AGAINST A PLAIN BACKGROUND (WHITE OR GREY IS USUALLY BEST)
> - TRY AND FILL THE VIEW FINDER WITH THE IMAGE
> - PUT A RULER BESIDE EACH OBJECT TO GIVE AN IDEA OF SCALE
> - PHOTOGRAPH MARKS, CHIPS, DENTS AND SCRATCHES

PHOTOGRAPHING

You may want to enlist the help of a professional photographer to photograph your collection, although if you observe a few simple guidelines it is quite a simple task to do it yourself. It is best to photograph objects using colour film outdoors in natural daylight. Choose a day when there's a light cloud cover, so the sunlight is not too harsh and the shadows aren't very noticeable. Standard 35mm 100 ASA print film, or a specially improved Polaroid camera are good options, although the older type of Polaroids, which are sometimes used by auction houses for research, are not generally useful as long term photographic records, because the colours can fade. For the clearest results the new digital cameras can be used. Many police stations have cameras available on loan, although you may have to supply the film. More details should be available from your local crime prevention officer.

To get the best results stand with the sun behind you, level with the object, not above or to the side, and close enough to fill the view finder. If the objects are very small, it is best to photograph them against a plain background; white is usually the best colour for this, unless the object itself is predominantly white, in which case use a grey or black background. It's also useful when photographing your collection to include a scale reference; a ruler placed beside each object is a good way of doing this. If the object is behind glass, stand slightly to one side to avoid unwanted reflections and glare.

Take at least one shot of each object, as well as close-up shots of any identifying scratches, bumps or marks on each piece. These detailed shots are especially important if the object is likely to be similar to many others. If you can show the crack on the ear of your Staffordshire dog, the hallmarks of your Victorian candlestick or the chip on the face of your carriage clock, they will provide an invaluable method of positive identification. As well as these individual photographs, it's also a good idea to take general shots of your room. These will help you to remember any smaller items which you may forget to list.

Remember to keep your photographs together in a safe place. Ideally, they should be filed in your inventory beside the entry for each object (see below). It's also a wise precaution to store a copy of photographs somewhere else for safe-keeping; your bank or with your solicitor would be ideal.

DOCUMENTING

Documenting your collection means keeping a record of every collectable object as you acquire it. It's a good idea to keep your records of each item in your collection all together in an inventory book.

Then, as your collection grows, you will find you have a useful source of reference as well as an interesting reminder of how your collection began.

Keeping a detailed record of each object in your collection is also an ideal way to show proof of ownership in the event of an insurance claim. So any new purchase should be documented and photographed as soon as possible after you have brought it home.

When beginning an inventory of your collection first make a list of every object you wish to include. Then write down the following information for each object:

- Where it came from.
- The date you bought or acquired it.
- The price you paid for it.
- The value for insurance purposes if your collection is insured.
- A full description of the piece, including its size, what it is made from, and any decorative features.
- A report of its condition, including cracks, chips, alterations or restoration. This should be updated whenever you have the piece restored.
- Anything else you know about the object's history.

It is also a good idea to keep the receipts of any items you have purchased in the same place as the inventory.

A detailed inventory of your collection is invaluable when claiming against burglary or damage.

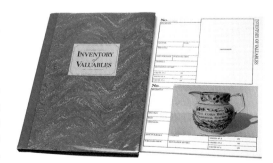

DISPLAY

Antiques can be displayed in a multitude of different ways, but it's important that the method you select should be appropriate to your lifestyle. You may long to display your collection of antiques throughout your home; however, if, for example, you have pets or children, fragile or potentially hazardous objects should probably be kept well out of harm's way – perhaps up on a shelf or out of reach in a cabinet. Bear in mind that not only can children or pets damage vulnerable and valuable objects, but that antiques can also pose a threat to their safety. Even something as seemingly innocuous as an old teddy bear may contain wires that could harm a small child.

However, so long as you take simple precautions, there is no need to feel frightened of your collection. Many types of antiques, such as furniture, glass and silver, can still be used for their original purpose, or adapted for modern-day living. Successful display should allow you to enjoy your collection as much as possible, whilst still conserving it in good condition.

Before you decide where to position your antiques, you should bear in mind how the piece was originally intended to be seen and used. Some pieces of furniture, for instance, were made to be placed against a wall, others were meant to be centrally positioned; try and display the piece in an appropriate manner. If you have a smaller object, say a sculpture, which is meant to be seen in the round, and you have nowhere suitable to put it, you could place it in front of a mirror, so that it can still be appreciated from every angle.

You may find you need to have shelves or cupboards specially constructed to house your collection. However, before you decide where to install special fittings, don't forget that nearly all types of antiques, with the exception of ceramics, silver and other types of metalware, should be displayed away from strong sunlight and direct sources of heat (see p36). So don't, for instance, display your samplers in front of a sunny window, and try to keep the backs of antique furniture away from radiators. If your room is a particularly sunny one, objects such as textiles and prints can be displayed behind non-reflective, light-resistant glass, which will allow you to enjoy them whilst protecting them from fading. If you need to mount old photographs, or printed ephemera, in order to display them behind glass it is best to use mounting tape rather than glue, which can irreversibly damage the objects themselves.

Among the many aids to the effective display of collections of antiques are pedestals, stands and hangers. Most of these can be purchased through department and good hardware stores. Other specialist pieces of display equipment are available by mail order through specialist magazines.

If you have a collection of vases or plates, or glass, you may consider having a series of small brackets built to display them. Make sure, however, that they all sit securely on their perches. If you are displaying plates on brackets, they will need to be propped up on plate stands. Before climbing up to put them in their final resting place, it's a good idea to test them on their stands at an accessible height, so you can check they are firm and unlikely to roll off. Plates and ceramic flatwares can also be simply hung on a wall. The best method for this is to use an acrylic hanger: these are transparent, adjustable and have no sharp points to scratch the surface of the piece. For more robust types of ceramic, modern plastic-coated wire and spring plate hangers are also suitable. These come in a wide variety of sizes, so make sure you choose the right one. If it's too small it could put the plate under strain and cause it to crack, and if it's too large the plate could fall down. To check the size is right put the hanger on top of the rack; it should be about 1in/2cm smaller than the diameter of the plate before you stretch it.

Shelves are also an effective and adaptable way of displaying a wide variety of antiques. If you are planning to put several heavy objects on a shelf, make sure it's suitably strong; take advice from your builder if necessary. Don't forget that objects which are openly displayed will need periodic dusting, so it's no good putting them somewhere where it will be impossible for you to reach them from time to time. If you don't want to have to dust so often, consider putting your collection in a glass cabinet or display case.

Small antiques are often more effectively displayed together, rather than dotted around a room. If you have a collection of small silver objects or boxes it might be a good idea to display them on an attractive tray, a dish, or even on a small table.

Antiques of different types look very attractive when displayed together, but always be careful before you place any objects directly on top of old furniture. Silver and metal objects, particularly pieces with feet, can scratch the surface of furniture, so if in doubt place them on a mat to protect the wood.

Finally, once you have displayed your collection, don't forget the importance of

Opposite Blue-and-white vases displayed on brackets.
Above A collection of porcelain displayed in an alcove.

lighting it effectively, but bear in mind once again that if you stand objects too close to powerful lighting they may be damaged by the heat. Nevertheless, a single spotlight positioned carefully on your display will invariably create a dramatic focal point in any room, whether it's a cluster of plates on a cottage wall, or a group of priceless porcelain figures on the mantelpiece of a stately home.

CARE & RESTORATION

Looking after your antiques correctly is essential if they are to remain in good enough condition for future generations to enjoy as much as you do. Nevertheless, there is a world of difference between caring for an antique correctly and attempting to restore it to mint condition. Almost all antiques reflect their age and you should not expect them to look too perfect.

In general, any restoration work reduces the value of a piece; limited wear and tear will nearly always be preferable and a slightly worn item is usually more

Porcelain restoration at West Dean College, Sussex.

valuable than one which has been over-restored. Nonetheless, if an antique is in danger of deteriorating further because of damage it has sustained, or if its imperfections are impairing your use and enjoyment of it, it may benefit from limited restoration. If this is the case, always consult a specialist restorer. Unskilled restoration can cause irreversible damage to an antique and may greatly reduce its value.

Nearly all antiques, apart from silver, ceramics and glass, should be protected from direct sunlight and heat. Sunlight can cause textiles, carpets, prints and furniture to fade. Direct sources of heat cause many substances, including wood and papier mâché, to expand. This may lead to warping and splitting in antique furniture, and can cause cracking or flaking in pieces made from a papier mâché core with a painted surface.

Prolonged exposure to cigarette, pipe and tobacco smoke can cause discoloration in many types of antiques which can be tricky to restore. So always keep antiques in a well-ventilated room, and protect them from excessive smoke.

Some general guidelines for caring for the main categories of antiques are listed below; further tips for the proper care of specific types of collectables can be found in Part 3.

FURNITURE

- Excessively dry conditions can cause veneers to lift, and joints to dry out. If you live in a very well heated home it may be worth investing in a humidifier which will help to protect your furniture. However, excessively damp conditions are also detrimental to furniture as they may cause the wood to rot.
- If pieces of veneer break off, don't just throw them away; keep them safely, as it is always preferable to use original veneers in restoration and their use may also reduce the cost of the repairs.
- Avoid silicone polishes and aerosol sprays; instead, use a small amount of good-quality wax polish. Don't polish a piece of furniture too often or the surface of the wood may become sticky.
- Never drag antique furniture even a short distance when you want to move it as this causes strain on the legs – pick it up instead. Don't risk picking a piece up by its carrying handle (these are usually more decorative than functional), or by the top if it has a protruding rim; always support the main structure.

CERAMICS AND GLASS

When ceramic pieces are cracked or damaged, the current trend is to leave damage showing, rather than attempt to disguise it completely. Cracked pieces may be stuck together with a suitable glue, but they should not be overpainted. Chips may be filled and coloured to match, but should not be overpainted.

- Pottery, porcelain and glass should occasionally be cleaned by hand with warm soapy water, and should be rinsed off well before they are left to air-dry.
- Decanters should be stored with the stoppers off.
- Do not secure loose lids or stoppers to the main bodies with adhesive tape or adhesive paste as these can easily damage any original gilding and enamel.

Restoration department at Sotheby's, London.

SILVER

Contrary to popular opinion, silver doesn't tarnish especially rapidly unless it's kept in a particularly damp atmosphere. Any proprietary silver polish may be used and a toothbrush may be handy to remove polish from nooks and crannies. Always make sure that you remove all traces of polish, or it can clog up decorated areas. Don't over-polish sliver, or you may erase decoration, and, eventually, wear the metal thin. You can wash silver, by hand, in warm soapy water. Don't put it in the dishwasher as the abrasive powder dulls the surface. Silver gilt doesn't need cleaning with polish; an occasional wash with soapy water should be enough.

- Try not to over-polish Sheffield and electroplate items as you will wear away the thin surface layer of silver.
- Never leave salt in cruets or cellars; salt may get under the glass liner and can cause corrosion spots.

CLOCKS

Most maintenance should be left to a specialist, although wooden cases can be lightly dusted and, occasionally, very lightly waxed. Brass and silvered dials are protected by lacquer and should never be polished or placed in contact with water or detergent.

- Any cleaning and oiling of a clock's movement should be carried out with great care by a specialist.
- Clocks with spring-driven and short pendulums can be carried from one room to another, but should be held upright. For long distance journeys the pendulum must be secured or removed. Longcase clocks should be dismantled before being moved.

CARPETS, RUGS AND TEXTILES

Carpets and rugs should be cleaned by brushing or beating (so long as they are not very frail).

- Placing underlay beneath an antique carpet absorbs wear and protects the pile.
- Sunlight can cause colours to fade and fibres to rot. Framed textiles can be protected by mounting them behind special light-resistant glass.
- Most textiles can be washed with warm soapy water, unless they are very fragile.

PART 3

COLLECTOR'S
COMPENDIUM

ABOVE MEISSEN BLUE–AND–WHITE SHAPED
RECTANGULAR DISH £4,140

LEFT DOLLS AND TEDDY BEARS ON DISPLAY IN AN
ANTIQUES SHOP

Of all the categories of antiques you can choose to collect, furniture is amongst the most popular. It is one of the largest and most diverse categories, with an enormous number of forms, styles and materials to consider. Furniture is also extremely practical; many pieces offer you the alternative of using them either for their original purpose, or of adapting them to modern-day living. Furniture differs from other types of antiques in that you probably won't want to collect it by the type of object – nobody normally wants a room full of only chests or tables – but you may discover that you have an affinity for a particular wood, period, or style of decoration. Whatever your preference, you need to familiarize yourself with the different decorative styles, methods of construction, and types of materials used, in order to determine whether the piece is "right" (in other words, in its original condition without any major alterations or additions) or "wrong" (which would mean that some major change has been made to it, or it's a fake).

The following pages discuss some of the most common types of furniture you are likely to come across, and give you hints about what to look out for. Once you've read them, visit as many auctions and dealers as possible before you begin to buy. Don't be afraid to examine pieces thoroughly; pull out drawers, get down on the floor and look under table tops, and lift up chairs to look at their legs. Remember there's no better way of learning about the subject than by hands-on experience.

BASICS

No matter what type of furniture you happen to be interested in, there are certain basic considerations which you need to take into account before you decide whether the piece you are examining is genuine, when it was made and how much it might be worth. Identifying the wood used, the type of construction, the decoration, the quality of workmanship and the overall condition are all crucial in helping you to make up your mind. Information about these fundamental issues, which can be applied to many different types of furniture, will be discussed over the following pages.

WOODS

The first furniture was made from solid wood with carved decoration. However as cabinet-making improved, a new technique of decorating furniture by applying veneers (thin sheets of wood) was developed. This was an economical way of using expensive woods, and allowed the maker to create decorative effects from the different grains and patterns (known as figuring) of the wood. Veneered furniture has a solid body (a carcass) which is made from a different (usually less expensive) wood. This secondary wood, as it is known, is most commonly pine or oak. Listed on the right are examples of the types of woods most frequently used for antique furniture.

AMBOYNA

Richly coloured wood with a tight grain, used during the 18th century and Regency periods, nearly always as a veneer.

BEECH

Brownish-whitish wood used in the solid from the 17th century for the frames of upholstered furniture, because it doesn't split when tacked. Also popular during the 18th and 19th centuries as a base for painted furniture.

CHERRY

Orange-brown wood popular for American Queen Anne and Chippendale furniture. Usually used in the solid.

CHESTNUT

Ranges in tone from light to dark brown,

much used during the 18th century for French provincial furniture made in the solid.

COROMANDEL

A dark, boldly figured wood, almost black in parts with pale striations, used mainly as a veneer for refined furniture of the Regency period.

EBONY

Dense, heavy, almost black wood, often used as a contrasting inlay in marquetry veneering.

ELM

Light brown-coloured wood, popular for Windsor chairs and provincial English furniture.

MAHOGANY

Rich golden-brown or red-brown coloured wood, it became popular in England from c.1730. There are several different types of mahogany; San Dominguan, Cuban (also known as Spanish) and Honduran are the most common.

OAK

Deep rich chocolate-brown, or paler golden-brown coloured coarse-grained wood used mainly in Britain from the Middle Ages to late 17th century. Also used as a secondary wood on good-quality furniture.

PINE

Soft pale honey-coloured wood used in England and America as a secondary timber, for drawer linings, and in the 19th century for inexpensive furniture (which was often painted).

ROSEWOOD

Highly figured dark red-brown wood with blackish streaks from the East Indies and Brazil. Used for decoration in the 17th century, it became popular during the Regency and Victorian periods in Britain for high-quality furniture.

SATINWOOD

Light yellow-coloured West Indian wood, favoured during the late 18th century. Usually used in veneers as it was expensive and sometimes embellished with painted decoration. Painted satinwood furniture was also popular in the Edwardian period.

VIRGINIA WALNUT

Dense, richly coloured wood resembling mahogany. Used in the solid and as a veneer on English and American furniture from c.1730.

WALNUT

Nutty or honey-brown highly figured wood noted for its excellent finish. Used in the solid on English and some French furniture from c.1660–c.1690 and as veneers from c.1690 until c.1735 when it was supplanted by mahogany. Walnut was also popular in America and the Victorian era.

YEW

Red-brown or honey-coloured hardwood used both in veneers or in the solid on the best English provincial furniture of the 17th and 18th centuries.

COLOUR AND PATINA

A rich mellow colour is one of the most important features of any piece of furniture. The *patina* is the glow the wood develops over the years from an accumulation of wax polish and dirt.

● Most furniture is not the same colour all over – grooves and carving will look darker, surfaces exposed to sunlight may be lighter.

● Deep *patina* is less favoured by the European market, where furniture is often stripped and repolished.

PROPORTIONS

The proportions are fundamental in assessing the quality of a piece, and deciding whether it's "right".

● A piece which looks too heavy on top, or has legs which are too big or small may well be a "marriage" (see p43).

● Small pieces are often more desirable.

CONSTRUCTION

Early furniture was made using mortise-and-tenon joints held by pegs or dowels (below) instead of glue or screws. This method was used until the late 17th century. Pegs were handmade and stand slightly proud of the surface.

- Later machine-made pegs are perfectly symmetrical and are either flush with the surface or slightly recessed.

- From the early 18th century, joints were dovetailed and glued (above).
- Until the end of the 18th century, when the circular saw was introduced, all wood was sawed by hand and has straight saw marks. After c.1800 circular marks may be visible on the surface of unfinished wood.

SCREWS

The earlier the screw the cruder it will be.
- The groove on old screws tends to be off-centre and the top irregular (top).
- The thread is also irregular and open and, unlike modern screws (above), runs the entire length of the shank.

DRAWERS

- Dovetails are the triangular joints which slot together on the corners of drawers. They became progressively finer (see p73) and can help with dating.
- Drawers had channels in their sides and, until the 18th century, ran on runners set into the carcass.
- Some drawers ran on the dust boards and had no runners.
- From the Queen Anne period the runners were placed under the drawer at the sides and ran on bearers placed on the inside of the carcass.

HANDLES

- Handles can provide a useful clue to dating, because styles changed from period to period (see p72).
- It's common to find pieces with replaced handles; this isn't serious but it's preferable to have handles in keeping with the rest of the piece.
- From c.1690 handles were secured by pommels and nuts.

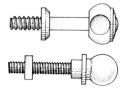

- Antique pommels were hand-cast in a single piece of brass (top). The thread goes only halfway up the shank, and the remainder of the shank is square-shaped. Modern pommels (above) are made from brass heads with steel shanks and the thread runs the whole length of the shank.
- The nuts used to attach handles in the 18th century were circular and slightly irregular. Modern nuts are regular and hexagonal.

FEET

Feet can give a useful guide to dating (see p72); however, centuries of standing on damp floors often causes feet to rot and may therefore have been replaced.
- Compare the wood of the feet with that of the rest of the body to decide whether or not they're original.

LOCKS

- Early locks are usually of wrought iron held in place with iron nails. From the 18th century locks were steel or brass and secured with steel screws.
- Locks are often replaced; this isn't serious although it's better to have original ones.

CARVING

Oak was relatively difficult to carve but as walnut and mahogany became popular carving became finer and more intricate.
- Original carved decoration adds to the desirability of a piece.

- Some pieces were adorned with later carving; these are far less desirable than those with original decoration.

VENEERING

The quality of veneering has an important bearing on price.

- Many pieces have *quarter-veneered* tops, where four pieces of wood create a pattern.
- *Banding*, strips of veneers laid around the edges of drawers, was also popular. Depending on the way in which the grain of the wood runs, banding is referred to as *straight banding*, *cross-banding*, *feather* or *herringbone banding*.

INLAY AND MARQUETRY

A pattern made from veneers of different coloured

woods (see p74). Inlaying was popular on English and Continental furniture from the 17th century and can add greatly to the value of a piece. Marquetry is the technique of cutting shapes in a veneer and first became popular in England in the late 17th century.

GILDING

The addition of gold leaf as decoration on a carved softwood frame (usually beech) has four stages. The wood is sealed and made perfectly smooth with a chalky layer of gesso; a layer of bol-coloured red or yellow is applied to give depth and richness to the gilding; the gold leaf is applied with a brush and glued in place; finally, the desired shine is created by burnishing the surface with an agate.

CONDITION

Furniture in original pristine condition commands the highest prices and is always extremely scarce.

- Don't dismiss pieces with blemishes – as long as the wood itself has not been damaged; surface spots can often be treated by a good restorer. The table (left) may look

rather scruffy but the wood itself is undamaged and could easily be repolished.

WOODWORM

Small round holes in old furniture are a common sight and show that the piece has at some stage been attacked by woodworm.

- These need not put you off, provided the infestation hasn't structurally weakened the piece.
- Active woodworm can be detected by pale-coloured powder in the worm holes, or on adjacent surfaces, and should be treated with a proprietary product as soon as possible.
- Check all your pieces periodically for signs of infestation.

MARRIAGES

A piece of furniture made up from separate items which did not originally belong together is termed a "marriage".

- The married parts may be of a similar period or one part may be later, or even modern.
- Marriages are nearly always much less desirable than pieces

in their original condition.

- Examine furniture in the way described on p40 to make sure it isn't a marriage.

ALTERATIONS

Furniture which has been altered is usually less desirable than that in its original condition. Among the most common alterations are large pieces which have been reduced in size. Freshly cut surfaces, repositioned handles, and plugged holes are signs of alteration.

FAKES

A piece of furniture can be described as fake if it deliberately makes you think it's older than it really is. Fakes made from new timber are usually easy to spot as the wood doesn't have the patina of age you would expect. Some fakes are made from old wood and these can be more tricky to identify. Beware of any piece being sold as 18th century or earlier if it has circular saw marks (see p42). These mean the wood was cut after c.1800 when circular saws were first used. Specific types of fake are dealt with in the following pages.

STYLES

BAROQUE

A carved beech stool, c.1690.

Originally a derogatory term derived from the Italian word *barroco*, meaning a misshapen pearl, baroque furniture is typically lavishly decorated with heavy carving, often including figural sculpture, cupids and elaborate curving shapes. The baroque style prevailed throughout continental Europe in the late 17th and early 18th centuries. Key designers of the period include Daniel Marot in Holland and England, Andrea Brustolon in Venice and Jean Le Pautre in France.

QUEEN ANNE

Uncluttered elegance and restraint are associated with the reign of Queen Anne (1702–14). Walnut was the prevailing wood of the period and cabriole legs made their first appearance. Chairs with these cabriole legs, as well as vase-shaped splats, curved backs, and rounded stiles, are the elements that best epitomize the Queen Anne style.

ROCOCO

A giltwood pier mirror in rococo style.

Developed in France in the early 18th century, the word 'rococo' comes from the French *rocaille*, which means a fancy stonework and shellwork for fountains and grottoes. Rococo furniture is typified by a lighter, more fanciful, decorative style than baroque, which came before it. Asymmetrical ornament is typical of rococo; favourite motifs include shells, ribbons and flowers. The rococo style spread throughout Europe between c.1740 and 1760. The designs in Thomas Chippendale's Directory of 1754 reflect the English vogue that emerged for the French, Chinese and Gothic tastes. There was a departure from classical order and a move towards fantasy and asymmetry.

LOUIS XV

A Louis XV painted armchair, c.1760.

The French high rococo style is synonymous with the early part of the reign of Louis XV, whose name is associated with curving shapes and asymmetric forms. Comfort became an important consideration, and the bergère was one of many chair forms to evolve. Chinoiserie and Oriental motifs were very popular in this period. Leading cabinet-makers included Jean-François Oeben, Bernard II van Reisenburgh and Charles Cressent.

NEO-CLASSICISM

An 18th-century shield-back mahogany armchair.

Interest in the new discoveries made at Herculaneum and Pompeii in Italy combined with a reaction to rococo exuberance to create a new style that dominated the second half of the 18th century. It was pioneered in England in the work of Robert Adam, and is also reflected in the designs of Hepplewhite and Sheraton. Neo-classical furniture is typically decorated with classical motifs, such as masks, swags and columns. Carving is in low relief and usually symmetrical. The furniture is characteristically light and elegant in appearance. Straight, tapering legs are typical of chairs at this time as are geometrical forms and the use of Greek and Roman ornament.

LOUIS XVI

A Louis XVI beechwood fauteuil, c.1785.

In France the neo-classical style partially overlapped the reign of Louis XVI, whose name is associated with furniture made from his accession until the Revolution (1789). In contrast to Louis XV, lines became straighter and more rectilinear. Upholstered chairs typically had padded oval backs and straight, tapered and fluted legs. Giltwood and painted furniture was popular, as were marquetry, exotic woods, lacquer, *pietre dure*, and figurative bronze mounts. Leading cabinet-makers included Georges Jacob, with makers such as Jean-François Oeben and Jean-Henri Riesener working in the rococo and the classical periods as well as in the intermediate 'transitional' style when rococo curves started to straighten.

GEORGIAN

A loose term applied to anything made during the reign of the first three king Georges (c.1715–1820). The period encompasses rococo, neo-classical, and Regency styles and was one in which the leading designers, such as William Kent, Thomas Chippendale, and Thomas Hope, had an increasingly powerful impact on furniture styles of the day through their design books.

REGENCY

A Regency chair, c.1815.

A term used to describe not only furniture made in the reign of the Prince of Wales as Regent (1811–20), but the new style that evolved from c.1790 and remained fashionable until c.1830. Compared with the furniture of the preceding neo-classical period, styles became heavier and more sober, inspired by classical prototypes, such as the klismos chair and the X-framed stool. The decorative motifs were drawn from Ancient Egypt, Greece and Rome. The key designers were Thomas Sheraton, Thomas Hope, Henry Holland and George Smith. The term 'Regency' should not be confused with the French *régence* style, which refers to a pre-rococo style of furniture made in the early 18th century. Mahogany was the favourite wood but rosewood, zebrawood and maple veneers were also used.

EMPIRE

The French equivalent of the Regency style became synonymous in France with the reign of Napoleon between 1804 and 1815. Only very simple lines and minimal ornament were used. Marquetry and carving were replaced by metal mounts, often in the form of either swans, military motifs – such as wreaths, eagles and trophies – or bees. Leading furniture designers of the period included Charles Percier and Pierre-François Fontaine.

VICTORIAN

An octagonal walnut Victorian library table, c.1860, by the English makers Gillow.

A wide variety of styles enjoyed a revival of popularity in the reign of Queen Victoria. Gothic Revival, Classical Revival, Rococo Revival, Renaissance Revival, Jacobean Revival and Japonisme all had their champions in Britain and North America.

Unlike previous periods the Victorians kept a style popular even when they rediscovered a "new" style, whereas in the 18th century, one style superseded another. Decoration of Victorian furniture is often elaborate with a profusion of carving; inlay and metal mounts were often made by industrial machines. Later, more stylized, Victorian, styles, including the Japonisme of E. W. Godwin, the Aesthetic Movement, forms of Arts and Crafts and Art Nouveau, all helped to drive out fussy Victorian ornament.

CHAIRS

Chairs are among the most essential pieces of furniture, and not surprisingly the finest antique ones – usually those made in the 18th century or earlier – can be very valuable. Prices for dining chairs are not only affected by quality and age, but also by the number of chairs in the set – the larger the set the more expensive each chair becomes. But if you choose a simple pattern you may be able to find odd numbers of chairs and build up a set piecemeal.

The first chairs were simply constructed like stools, with a plank of wood at the back which sometimes had carved decoration. During the second half of the 17th century walnut replaced oak as the favourite wood and chairs were often elaborately carved with scrolls on stretchers and legs.

Mahogany chairs became popular during the 18th century, and chair styles reflected designs published by leading designers such as Chippendale, Hepplewhite and Sheraton. Pattern books of their designs were circulated nationwide to many local cabinet-makers, who reproduced the designs, often in much simplified form. Nowadays, when a chair is described as "Chippendale", "Hepplewhite" or "Sheraton" it usually means it is based on one of their patterns rather than made by the cabinet-maker himself.

DATING CHAIRS

18thC

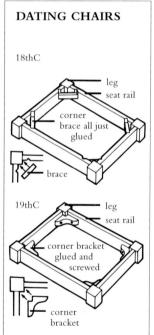

leg
seat rail

corner brace all just glued

brace

19thC

leg
seat rail

corner bracket glued and screwed

corner bracket

Before the 19th century, chair seat frames were strengthened with glued corner braces. After c.1840 shaped and screwed triangular brackets were used.

▼ EARLY OAK CHAIRS
Carving can help identify a chair's origins. This one dates from c.1640 and is carved with the dragon crest and scrolled arms typical of the Gloucestershire region. £1,500–5,000.

▲ WALNUT CHAIRS
This c.1720 walnut chair has the cabriole legs and drop-in seat characteristic of chairs of the period. However, high-quality chairs of this date would not normally have had stretchers so this one was probably made by a provincial maker rather than a major name. £300+

THOMAS CHIPPENDALE

Many of Thomas Chippendale's chair designs featured pierced splats carved with scrolling foliage and incorporating Gothic elements, just as seen on this c.1765 chair. Ribbons and chinoiserie details were also popular motifs which he used freely. £750+

WHAT TO LOOK FOR

- Examine each chair carefully for signs of genuine wear and the patina of age – nearly all types have been reproduced.
- If the colour of one part looks very different it may be replaced.
- Thick brown varnish often indicates a chair trying to look older than it is.

▼ REGENCY CHAIRS

This c.1800 painted chair, with gilded decoration, slender arms and ebonized and tapered front legs is typical of the early Regency period. Later chairs were more heavily proportioned. £500–2,000

▲ WINDSOR CHAIRS

Windsors are made from country woods such as elm, oak, ash and yew and usually date from after c.1700. Yew Windsors, like this one, made c.1810, are the most sought-after. The curved crinoline stretcher between the legs is unusual at this date. £500+

▼ BALLOON-BACKED CHAIRS

The value of this c.1860 Victorian walnut balloon-back chair is increased by its fine proportions and desirable needlework seat. £300–400

DINING CHAIRS

The designs of George Hepplewhite and Thomas Sheraton dominated the appearance of chairs in the last quarter of the 18th century. Hepplewhite's shield-back chair design was one of his most popular, while Sheraton introduced square-backed chairs of lighter proportions. Chair seats became narrower at the end of the 19th century, as the demand

	GEORGE III	EARLY 19TH CENTURY	MID-19TH CENTURY
	MAHOGANY DINING CHAIR c.1780	MAHOGANY DINING CHAIR c.1825	VICTORIAN SALON CHAIR c.1860
WHERE, WHEN, WHY	Decorative motifs drawn from Classical antiquity, such as the anthemion flower on the pierced back splat of this chair, are characteristic of chairs made in the third quarter of the 18th century in England, after designs by Hepplewhite.	Made between 1810 and 1840, the Regency to early Victorian period, a curved top-rail and the outswept back legs reflect the influence of ancient Greek seating. The seat is stuffed but not sprung.	Salon suites of six side chairs with matching settee and armchairs originated in Europe and were popular from c.1850 to 1910 in England. It is rare to find these in sets of more than six, or with arms.
WHAT TO LOOK FOR	● Detailed carving on the back splat – a sign of quality. ● Original stretchers. ● Drop-in seats – they are easier to re-upholster than the fitted variety.	● Circular tapering reeded legs, or outward curving sabre legs; chairs of lesser quality have simpler legs. ● Sets of six chairs with two matching armchairs.	● Balloon backs with cabriole legs more sought after than those with straight legs. ● Walnut and rosewood, followed by mahogany, are the most desirable woods; stained beech is considered less valuable.
PRICES	£150–200 each for single chairs. £4,000–5,000 for a set of six with two matching armchairs.	£2,000–3,000 for eight. £6,000 for six with two matching armchairs.	£800–1,200 for a set of six in mahogany with cabriole legs. £1,000–1,500 for eight with turned legs.

grew for chairs that would fit into smaller rooms. Mahogany remained the wood that was commonly used for formal dining chairs, but walnut and rosewood were also used to produce quality sets. While Gillow – leading 19th-century furniture makers – favoured oak, many less expensive chairs were made from stained beech.

ART NOUVEAU	EDWARDIAN	THONET CHAIRS	
STAINED BEECH CHAIR c.1900	MAHOGANY DINING CHAIR c.1900	BENTWOOD CHAIR c.1900	
Old decorative forms were interpreted in new ways in Art Nouveau chairs made in the early 20th century. Here, the form of turning and tapering and the elongated proportions are characteristically Art Nouveau.	In England the chair designs of Sheraton and Hepplewhite became fashionable again in the late 19th century. The proportions in later versions tend to be less generous, with thinner arms, legs and splats.	Michael Thonet was an innovative 19th-century German designer who developed a technique for mass-producing bentwood furniture. By 1900, he had factories throughout Europe and America that made over six million chairs from beech that had been steamed, bent and stained.	WHERE, WHEN, WHY
● Sculptural and unusual designs. ● Chairs more akin to a design by a well-known designer e.g. Mackintosh, Voysey or Mackmurdo. ● Original upholstery (although this does not always add value).	● Stringing, popular in the Edwardian era, but rare in 18th century, is found on better-quality chairs, often made of East Indian satinwood. ● Reasonably sturdy proportions – some have spindly appearances.	● The original Thonet brand mark or label under the seat rim or that of the lesser-known maker, Kohn. ● Good condition – these chairs are quite easy to find and, therefore, not worth buying if damaged.	WHAT TO LOOK FOR
£200–300 for the set of six beech chairs (above).	£1,500–2,000 for a set of eight with two armchairs.	£10–20 for a single chair.	PRICES

COUNTRY CHAIRS

Country chairs, many of which were made in remote rural areas, developed independently from the fashionable seating featured on the preceding pages.

Country chairs are always made of solid wood from indigenous trees: elm, yew, oak, ash and beech. The wood used can have a significant bearing on the price. Chairs made entirely or partly from yew are particularly sought after, while beech is more common. Dating can be a tricky business because designs changed little between the 18th and early 20th centuries, although examining the patina of the wood and the decorative details can be of considerable help.

If the chair combines decoration typical of different periods, always date it by the latest decorative detail.

▶ **STYLES**
Most country chairs vary more because of where, rather than when, they were made. The elaborately arched splats on this oak chair are typical of chairs made in South Yorkshire and Derbyshire, while the bobbin turning on the front stretcher dates the chair to the late 17th century.
£1,000–1,500

▼ **SETS**
The number of chairs in a set can affect the price dramatically. This simple ash and elm early 19th-century Windsor is from a set of five that would cost £600 to £900. If there were six chairs, the set would cost about £800 to £1,200; at the other end of the scale, you might find a single one for £100.

◀ **LADDER BACKS**
The six horizontal splats on this rush-seated early 19th-century ash armchair are responsible for its name: "ladder back". The rush seat looks a little sagged but could be restored without affecting the piece's value.
£250–350

EXAMINE A WINDSOR CLOSELY, AS THE COMBINATION OF WOODS CAN AFFECT VALUE. THIS ARMCHAIR, MADE FROM SOLID ASH AND ELM, IS WORTH £300 TO £400. IF IT INCLUDED YEW, IT WOULD BE MORE DESIRABLE AND COST £600 TO £900.

As with most country chairs you will find, this one has an elm saddle-shaped seat.

The heavy turned legs date the chair to c.1825–50; an earlier chair would have cabriole legs. The turning on the back legs should match that on the front – if it does not, it could be a sign that some of the legs are replacements.

The higher and more elaborate the back, the more expensive the Windsor will be – this splat is fairly simple.

Check the splat, top rail and arms for cracks; you should be especially careful if they are made from yew, which is more brittle than ash.

The crinoline stretcher, more commonly seen on 18th-century chairs, adds value.

HOW DID WINDSORS GET THEIR NAME?

According to one legend, George III, out riding near Windsor Castle, was caught in a storm and took refuge in a cottage. He took such a liking to the seat he rested on that they became known as "Windsor" chairs. A more mundane explanation is that the chairs were originally made in the area surrounding Windsor.

CHAIR STYLES

The changing styles of chair backs, legs and feet can help collectors to date chairs. The illustrations show a selection of the more commonly seen designs. However, as most of these were repeated in later periods, the style of a chair must be seen only as a guide to its age, not as proof of its authenticity.

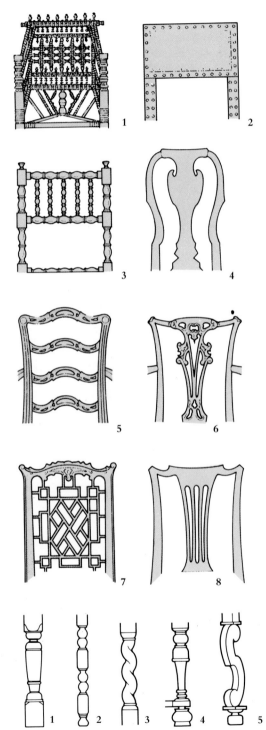

CHAIR BACKS

1 Early 16thC bobbin frame
2 Cromwellian padded
3 Late 17thC bobbin turned
4 Early 18thC Queen Anne hoop-back with urn-shaped splat
5 Ladder-back with horizontal pierced splats, c.1760
6 Chippendale-style with carved splat c.1760
7 "Chinese" Chippendale chair c.1760
8 Plain mahogany Chippendale-style chair c.1760
9 Late 18thC Hepplewhite-style shield back
10 Late 18thC Gothic-style chair
11 Late 18thC lyre-back
12 Early 19thC country-style ladder back
13 Late 18thC hoop-back with wheatsheaf
14 Sheraton-style arm chair c.1790
15 Early 19thC Sheraton-style square framed
16 Late 18thC Gothic Windsor
17 Early 19thC spindle-back
18 Early 19thC plain Windsor

19 Regency with key pattern c.1820
20 Regency rope twist c.1820
21 Early Victorian c.1940
22 Gothic square-backed c.1830
23 Victorian carved balloon-back c.1850
24 Mid-19thC Victorian Carolean

LEGS AND FEET

1 16thC baluster
2 Late 17thC bobbin turned
3 Second half 17thC barley-twist
4 Inverted cup baluster c.1675–1700
5 Late 17thC double scroll
6 Early 18thC cabriole
7 Early 18thC carved cabriole
8 18thC shell-carved cabriole
9 Early Georgian carved cabriole
10 Mid-18thC cabriole with claw-and-ball foot
11 Chamfered c.1750–80
12 Mid-18thC blind fretted
13 Late 18thC turned
14 Early 19thC sabre
15 Victorian Carolean c.1845
16 Mid-19thC reeded

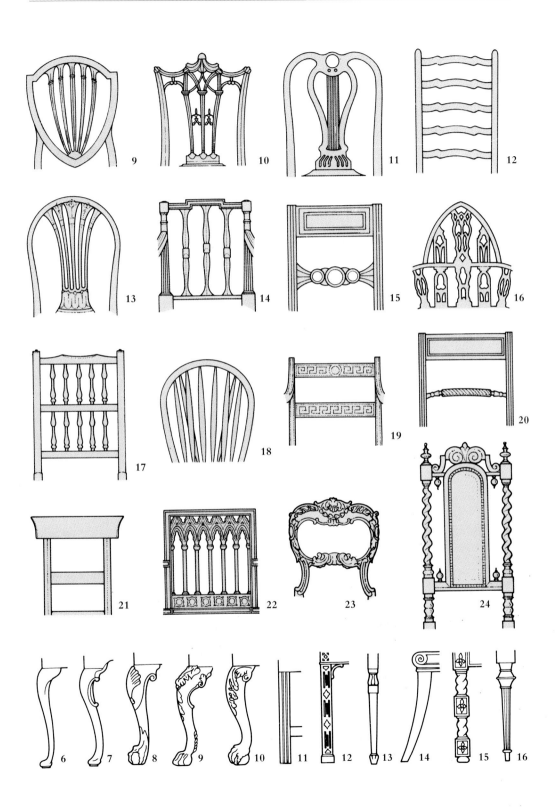

UPHOLSTERED CHAIRS & SOFAS

No home would be complete without comfy sofas and chairs, and antique upholstered furniture can sometimes be less expensive than modern counterparts – and surprisingly comfortable as well.

Among the most popular types of chairs are winged armchairs with simple cabriole legs and side panels to keep out chilly draughts.

These were first made in the early 18th century and the design has remained virtually unchanged to this day. The wooden frame is the most important part of antique chairs and sofas, so never buy a chair with a severely damaged frame. Don't worry too much about the condition of upholstery – as this can usually be restored.

WING ARM CHAIRS

◀ SIGNS OF AGE
The marks left by the original upholstery nails are still clearly visible on the side of the chair and are a good indication that it is an original and not a more recent reproduction.

▲ BEFORE
Although this arm chair (shown on the right after it had been re-upholstered) looks terribly tatty, being able to see it like this is a bonus – you can make sure the wood is original and hasn't split or been weakened by woodworm.
● If the chair is recently re-covered, ask if there are photos of the frame.

▶ AFTER
It's very rare to find a chair with its original covering but provided the fabric is in a style appropriate to the chair the re-upholstering doesn't greatly affect value – this 18th-century chair is covered in a suitable silk damask. £5,000+

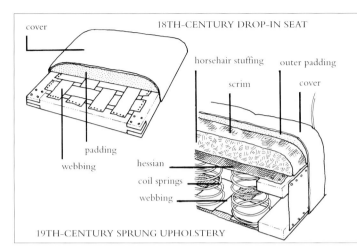

18TH-CENTURY DROP-IN SEAT

cover

horsehair stuffing outer padding

scrim cover

padding

webbing

hessian

coil springs

webbing

19TH-CENTURY SPRUNG UPHOLSTERY

WHAT'S INSIDE A CHAIR?

Before c.1830 the upholstery on chairs was made from thin layers of horsehair and padding supported by webbing covered with fabric. Upholstery using coiled metal springs covered with padding and webbing was made from c.1830.

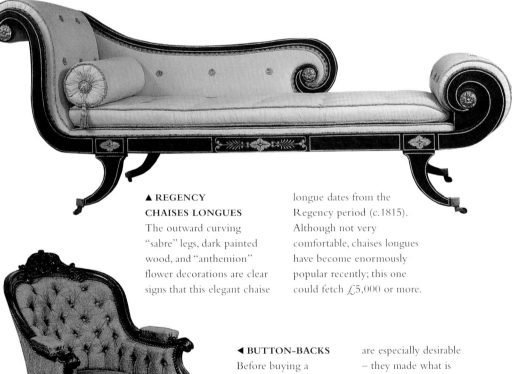

▲ REGENCY CHAISES LONGUES

The outward curving "sabre" legs, dark painted wood, and "anthemion" flower decorations are clear signs that this elegant chaise longue dates from the Regency period (c.1815). Although not very comfortable, chaises longues have become enormously popular recently; this one could fetch £5,000 or more.

◀ BUTTON-BACKS

Before buying a Victorian button-back, turn it upside down and look for a manufacturer's mark or label; these can add greatly to value – Howard & Sons' labels are especially desirable – they made what is considered the "Rolls-Royce" of chairs! This particular armchair is worth over £3,000, but it is possible to find other examples from around £500+.

OPEN ARMCHAIRS

During the 18th century, the increasing importance attached to comfort and luxury led to the development of a wide range of sumptuously upholstered open armchairs. Although seats were generally stuffed rather than sprung, many had loose feather-filled cushions that made them very comfortable.

Armchair design was led by the French. Many English armchairs produced in the 18th and 19th centuries are based on French prototypes of the Louis XV and Louis XVI periods. Pairs are particularly sought after and will usually cost more than twice the price of a single constituent chair.

▶ **WALNUT ARMCHAIRS**
The shell that you can see at the top of the cabriole legs and on the centre of the back splat of this French walnut armchair, made about 1720, is one of the most popular motifs to be found on early 18th-century furniture. This piece is worth £3,000 to £5,000.

▲ **FRENCH OR ENGLISH?**
When it comes to mid-19th-century furniture, deciding whether a piece is English or French can be difficult. The chair on the left, in the Louis XV style, was made by the popular English makers Howard & Sons in the 1860s. The construction of the Louis XVI-style chair on the right suggests that it was made in France, but in fact it carries a Howard & Sons' label, probably because it was retailed or repaired by them.
£800–1,200 (left)
£700–1,000 (right)

► **BUTLERS' CHAIRS**
Although the seat
is not upholstered,
this interesting, late
19th-century oak chair,
with original buttoned
moquette upholstery, is
very comfortable. The

chair was probably
made for the sitting-
room of a head butler
in a grand house; today
it would be equally
practical for sitting at
a desk.
£200–300

▼ **WHAT'S IN
A NAME?**
Chairs made by leading
manufacturers in the
19th century were
occasionally marked
with their names.
If you can find the
manufacturer's stamp (it
is often under the seat
rail or inside the back
leg), it can dramatically
increase the value of

the chair. Although this
walnut armchair, made
about 1865, is battered
and worn, it would be
worth buying and
restoring because it is
stamped by Gillow,
leading makers of the
period.
£2,000–3,000
(in this condition)
£3,000–4,000
(restored)

NAMES TO LOOK OUT FOR
Gillow (Lancaster)
Howard & Sons (London)
Krieger (Paris) (stamped on the arm)
Lexcellent (Paris)
Maple (London)
Thomas Schoolbred (London)

▲ **CASTERS**
French chairs often
had wooden casters so
that they would not
scratch wooden floors.
In England, where
carpets were generally
favoured, casters in the
18th century were
often made from brass
with leather-bound

wheels (as in the detail,
left). Later, in the 18th
century, they were
just brass wheels.
Some were stamped
by their makers
(Cope & Collinson
are particularly well
known). In the 19th
century, less expensive
chairs were made with
ceramic casters, which
are of less interest to
collectors. Note: you
should never remove
the old casters from a
chair, as this will reduce
its value.

STOOLS

A status symbol, an extravagant accessory, a seat, and something to put your feet on – the humble stool has played a multitude of roles since it first appeared in ancient times. At medieval court the stool showed rank – only honoured guests could use them – the king sat on a throne, everyone else stood.

Among the most elegant and expensive stools are those inspired by antiquity. Robert Adam designed a stool modelled on a Roman cistern (a water tank), and the X-form stool, used by Ancient Egyptians, Romans and Greeks, became enormously popular in the Regency period (the Ancient Egyptians made a wide range of stools in materials ranging from papyrus and wicker to wood and ivory).

American stools often reflect European designs. The joint stool, for example, which was usually made of oak, was produced from the 17th century onwards in both continents.

A good 18th-century or Regency stool might cost several thousand pounds, but you can often find 19th- and 20th-century pieces for about £100.

◀ **18TH-CENTURY STOOLS**
You can tell from its deep sides that this simple walnut stool, made c.1730, was once a commode (the sides hid the chamber pot). The 18th-century crewelwork covering is a plus, even though it is not original to the stool.
£800–1,200

HOW OLD ARE THEY?

The earliest form of stool commonly seen today, the joint stool, was first popular in the 17th century (far left); it was also reproduced in large numbers in the 1930s (left). There are a number of signs of age that you should look for, including:
● a mellow sheen with variations in tone where the stool has been exposed to wear;

● genuine wear on the stretchers – here, the modern version's stretchers are artificially worn in the centre;
● irregular-shaped pegs that stand proud; but beware – copies have machine-cut pegs that are sometimes left proud to give an impression of shrinkage;
● a dry appearance underneath.

◀ X-FORM STOOLS
X-form stools, popular in the late 18th century, are often of superior quality and therefore expensive. This is one of a characteristically refined pair, made c.1800, with dished mahogany seats and elegant scrolled ends; a pair would be worth £3,000 to £4,000.

▲ PIANO STOOLS
Piano stools were first seen in the late 18th century; this rosewood example can be dated to c.1835 by its heavy proportions and the scrolling, rococo-style carving on its legs. £200–300

▲ MOORISH STOOLS
Large quantities of Moorish-style furniture were made throughout the Middle East (and especially in Cairo) for export to the West during the late 19th century. Most pieces feature elaborate turning, derived from Musharabyeh panelling (which is used for Oriental screens). This stool is made from stained softwood and would be relatively inexpensive; look out for walnut versions, which can be worth four times as much. £100–200

▲ POUFFES
The home-worked top of this horsehair-stuffed pouffe was probably made by a middle-class lady in the 1870s. Pouffes are among the least expensive stools available; this one might cost you £200.

DINING TABLES I

PEDESTAL TABLES
Elegant pedestal tables are so practical and popular that they have been made continuously from the 18th century to the present day. Value depends largely on age and number of pedestals. A 19th-century one such as this

might cost from £3,000 upwards, a modern version £300–500.

BEFORE YOU BUY IT...
fit any extra leaves in the table to check that they haven't warped.

SIGNS OF AGE
- solid mahogany tops (usually without cross-banding or inlay)
- "reeded" edge to tops
- brass casters – plain or cast as lion's paws.

There are many different types of dining table to choose from, depending on what size you require – and how much you want to spend. Remember to look at the grain of the wood on the top – an attractively grained top is a definite plus but will increase the price. If you're on a limited budget don't dismiss tables which have marked tops – so long as the wood has not been damaged it can probably be restored to its former glory. Don't forget to sit down at the table to make sure it feels a comfortable height and the legs don't get in the way of yours.

WHAT TO LOOK FOR
- Signs of wear on the legs and top – scratches and marks are a sign of genuine age and to be expected.
- Legs of more or less the same colour – if one is noticeably different it might be a later replacement.
- Flaps which match the rest of the table reasonably well – those used only occasionally may not have faded as much as the rest of the table but their figuring should be similar.

(see p43)

◀ **REFECTORY TABLES**

These are among the earliest dining tables; most date from the 17th–18th centuries, but there are also fakes around – many made from old floorboards. Look for circular saw marks – these show the table is not as old as it seems and has been tampered with since the 19th century. This one dates from c.1620 and is worth over £10,000.

▶ **DROP LEAF TABLES**

Drop leafs with simple pad feet like this are among the most affordable types of 18th-century tables; this one would cost around £500+.

▲ **D-ENDED TABLES**

Adaptable D-ended tables come in several sections; the ends can be used as side tables. £1,500–4,000

▶ **GATELEG TABLES**

Hinged "gates" pull out to hold up the flaps on these 17th/18th-century tables – hence their name. The most expensive ones seat six or more. £1,000+

BEWARE

Some tops are "married" (see p43) to different bases: look carefully under the top – marks which could have been made by different supports should make you suspicious.

DINING TABLES II

A variety of new and ingenious extending dining tables emerged in the early 19th century. The Cumberland action table stored the extra leaves and legs within a deep apron under the top. Robert Jupe, the innovative furniture maker, patented a capstan (rotating) circular extending table in 1836; when the top was twisted the segmented top opened, allowing the extra pieces to slot in. Other dining tables were extended with winding handles and telescopic sliders.

Prices for the best designs have rocketed in recent years. Circular tables have become especially fashionable, but you can still find some large and less spectacular Victorian tables for about £1,000. The elaborateness of the supports can affect price; the best have heavily carved pedestals or legs.

▶ **CIRCULAR TABLES**
This extending table dates from about 1880. The small supports pull out to hold segmented leaves around the edge. Missing these leaves it is worth £1,500 to £2,000; with them it would fetch between £5,000 and £8,000.

◀ **RECTANGULAR TABLES**
The two end sections of this Regency table pull open on a box frame to allow extra leaves to be inserted. Made c.1820, the table still has its original leaves and would fetch £4,000 to £6,000.

WOODS
Most 19th-century dining tables have tops made from solid mahogany, some with veneered friezes; solid oak was a less common alternative. Veneered tops are often found on reproduction tables.

WHAT TO LOOK FOR
• Make sure that the opening mechanism works well.
• Check that the legs are sturdy.
• Look for a well-figured top – this increases desirability.
• Elegant legs, such as the reeded ones on the table above, add visual appeal.

► **SPLIT-PILLAR TABLES**

The central pillar of this table splits in two and can hold three extra leaves. The grand C-scroll legs are typical of the rococo revival style of c.1840; similar tables were made in north Germany. £6,000–8,000

◄ **VALUE**

While superior designs have risen dramatically in value, prices for less exceptional examples have remained steady. Made c.1860, this table extends with a winding handle to take three extra leaves; it measures 9ft 10in/3m and seats 12 comfortably. £2,000–3,000

▲ **CRÈME DE LA CRÈME**

Extending tables made by the cabinet-maker Robert Jupe have attracted top prices recently. Only a decade ago they sold for £2,000 to £3,000, they change hands now for between £70,000 and £80,000. This William IV version, made c.1835, recently sold for £78,000.

MEDIUM-SIZED TABLES

The Pembroke table, the forebear of the sofa table, was introduced in the mid-18th century. It was named after the Countess of Pembroke, who supposedly ordered the first one. Pembrokes have rectangular, circular, serpentine or oval tops, with flaps supported on small, hinged members called "flys".

The term "Pembroke" table was used interchangeably with "breakfast" table. They were used for light meals – breakfast and tea – or as work tables. The sofa table, which was a longer, narrower version of the Pembroke, was designed to stand in front of a sofa and was used by ladies for writing, drawing and reading. The first ones appeared in the 1790s and were made of mahogany. Various exotic woods were also used for creating veneers. Marquetry decoration of Neo-classical design is found on finer pieces.

Centre tables are similar in form to sofa tables, but they do not have the flaps at each end. Library tables tend to be very grand and expensive – the most elaborate versions have hinged tops for showing maps and prints.

▶ PEMBROKE TABLES

Sheraton-style Pembroke tables were widely copied in the late 19th and early 20th centuries. If you think that you have found one, examine the thickness of the veneers – later reproductions are covered in thin, machine-cut wood. This one is genuine: it was made c.1790 from mahogany and has satinwood banding – it is worth £1,200 to £1,800; later copies fetch £300 to £500.

◀ SOFA TABLES

The position of the stretcher on a sofa or centre table can give an indication of the table's date. The high stretcher on this painted satinwood table points to an early date of c.1790. A decade later stretchers were lower or had been replaced by central pedestals. Note the low stretcher on the library table opposite. £3,000–4,000

CARE
Original leather tops tend to become scuffed and worn, but always try to save them by having them recoloured and repolished, rather than replaced.

▶ **LIBRARY TABLES**
Library tables such as this one, made c.1850 of walnut, usually have leather tops. This one reflects the eclectic Victorian style: it mixes rococo C-scrolls and Elizabethan motifs.
£2,000–3,000

◀ **PROVENANCE**
An illustrious provenance will always boost the price of any furniture. This well-worn Victorian oak centre or library table would normally sell for £3,000 to £5,000. However, because it was sold in a well-publicized house sale at Stokesay Court, Shropshire, it made more than double the top estimate, selling for nearly £6,500.

▶ **CONTINENTAL TABLES**
This Spanish kingwood veneered centre table, made c.1860, is similar to contemporary French tables. Restrained though heavy, it is clearly of high quality.
£2,000–3,000.

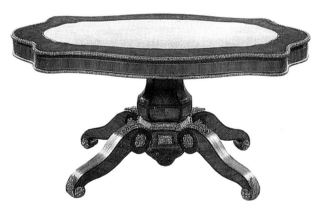

SMALL TABLES I

Small tables tended to be simply made from solid wood until the late 17th century. Over the next two hundred years, as society became more sophisticated and interiors more refined, cabinet-makers produced an enormous variety of smaller tables, adorning them in a myriad ways: carving, gilding, marquetry, metal mounts and porcelain plaques are just some of the decorations that you will find on small tables made during the 18th, 19th and 20th centuries. Condition,

ease of use (in other words, how practical they are in today's homes) and appearance are important factors in determining the value of all kinds of small table. Those made in the 18th century are often very elaborate and were produced for the wealthiest homes.

Many types of small table were used for serving tea or coffee, which were then seen as expensive commodities that deserved to be presented on a suitably extravagant stage. Console and pier tables were decorative

	SIDE TABLES	LOWBOY SIDE TABLES
	OAK SIDE TABLE c.1660-80 £1,000-1,500	OAK LOWBOY c.1740 £1,800-2,800
HOW, WHEN, WHY	The forerunners of serving tables, side tables were made from the 16th century to stand against walls. Their backs are plain and there is often a drawer in the front frieze. The rectangular tops were made from planks.	Made from c.1700–50 for writing or dressing, lowboys usually have stretcher-less cabriole legs. The three top drawer fronts are often dummies applied to a single drawer.
WOOD	This varies according to date, but oak was commonly used.	Lowboys were made from oak, walnut or mahogany.
WHAT TO LOOK FOR	• Attractively shaped legs – these double baluster legs are a bonus. • Shaped stretcher (if there is one) – this X-frame stretcher adds charm and value. • Good patination – this adds greatly to value whatever the wood. • Original or appropriate handles – these pear-drops are replacements, but in keeping with the date of the table.	• Decorative details, such as ogee arches, or a frieze, as seen here. • Re-entrant corners (shaped corners on top). • Tops with moulded edges. • Outlines of overlapping drawer fronts on the carcass indicate authenticity.

objects, designed for the large rooms of grand Georgian houses; they were expensive items when made and have remained so.

It is hard to find small tables made in the 18th century for under £1000, and prime examples may fetch tens of thousands of pounds. If your budget is limited, however, you need not despair. The most successful 18th-century designs for small tables were often repeated in the late 19th century. These later versions are often extremely well made and offer you the opportunity to buy the elegance of 18th-century style at only a fraction of the cost. While a set of Georgian quartetto tables might cost £3,000 to £4,000, it should be possible for you to find an early 20th-century set for about £600 to £800.

Small tables are, in general, one of the most popular types of furniture. Their very portability means that they are taken from home to home rather than sold, which keeps both demand and prices high.

SILVER TABLES	CONSOLE TABLES	
MAHOGANY SILVER TABLE c.1755 £15,000–25,000	FRENCH c.1750 GILTWOOD CONSOLE TABLE £3,000–5,000	
Tables with galleried edges were designed by Chippendale in 1754; they were used for displaying objects and for serving tea in the 18th century. In the 19th century, French-style tables with metal galleries were popular.	With no back legs to support it, the console table was permanently fixed to a wall in an entrance hall or grand salon, often with a mirror above. Made from the 18th century onwards, they often came in pairs.	HOW, WHEN, WHY
Mahogany was used in the 18th century, and various woods after that.	Console tables are frequently found in giltwood or japanning, and often have marble tops.	WOOD
● Pierced galleries on 18th-century tables should be made from three thicknesses of laminated wood. ● Wide casters on 18th-century tables. ● Arresting decorative form – the delicate domed stretcher with urn finial is particularly attractive. ● Good-quality metal mounts on 19th-century versions.	● Original marble top in good condition. ● Pairs. ● Attractive carving, especially on the faces of figures – many (such as this one) are very ornate in the Italianate manner with swags, garlands, putti etc. Outspread eagle bases are also sought after.	WHAT TO LOOK FOR

SMALL TABLES II

PIER TABLES	TEA TABLES	COACH TABLES
ROSEWOOD PIER TABLE c.1820 £2,000–4,000	MAHOGANY TEA TABLE c.1820 £800–1,200	MAHOGANY COACH TABLE, c.1870 £400–600

	PIER TABLES	TEA TABLES	COACH TABLES
HOW, WHEN, WHY	The pier is the wall space between two windows. Pier tables were made, usually in pairs, from the 18th century. They are similar to console tables, but have back supports.	Tables for serving tea date from the 18th century onwards (when tea-drinking became fashionable). Shapes vary – this one resembles a card table but, when opened, has a veneered top.	First popular in the mid- to late 19th century, coach tables are a variant of butlers' trays that could fold flat vertically when not in use. They were used for picnics in the garden or for eating in trains or mail coaches.
WOOD	Expensive woods were used, such as rosewood, mahogany and giltwood.	Mahogany was usually used for tea tables; japanning was popular in the 18th century.	Coach tables were commonly made from solid mahogany and had little decoration.
WHAT TO LOOK FOR	● Decorative appearance – semi-circular or serpentine shapes are desirable. ● Regency versions often have mirrors below to reflect light – original glass is a bonus. ● Original or traditional gilding. This one has been over-painted with gold and looks gaudy, detracting from its value.	● Well-figured wood. ● Swivel tops – these were added to some to make serving easier. ● Good decorative detail – the canted sabre legs on this one are an attractive feature. ● Original casters – these lion's paws are typical of the date.	● Examine the hinge on the folding flap to make sure that it is in good condition. ● Check that the top and base belong together – look underneath for any signs of tampering. ● Make sure that the legs and stretchers (if there are any) are sound.

OCCASIONAL TABLES	DISPLAY TABLES	QUARTETTO TABLES	
OCCASIONAL TABLE c.1880 £2,000–3,000	SATINWOOD DISPLAY TABLE c.1890 £1,000–1,500	MAHOGANY QUARTETTO TABLES, c.1910 £400–600	
The opulent French style of the 1720s and 1730s was enormously fashionable from 1830 to 1930; large numbers of small tables in the Louis XV manner such as this one (also known as *guéridons*) were made in England and France.	These are small tables with hinged glass tops that were used to display precious ornaments. Many were made in the last 15 years of Queen Victoria's reign and in the Edwardian era. French versions are called *vitrines*.	Nests of graduated tables were first made c.1780–1820 in England and revived in the last years of the 19th century. Practical for modern-day interiors, they have remained popular in the 20th century.	HOW, WHEN, WHY
Various woods were used and often combined to produce marquetry decoration.	Decorative woods – usually veneered and then sometimes painted – were used.	Mahogany was most common; papier mâché was used in the 19th century; satinwood is rare.	WOOD
● The top and platform stretchers should be of matching form; here, both are serpentine squares. ● Marquetry that is in good condition, with no pieces missing. ● Good-quality metal mounts. ● Sèvres-style porcelain plaques painted with attractive subjects.	● Elegant shape – the cabriole legs on this one are typical of the 1890s and reflect quality. ● Check that there are no chips or cracks in the glass – it could be expensive to replace. ● Attractive decoration – whether painted, gilt metal, marquetry or giltwood.	● Solid, generous proportions if they are Georgian – later versions tend to have thinner legs and lighter trestles. ● Reasonable condition – they are vulnerable to damage. ● Attractive painted decoration – in the French or neo-classical style.	WHAT TO LOOK FOR

CARD & GAMES TABLES

Fortunes were won and lost at cards in the 18th century and, from c.1690 onwards, numerous tables were produced especially for card-playing. As backgammon, chess and tric trac (a variation on backgammon) became popular, tables were made to accommodate these different games.

Tric trac tables often resemble Pembroke or sofa tables but for their removable panels: these panels conceal wells that are divided in two. Prices for card and games tables reflect the demand for all small tables that fit well in modern sitting-rooms. Various woods were used, as well as papier mâché.

A high-quality 18th-century concertina action table will fetch over £40,000. Less spectacular pieces, such as the ones shown below, are in the £500 to £12,000 range.

▼ **CONDITION**
The walnut veneer on this card table, made c.1710, is starved of colour; note also that the top has warped, probably because it has been over-exposed to sunlight. Nevertheless, the fact that it opens in a highly elaborate way, known as a 'concertina action' (see detail below), means that it would still be worth around £8,000 to £12,000.

▼ **DEMI-LUNE**
The D-shape or 'demi-lune' is a common shape for card tables and was particularly popular c.1780 (when this one was made). This table is slightly superior to most – both back legs open in a double gateleg action.
£800–1,200

CONCERTINA ACTION
The back legs of the table, attached to a hinged frieze, pull out to support the top when it is unfolded (as shown in this detail).

► **STYLE**

With its serpentine top and cabriole legs, this card table, made c.1770, was inspired by French designs of the 1750s. An English furniture maker, John Cobb, is often associated with this elegant style. £2,500–3,500

► **LATER CARD TABLES**

By the early 19th century card tables with central supports (and no legs to disturb the players) had become popular; today they are relatively inexpensive. The reeded baluster support on this swivel-top rosewood table, made c.1830, is typical of furniture made in the reign of William IV. £1,200–1,800

▼ **PAPIER MÂCHÉ TABLES**

This papier mâché chess and writing table, made c.1840, would originally have had an upper part with shelves and drawers that had to be removed before the inlaid mother-of-pearl chess board could be used. Because the top is missing, this piece is worth £500–800; with its top, it would fetch twice as much.

PAPIER MÂCHÉ

Made from sheets of wet paper that were pasted together and pressed in moulds, a great deal of papier mâché furniture was manufactured in the Birmingham area between 1820 and 1870. Once dried, the furniture was coated with layers of (usually) black lacquer and then decorated with gilt, painted decoration and thin slivers of mother-of-pearl.

The manufacturers Jennens and Bettridge are particularly associated with papier mâché furniture; the appearance of their stamp on a piece will add some value.

CHESTS

Chests of drawers are among the most indispensable pieces of furniture for storage and, not surprisingly, have been made in huge numbers over the centuries. They are still among the most easily available and inexpensive pieces of antique furniture – although of course there are rare and expensive ones as well.

A chest has many of the elements found in other types of furniture – drawers, feet, handles and so on – and if you're keen to learn how to date and authenticate any type of antique furniture, examining a chest carefully can teach you a great deal.

STYLES OF FEET

Feet can give a useful clue to the date.

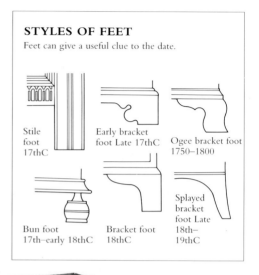

Stile foot 17thC

Early bracket foot Late 17thC

Ogee bracket foot 1750–1800

Bun foot 17th–early 18thC

Bracket foot 18thC

Splayed bracket foot Late 18th–19thC

HANDLE STYLES

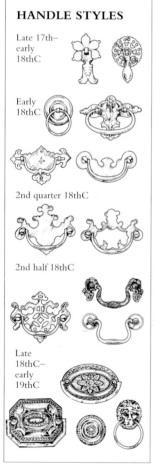

Late 17th–early 18thC

Early 18thC

2nd quarter 18thC

2nd half 18thC

Late 18thC–early 19thC

◀ **WALNUT CHESTS**
Size has an important bearing on the price of all chests. Although this walnut-veneered 18th-century chest is in a sorry state, it's desirably small (2ft 6in/77cm wide) and so is still worth £2,000–4,000.

◀ **MAHOGANY CHESTS**
Mahogany chests, such as this (made c.1765), are more common than walnut ones and so are usually less expensive. This chest is of exceptionally high quality, but even so need not cost much more than the battered walnut one above. £2,000–4,000.

WHY DO DEALERS LOOK IN DRAWERS?

When looking at a chest (or any piece with drawers) always pull each one out and examine it carefully. Marks in the wood, tiny holes and joints all have things to tell us. Look for marks on the dustboards inside – if the chest is original the marks of the runners should correspond with marks on the bottom of the drawer. From c.1790 drawers were strengthened by baseboards running from side to side with a central rib.

CONSTRUCTION

Examine the dovetails – they can tell you when the drawer was made. The earliest drawers have three coarse dovetails; later drawers usually have four or five finer ones. Don't just look at one drawer – check them all to make sure that they're all made and worn in the same way.

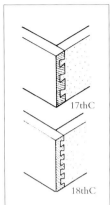

17thC

18thC

This mahogany chest was made c.1790; the bow-fronted style remained popular throughout much of the 19th century.
£500–3,500

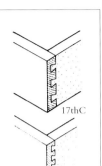

HANDLES

Check drawers inside and out for marks, such as holes or the outline of an old handle shape, where different handles might once have been. However, don't be put off if the handles have been replaced – it's very common and should not decrease desirability.

UNDERSIDES

Don't expect chests to be neatly finished all the way round. They were made to stand against a wall and their backs and undersides are usually made from rough unpolished boards.

FEET

The feet are most prone to wear and are often replaced, so check the colour and grain of each one. These feet are original and look appropriately battered.

DRESSERS, CABINETS & CREDENZAS

In the minds of most collectors antique dressers epitomize a particularly "country" style and an image of rustic charm. They give instant atmosphere to a room and can look equally impressive standing in a dining room, kitchen or hall – or wherever else you might care to put them. Dressers vary greatly in price according to the style you are looking for; those made from simple pine during the 19th century, or later, are most likely to be affordable; early ones, especially those made of oak, are usually very much more expensive.

In contrast to dressers, cabinets are considered to be among the most refined – and therefore valuable – pieces of antique furniture available. They were made in the 17th and 18th centuries and were specifically designed to store precious curiosities, and became status symbols reflecting the wealth and taste of their owner. Cabinets can create a dramatic focal point in any room – but unless you are extremely lucky, you will probably have to dig deep in your pocket to be able to afford an early one.

If your budget means that you seek a more affordable elegance, look out for 19th-century credenzas. Like cabinets, credenzas were made to display collections of valuables, and they are often highly ornate and decorative. Unlike most early cabinets, however, some are still available at relatively inexpensive prices.

▼ CABINETS

Legs on cabinets have often been replaced. Even though the stand of this c.1690 oyster laburnum marquetry cabinet is actually a later replacement (it has a harsh glossy finish quite different from the mellow sheen of the rest of the piece), the cabinet is still very valuable and worth around £7,000–9,000.

MARQUETRY

Marquetry

Oyster veneer

Stringing

Cross banding

Secondary wood

Marquetry, like that seen on the 17th-century cabinet above, always adds to value. Terms used to describe the different techniques are:

- **Oyster veneering:** slices cut across branches to make patterns like an oyster shell.

- **Cross-banding:** border with a grain at right angles to the main veneer.
- **Parquetry:** geometric pattern of small pieces of veneer.
- **Stringing:** narrow line of inlaid wood.

DRESSERS
Beware of dressers where the base and rack have been "married" and did not originally belong together.

Not all dressers had racks so watch for anything out of place. Compare the colour and patina of wood on both parts – here the colour of rack and

base are similar, showing that they belong together. Look for the outline of the rack on the base, such as you can see here. £3,000–5,000.

▶ **CREDENZAS**
Some credenzas, especially ebonized examples, can still be bought for under £2,000 – a bargain considering their usual good quality, especially when you compare them with the cost of earlier similarly elaborate pieces. This one, however, is worth around £2,500–3,500 and has many desirable features:
- walnut veneers
- original glass
- gilt mounts
- attractive inlay.

CORNER CUPBOARDS

Although they are undeniably attractive, corner cupboards can be a furniture dealer's nightmare. As rooms have become smaller, spare corners are harder to find and these cupboards have become more difficult to sell. Consequently, prices for them never seem to rise at the same rate as for other types of furniture. If you are lucky enough to have a corner to spare, you will find corner cupboards are very good value – even a pair of 18th-century corner cupboards can be fairly modestly priced. Most such cupboards on the market today date from the 18th and 19th centuries.

◀ STYLES
This unusual but pretty corner cupboard, made c.1770, looks like a corner washstand and may have been intended for a wash basin, jug or chamber pot. Apart from the top, all the lines are serpentine, and this stylistic feature makes the cupboard more valuable.
£1500–2,500

▲ HANGING CUPBOARDS
The simplest form of corner cupboard is the hanging variety with solid doors that was made from c.1700 until the mid-19th century; it was made in oak, mahogany and pine. If you look inside the cupboard and you are lucky, you might find that, as on this pine cupboard made c.1770, the original painted finish has survived.
£600–800

▶ CORNER BOOK CABINETS
This mahogany corner book cabinet, c.1910, was probably made in Germany, perhaps to fit around a column with three similar cabinets. The open shelves make this one of the most practical types of corner cupboard.
£2,500–3,500

STANDING CORNER
CUPBOARDS WERE
POPULAR IN THE
GEORGIAN PERIOD.
THIS MAHOGANY
VERSION DATES
FROM C.1785 AND
IS WORTH ABOUT
£2,000 TO £3,000.

The cornice hides the
top, which would be
left unfinished.

These attractive bars
add to the value of
the cupboard, as does
the bow-front.

Shelves either follow
the line of the outer
carcass (here they are
curved), or they are
quite elaborately shaped.

Open the door and look
obliquely at the glass.
If you can see ripples
and impurities, the glass
is probably original –
this is a bonus but
not essential.

By the late 18th
century, doors were
hinged on the inside.
On earlier 18th-century
and provincial corner
cupboards the hinges
are on the outside
of the doors.

BEWARE
Look out for
marriages, where
tops and bottoms
do not belong
together. Also,
some hanging
corner cupboards
may simply be
the top halves of
standing corner
cupboards.

DISPLAY CABINETS

A display cabinet is actually a vitrine; in other words, a cupboard with large glazed panels. Even though today they are often described as display cabinets, it seems likely that cabinets made in the 18th century were originally intended as bookcases. The fact that they were made for books is one reason why the shelves on even the most sophisticated Georgian cabinets do not necessarily line up with the glazing bars. Cabinets that were designed specifically for displaying objects only became common in the latter part of the 19th century.

▼ INLAYS

The satinwood and tulipwood crossbanding on this display cabinet is often thought to be a later feature, but it was extremely popular on provincial pieces that were made in Scotland and in the north of England c.1800.

£4,500–6,000

▲ DATING

The distinct contrast in graining and colour between the top and the base of this walnut-veneered cabinet points to the fact that they did not start life together. The top has simple, heavy glazing bars, typical of the early 18th century, and it probably came from a bureau or cabinet. The serpentine drawers, in contrast, would have been extremely rare at this date. The idealized Queen Anne-style stand was made during the 1920s.

£800–1,200

BEWARE

Many continental and 20th-century English display cabinets include panels of serpentine glass: make sure before you buy one that none of the glass panels is chipped – they can be very expensive to replace.

▶ MIRRORS

Mirror backs became popular features on display cabinets made from c.1850 onwards because they enabled you to see both sides of the objects that were being displayed; they also increased the light in the room. The thin legs, moulding and stringing, and the exaggerated swan-neck crest on this cabinet, which was produced c.1900, are weakened versions of late 18th-century styles.
£700–1,000

▲ ART NOUVEAU CABINETS

Probably called 'Queen Anne' by its retailer, cabinets of this type were mass produced in the 1920s; they are becoming difficult to find in good original condition, however, and are probably sound investments for the future. The dramatic black roses are typical of the Art Nouveau style that waned just before World War I.
£500–800

▼ ART DECO CABINETS

This walnut cabinet, made c.1930, is based on the radios of that period; it was designed by the Gordon Russell Workshops. A cabinet such as this would give an instant sense of the Art Deco period to any room. It would be good value at between £400 and £500.

CUPBOARDS & WARDROBES

The late 20th-century passion for fitted furniture has caused a fall in demand for antique wardrobes and cupboards. As a result, they often cost much less than their built-in modern equivalents – and you can take them with you when you move. Apart from being practical for storage, old wardrobes, especially those from continental Europe, are often extremely handsome pieces of furniture.

By the end of the 19th century, wardrobes tended to be made as parts of bedroom suites, not as individual pieces. The old "clothes presses" were, by then, being used to store linen rather than clothing.

▼ WARDROBES
This classic mahogany wardrobe, made c.1780, would be a decorative and practical addition to any bedroom. Inside there are sliding trays above drawers, and a hanging space on each side. With wardrobes of this kind, the internal fittings have often been altered or removed, but, as long as this has been done in a sympathetic manner, the change should not greatly affect the value of the furniture.
£3,000–4,000

▲ FRENCH ARMOIRES
This oak and chestnut armoire, made c.1780, dates from the reign of Louis XVI. The long outset brass hinges and cockerel-head escutcheons are typical of the stylish metalware to be found on French furniture. The rococo carving also makes this a very attractive piece and it is worth around £3,000. A less elaborate version could be found for around £1,000.

BEWARE
• Some bookcases are wardrobes on which the solid doors have been replaced with glazed ones. This is acceptable if the piece is correctly described and priced fairly.
• When the popularity of the clothes press waned in the early 20th century, many had their tops cut off and discarded; the bottoms were converted into oddly proportioned chests of drawers.

► **CLOTHES PRESSES**
The word "press" in this sense means a cupboard with shelves. Clothes presses with double doors, open shelves and low chests of drawers are usually made from mahogany and date from the Georgian period. This one is a provincial version made in Wales or Cheshire c.1780. In smaller country houses these cupboards were generally used to store the clothes of the whole family.
£2,000–3,000

◄ **DUTCH ARMOIRES**
Dutch armoires made in the 18th century, such as this one, made from oak c.1770, were always plain. If you find one with marquetry inlay, it is probably a modern reproduction, or it might have been "improved" in the 19th century. Reproductions fetch about £2,500; a genuine piece from the 18th century, even with later inlay, might fetch £10,000.

WHAT IS THIS?
At first glance, this cupboard looks like the base of a 1770s press cupboard. However, if you look closely you will see that the proportions are wrong. In fact, it has been made up more recently from old bits of 18th-century wood to act as a video or TV cabinet. While it might be practical, it is not a piece that will increase in value.
£300–400

SIDEBOARDS & DINING ACCESSORIES

Even after you have chosen your table and chairs, no matter what your preferred style, there's a wealth of other antique accessories available for the dining room.

Large pieces, such as serving tables and sideboards, became extremely elegant and sophisticated during the 18th century, and many are now very expensive. Much more reasonably priced are the wealth of 19th-century sideboards available; and surprisingly the largest examples are often also the most affordable.

You can also find an extraordinary array of smaller dining room accessories, such as wine coolers, urns, knife boxes, cellarets and dumb waiters. Most were originally made with a very specific function in mind but can nevertheless be surprisingly versatile. These days wine coolers are more often used as containers for flowers than for wine, but they are still highly collectable.

▲ URNS
You might think that these attractive urns are purely decorative; in fact they open up and some were fitted out to hold knives, while others have spouts for iced drinking water. Pairs of Georgian urns are especially desirable. These ones were made c.1775 and would cost around £5,000–7,000.

18TH-CENTURY SIDEBOARDS
Check the legs haven't been altered; turned legs on 19th-century sideboards are sometimes replaced with 18th-century-style tapered ones to make a piece seem older – and more valuable.
£3,000–5,000

◄ CELLARETS
Most 18th-century sideboards, such as this, made c.1790, have a cellaret – a deep lead-lined draw, designed to hold bottles of wine for short periods before they were served.

◀ LATER SIDEBOARDS
Provided you have the room, you can still find some larger 19th-century sideboards in reasonable condition for £1,000–1,500; this one dates from c.1815, and would be worth £2,500–3,500.

HOW OLD IS IT?
This Gothic Chippendale-style side table might look 18th century but in fact was made c.1910. One telltale sign is the dull flat sheen of the wood – an older piece would have a mellow glowing patina. £1,500–3,000

CELLARET OR WINE COOLER?
Wine coolers were used for cooling bottles in ice before their contents were drunk. They rarely have lids and may have a plug in the base. Lidded containers for storing wine, such as this, are properly described as cellarets, but the terms overlap. £1,500+

▶ Wine coolers and cellarets can usually be dated from their style.

c.1760

c.1790

c.1770

c.1815

DESKS & BUREAUX

There are many different types of "writing furniture", but perhaps the best known is the bureau, basically a desk with a hinged flat that folds up when not in use. Made in quantity from the 18th century, bureaux are generally oak, walnut or mahogany, sometimes lavishly decorated with lacquer or marquetry. They were often combined with bookcases and cabinets to become bureau bookcases or bureau cabinets. Like ordinary cabinets, these were as much to display the wealth of their owner as for any practical purpose. Many bureaux have a strong architectural feel and were designed to co-ordinate with the architecture of the room in which they stood. Other forms of writing furniture included writing tables, kneehole desks and the curiously shaped davenport.

▼ 18TH-CENTURY BUREAUX

This early 18th-century bureau has many typical features which you should look for:

- small size – those wider than 42in/107cm are less desirable
- attractive walnut veneers
- bun feet, although most are replacements.

Circular saw marks in the baseboard (below) show that a bureau originally had bracket feet (even if it now has bun feet).
£3,000–6,000

LACQUER & JAPANNING

Chinese and Japanese lacquer became popular in the 17th century, and soon English cabinet-makers began to produce their own "Oriental"-style lacquer called japanning. Black was the most common colour; red, as on this desk, is much rarer.

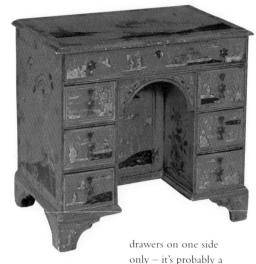

▲ KNEEHOLE DESKS

Kneehole desks are sometimes converted from chests of drawers, so check that the drawers look complete and that veneers match. Avoid a desk with drawers on one side only – it's probably a converted washstand!

- Most desks are made from walnut, mahogany or pine. The wood of this one is covered with red japanning which means that it is worth £10,000+

DATING
Pediments can help with dating

Double dome top
1690–1720

Broken pediment
1730–1800

American
bonnet top
1730–1760

Swan-neck
pediment
1760–1810

Regency top
1800–1830

Moulded dentil
1780–1810

▼ DAVENPORTS
There are two main types of davenport. Early ones were quite plain and had an upper section which pulled forward to provide the writing surface. By c.1840 many had the desirable "piano-rise' top (which opens like a piano) and a recess case, like the one shown here. Expect to pay more for good-quality woods, like satinwood, rosewood, or the burr walnut of this piece which is worth about £3,000–4,500.

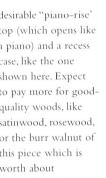

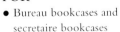

WHAT TO LOOK FOR
- Bureau bookcases and secretaire bookcases
- Bookcases should be slightly smaller than their base, but made of matching wood.
- **Beware** of bases and tops which are flush sided – they could be a marriage or cut-down library bookcase.

▲ SECRETAIRE BOOKCASES
The secretaire bookcase first became popular in the late 18th century. When the deep top drawer is open the front "drops" to form the writing surface. The fine-quality interior of this piece will be reflected in the price – about £15,000 – a lesser one might be as little as £1,500.

PEDESTAL DESKS

The English pedestal desk, still a popular type of office furniture, was introduced in the 1670s. Georgian and Regency pedestal desks with leather-lined tops and well-figured veneers offer elegance and utility. Some were designed to be free standing and have drawers on one side and cabinets on the other; some are known as partners' desks and can be used by two people at the same time. Partners' desks usually have drawers on both sides of the frieze, and their pedestals have drawers on one side and cupboards on the other. The cupboards sometimes have dummy drawer fronts.

◄ KNEE-HOLE DESKS
Small desks such as this one, made from mahogany c.1800, are sometimes called knee-hole desks. This one is a partners' desk because the opposite side has cupboards and drawers. £3,000–4,000

▼ SERPENTINE DESKS
This is a late Victorian copy of the grandest form of 1740s Georgian partners' desk. The serpentine-shaped top raises the value to between £20,000 and £25,000. If it was a Georgian piece, it could make £100,000 or more.

CONSTRUCTION
The back of a pedestal desk was either plainly veneered, so that it could stand by a window, or, if it was to stand against a wall, left unfinished.

◀ GILLOW DESKS

The Victorians "improved" the simple Georgian pedestal design by adding a gallery and banks of drawers on top, and an upholstered footrest in the space between the pedestals. This fine-quality desk was made by Gillow of Lancaster c.1870. Typically, the central drawer is stamped with the firm's name.
£2,500–4,000

▼ KIDNEY-SHAPED DESKS

The kidney form was and still is a popular shape usually seen on small drawing-room pieces. This late Victorian example, constructed c.1900, is made of mahogany decorated with engraved boxwood inlay.
£4,000–5,000

QUALITY FEATURES

- Metal mounts or carved decoration.
- Good-quality locks – perhaps marked by the locksmith.
- Desirable shapes: serpentine or kidney.

PINE KITCHEN FURNITURE I

From the late 18th century onwards, pine was either used for the backs, carcasses and drawer linings of pieces veneered with more expensive timbers, or for cheaper furniture that was then painted.

Much early pine kitchen furniture was actually built into a room. As the fashion for stripped pine grew in the 1960s, many pieces were removed from their original locations and converted into free-standing pieces.

It is rare to find a piece of pine furniture in its original condition; most has been adapted, stripped or converted to suit modern tastes. These pieces, however, can be just as valuable. Watch out for pine furniture that is made from old floorboards; it is worth buying, but do not pay the price of a genuine antique.

▶ DRESSERS

Made of 19th-century pine, this high dresser has been adapted to 20th-century use. The classical upper part of the dresser with its heavy pilasters is not reflected in the base, which is simpler in style. The eight-bottle wine-rack is a modern idea – an addition that would not be seen on early pieces.
£2,000–2,500

◀ SIDE CABINETS

This quirky side cabinet, made c.1900, could be mistaken for a table with cupboard doors added. Although the wood is rather stark and newly stripped, this is a utilitarian piece that with use and polish would develop patina and hold its value.
£300–400

► **FRENCH STYLE**
This side cabinet, with
its elegantly panelled
cupboard door, is
reminiscent of French
provincial furniture.
Made c.1900, there
would probably have
been a deep plinth
running around the
base. The feet look
as if they are fairly
recent additions.
£300–400

◄ **SIDE TABLES**
Made during the last
twenty years of the
19th century, this table
would fit comfortably
into a sitting-room,
bedroom or kitchen.
The drawer handles are
later additions; turned
wooden handles might
be more in keeping
with the piece's style.
£250–350

► **SMALLER PIECES**
As the fashion for
country-style kitchens
has grown, small pine
"kitchenware" has
become increasingly
difficult to find.
This washboard is
inexpensively made
with a rudimentary
frame and ribbed glass.
£50–75

**WHAT TO
LOOK FOR**
Other small kitchen pieces
you might find include:
● meat safes;
● plate racks;
● clothes airers;
● spoon racks.
Beware: plate racks and
airers are in short supply
and reproductions have
been made.

PINE KITCHEN FURNITURE II

As with the pieces featured here, most pine furniture that you see today has been stripped of its original finish, although nearly all pine furniture was painted when first made. The techniques for decorating pine were often inventive and included scumble (softening the painted finish by applying an opaque top coat of a different shade), *faux* marbling, and graining to simulate expensive woods. In recent years there has been increased demand for old pine with its original painted finish and such pieces command a premium.

◀ SETS OF CHAIRS
This armchair, made during the mid-19th century, would be desirable on its own, but even more so if it was part of a set. Individually, this chair would be worth £300 to £400, while a set of six chairs and two matching armchairs could fetch between £3,000 and £4,000.

▶ LADDER-BACKS
Rush-seated ladder-backs such as this one are another popular style of pine kitchen chair. A single chair is of relatively little value (it would sell for around £50), but as part of a set of six or more the same chair might be worth twice as much.

▲ HIGH-BACK CHAIRS
This is the most common style of high-back pine arm chair, constructed with a shaped, flat-slatted back and turned legs and stretchers.
£300–400

◀ **EXTENDING TABLES**
On late Victorian and Edwardian extending tables such as this, the winding mechanism is usually reliable. Make sure that the leaves are original by comparing the colour and grain of the wood. Tables of this design are likely to be found in a more sophisticated walnut or mahogany. Pieces in these woods will cost 50 per cent more than those made in pine. £1,000–1,500

▼ **KITCHEN TABLES**
Before buying a plank-top table try sitting at it first. A table with a deep frieze, such as this one, made c.1900, can be uncomfortable if it has been reduced in height, particularly if you are a tall person. About 30 in (76cm) will be high enough to suit most people. £1,000–2,000

BEWARE
Check the joints of stripped pine furniture very carefully for strength and firmness; if the piece has been stripped in an acid bath, any glued joints may be seriously weakened.

MISCELLANEOUS FURNITURE

Antique furniture is not confined solely to the main types covered on the previous pages. There is also an extensive array of other interesting and attractive pieces, which, although they do not fall into any particular category, are nonetheless extremely popular with antiques collectors.

▶ MIRRORS

Don't confuse carved giltwood mirrors, such as this one, made c.1750, with later gilded composition ones. If you can see a cement-like substance over a wire frame on any undecorated areas, rather than wood, it is a composition mirror – and it will therefore be worth only a fraction of this giltwood mirror's £3,000+ price.

▲ OAK COFFERS

You can still find plain 17th- and 18th-century coffers for a few hundred pounds. Original carving, as seen here, adds to value; but be suspicious of any carving that seems unusually regular and stiff – it could well have been added in the 19th century.
£1,000–3,000

◀ FIRE SCREENS

Because many 17th- and 18th-century ladies' cosmetics were made with wax, fire screens, such as this short pole screen with a tapestry panel, were developed to provide essential protection from roaring fires, and stop their make-up melting and dripping down their faces! £500+

◀ BEDS

Nothing can give a more sumptuous look to a bedroom than an antique bed, but before you buy one remember they are often smaller than modern beds so you may need to have a mattress specially made. Nearly all four-poster (tester) beds have been changed in some way. Many are composites from different periods. This one has panels dating from c.1600 combined with later additions. £5,000

▼ STOOLS

Although the stool is the simplest type of seat furniture, don't expect to find them all at rock-bottom prices – they can be surprisingly valuable.

This pair of French mid-18th century X-frame stools would be worth over £3,000 – but you could well find a Victorian or Edwardian stool for much less.

▲ COMMODES

Originally dubbed "night tables" during the prudish Victorian era, cupboards for chamberpots were renamed "commodes" – the name has stayed the same ever since. £850–2,500

GARDEN FURNITURE I

Eighteenth-century paintings sometimes show ladies and gentlemen outside with what would appear to be Georgian garden furniture. In fact, in the days of servants there was probably little difference between the furniture made for indoor use and that made for outdoor use. Purpose-built garden furniture was made, for the most part, from the Victorian era onwards as conservatories became increasingly popular.

Garden furniture changed dramatically after the improvement of iron casting, which was pioneered by the Coalbrookdale Iron Company in the 1840s. Garden furniture is very popular, and as values have risen, it has increasingly fallen prey to thieves.

COALBROOKDALE

Coalbrookdale of Ironbridge, Shropshire, the leading manufacturers in Britain of cast-iron garden furniture in the 19th century, made a popular range of ornately cast benches, tables and chairs. Many of the designs popularized at the Great Exhibition of 1851 were based on naturalistic forms such as nasturtiums, ivy, horse-chestnut leaves, ferns and oak leaves.

▲ RARITY

Coalbrookdale seats were listed in the company's catalogue and certain designs are less common and therefore more valuable than others. This Medallion pattern seat, produced c.1870, is one of the rarer examples. Original paint is almost impossible to find, but should always be kept if in acceptable condition.
£7,000–8,000

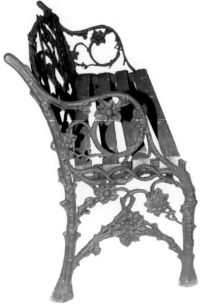

◀ SEATS

Cast-iron seating was fitted with metal, pine or oak slatted seats. This passion-flower cast-iron bench by Haywood of Derby, made c.1860, has had its slats replaced. This is a fairly common alteration that does not greatly affect value.
£1,500–3,000

BEWARE

The rising value of cast-iron furniture has led to many reproductions. This Gothic pattern seat, made in the 1990s, is a replica of an 1860s Coalbrookdale design. Some reproductions include the date of the "original", but seek expert advice if you are in doubt. £700–900

SIGNS OF AUTHENTICITY
● Crisp casting.
● Registration or 'kite' stamp – this may be indistinct even on a genuine piece.
● Foundry mark.

◄ WOODEN FURNITURE

This green-painted country chair dates from c.1830 and, although it is equally at home in the kitchen or the garden, it should always be stored indoors. Wooden painted furniture has little resilience to wet weather, and not much has survived. £300–400 (painted; much less if stripped)

▲ GARDEN SETS

By the early 20th century, garden furniture such as this teak 1930s set became increasingly practical, if less elaborate. This sturdy set, with its six chairs, was cleverly designed to hold a parasol; note, too, that the chairs can be tucked under the table to keep them dry in wet weather. £800–900

GARDEN FURNITURE II

The most expensive garden furniture is that made from marble or stone. Most marble furniture originated in Italy, but stone seats and benches were also carved from local materials by stonemasons throughout Europe. Coade stone, which is an early type of reconstituted stone made by a method that has been kept secret since the 18th century, is also extremely valuable. Among the more affordable garden furniture is a wide range of attractive, metal bent-wire pieces, produced in France at the beginning of the 20th century, that can often cost less than the modern equivalent. The market for 1940s metal dining tables and chairs is growing, and prices are rising.

BEWARE

Just because a piece looks weathered, it does not necessarily mean that it is old. You can achieve the moss-clad look in a matter of weeks if you paint a modern piece of stone furniture with sour milk! (Note that this will result in a decreased value.)

▲ MARBLE

Garden furniture made from Italian marble became extremely popular in the 19th century. It was bought by tourists in Italy as a souvenir and, later, as demand grew, widely exported for sale to other countries. Quality varies, and you can buy plain tables and benches for around £1,000. The attractive carving on this one raises its value.
£2,500–4,000

WHAT TO LOOK FOR

● Carrara marble statuary.
● Stone benches – these are less expensive but can be very attractive when they are weathered.
● Early types of reconstituted stone.
● Avoid modern stone or cement.

◀ **SPRUNG CHAIRS**
The flat, curving strips of metal that form the back and seat of this French chair create sprung supports that are much more comfortable to sit on than most metal seats. Made c.1900, the price of this one is reduced because it is in need of repair. In better condition it might cost half as much again. £60–80

▼ **VALUE**
A single, stylishly designed wire chair, such as this one made in France in the 1920s, would cost £30 to £40; a set of six would multiply the value and be worth between £300 and £400.

▲ **WIRE SETTEE**
This attractive and affordable French garden settee, produced c.1900, is made from industrial heavy-gauge wire, but there is a clever attention to detail in the way the tendrils weave in and out, lightening the overall effect. £300–400

▶ **CONDITION**
When you buy any type of metal furniture, make sure that the wire is strong – the welding is vulnerable to damage from rust. Metal garden furniture will last longer if you repaint it regularly and this does not reduce the value of less expensive pieces. £50–60

WICKER & BAMBOO

Wicker and bamboo are light and relatively inexpensive materials – this makes them ideal for conservatory and garden furniture that is frequently moved. Bamboo furniture with Oriental-style lacquer tops became extremely popular in the Edwardian period, and large numbers of inexpensive small tables were made in Japan for the Western market. Wicker furniture enjoyed a peak of popularity between 1920 and 1940. During this period the name Lloyd Loom became synonymous with an innovative type of wicker furniture made from twisted paper fibres that were reinforced with metal wire.

Bamboo furniture was popular during the Regency period, when it was used to furnish chinoiserie interiors. Beech was often carved in imitation of bamboo.

◀ BAMBOO TABLES
This bamboo tea table, with folding trays and lacquer top decorated in traditional colours, typifies the type of furniture made at the beginning of the 20th century. Few items of this type have survived in such good condition but, even so, it would not be very expensive. £80–120

▲ LLOYD LOOM
Lloyd Loom was the brainchild of the American Marshall B. Lloyd, who developed a method of producing furniture from bentwood frames covered in a machine-made, twisted paper fibre. Many different styles were manufactured but this design is probably the most famous. This example was manufactured c.1935 and is worth £60 to £80. Previously, wicker furniture was handmade from natural materials, such as cane and rattan, which were less robust and impossible to mass-produce.

BEWARE
Lloyd Loom furniture is simple to identify. An ordinary magnet will enable you to tell if a chair was made by Lloyd Loom or if, like this example produced during the 1930s and 1940s, it was made from bamboo. A genuine piece contains metal wires within the upright strands, and this is why a magnet will stick to it.

▶ MODERN LLOYD LOOM

Modern furniture in classic Lloyd Loom styles is being produced today, but it is usually easy to identify. This is because all Lloyd Loom was originally marked with a label that varied according to the date of manufacture; many of the pieces were also date stamped. Labels are usually attached to the frame of seating, or to the underside of items such as linen baskets and tables.

LABELS

The Lusty company secured the franchise to produce Lloyd Loom furniture in England. This label was used between 1937 and 1940.

RANGE

A huge range of general household furniture was made by Lloyd Loom, including tables, linen baskets, dressing tables, chests and small cabinets.

20TH-CENTURY DESIGNERS I

Great changes in furniture design occurred during the 20th century as new manufacturing techniques and materials were introduced. Many of the leading designers such as Marcel Breuer, Ludwig Mies van der Rohe and Le Corbusier were also established avant-garde architects. Their furniture was tailor-made for modern homes, where space was often at a premium, so folding and stacking furniture features prominently.

Much 20th-century furniture was designed to be mass-produced, rather than handmade by craftsmen in the 18th-century tradition.

Novel, inexpensive materials, such as tubular steel and moulded plywood, were used in simple and streamlined forms, with minimal surface decoration.

From the second half of the century onwards the availability of plastics and fibre-glass allowed designers to go beyond the purity and precision of the machine aesthetic and produce biomorphic shapes and organic designs – almost any concept, no matter how bizarre, could be realized. At last designers were able to break away from derivative forms and invent new styles of furniture.

◀ **CHARLES EAMES**
The American designer Charles Eames originally designed this moulded, rosewood-veneered plywood and leather-upholstered lounge chair and ottoman (designs '670' and '671') as a television chair for the playwright Billy Wilder. The set was commercially produced by the American manufacturer Herman Miller in 1956; usually upholstered in black (less often in tan and only rarely in white), it is still being reproduced today. Miller originals are worth £1,000 to £1,200; reproductions, oddly, fetch between £2,500 and £3,000.

UPHOLSTERY
- The original upholstery is always desirable – but not always practical.
- Re-upholstering carried out by the original manufacturer will not affect value and is a good selling point.
- Black or dark blue leather is usually more desirable than tan.
- White upholstery is particularly rare.

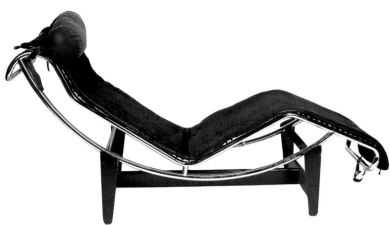

◀ **LE CORBUSIER**
The French architect
Le Corbusier designed
this tubular-steel *chaise
longue* with Pierre
Jeanneret and Charlotte
Perriand in 1928. It
was made in very
limited numbers by
Thonet Frères, Paris.
In the 1960s and 1970s
it was reissued by the
firm Cassina, and most
of those for sale today,
at £700 to £1,000,
date from this period.
New pieces by Palazetti
cost about £800.

▶ **GRAND COMFORT**
From a 1928 design by
Le Corbusier, Pierre
Jeanneret and Charlotte
Perriand, this tubular-
steel and leather chair
was originally made by
Thonet Frères and later
by Heidi Weber (1959)
and Cassina (1965). A
new version costs more
than a 1960s chair, at
£600 to £1,000.

◀ **SOFT PAD CHAIRS**
These chairs were
originally designed by
Charles Eames in
1958 as part of his
Outdoor Series.
Herman Miller
produced a version
intended for luxurious
offices in 1969; the
design is still produced.
A vintage high-back
example (right) would
sell for £600 to £900;
a side-arm chair (left) is
worth £300 to £400.

20TH-CENTURY DESIGNERS II

There seems little doubt that 20th-century furniture is one of the most promising collecting areas of the future. In recent years it has risen steadily in popularity in the UK, in continental Europe and in the USA. Auctions that are devoted to this field are now held by Phillips and Christie's South Kensington. To capitalize on this market you will need to collect with care – look out for innovative designs that are attributable to recognized designers.

Remember that designs tend to be more collectable once they have gone out of a production. If you are tempted by a design that is still being produced, always try to find a vintage example – it might be more expensive now but you will find that it turns out to be the more valuable collector's item.

There is a booming cottage industry in 1990s Britain, with many young designers and craftsmen making innovative furniture for home and international markets.

▶ **MAURICE CALKA**
The biomorphic "Boomerang Desk", by the French sculptor Maurice Calka, came in three variations; the design won the Grand Prix de Rome in 1969. The desk was one of the icons of late 1960s furniture and because it was only ever made in limited numbers it is extremely collectable.
£5,500–7,500

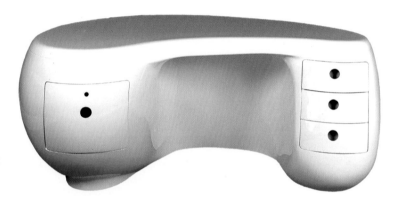

NAMES TO LOOK OUT FOR
- Alvar Aalto (Finland)
- Harry Bertoia (United States)
- Wendell Castle (United States)
- Arne Jacobsen (Denmark)
- Pierre Paulin (France)
- Ernest Race (England)
- Marcel Breuer (Germany)

◀ **VERNER PANTON**
The innovative Danish designer, Verner Panton, dreamt up this sculpture for the "What is Design" exhibition held at the Louvre, Paris, in 1969. The 12ft/364cm high "Living Tower" seat took four people: one on top, two on the projecting limbs, and one reclining on the bottom!
£3,500–5,500

◀ JASON CHAIRS

Designed by Carl Jacobs, another leading Danish designer, "Jason Chairs" were designed to stack easily and were produced commercially by Kandya Ltd in the 1950s. Most were made in naturally coloured laminated wood; the painted finish on the examples seen here is rarer.
£50–60 (each)

◀ JOE COLUMBO

Italian designer Joe Columbo's furniture is notable for its elegant use of plastics, and his designs reflect his concept of a Utopian environment. "Elda", this extravagantly upholstered lounge chair, was designed for the manufacturers Comfort in 1963.
£400–600

▼ HARP CHAIRS

20th-century designers have concentrated on seating far more than on other types of furniture; in modern homes the storage cupboards and shelving tend to be built in. The "Harp" chair is an unusual and surprisingly comfortable seat, designed by Jorgen Hovelskov of Denmark in 1958.
£200–300

▶ TULIP CHAIRS

Sculptural tulip chairs and matching tables were designed by the American designer Eero Saarinen in 1956. They were made by Knoll with moulded fibreglass seats and slender aluminium pedestal bases.
£40–50

Ceramics can be broadly divided into two main groups: pottery, which is opaque when held to the light, and porcelain, which is translucent. Within these two categories there is a huge range of different types of wares which have evolved over the centuries as new manufacturing techniques were developed.

If you're just beginning your collection the multitude of English pottery wares produced during the 19th century could be an ideal starting point. During this period factories in the Staffordshire area produced an enormous number and variety of inexpensive household and decorative objects. At the time these pieces cost a few shillings or less and they are still abundantly available and, although collectable, they have remained relatively inexpensive.

Porcelain has long been highly prized by collectors and as a result tends to be more expensive than pottery. The field is divided into two main groups: hard-paste porcelain and soft-paste porcelain. Many pieces have manufacturer's marks of some type. These can provide useful information about both origin and date, but they are no guarantee of authenticity. Many factories copied others' marks to make their products more desirable, and in China pieces were often marked with earlier dates to show respect for earlier potters.

Value is usually a matter of size, age, rarity, decorative appeal and, above all, condition. European 18th-century porcelain tends to be very highly priced but you can often buy damaged pieces for a fraction of the cost of those in perfect condition.

BASICS

When you first examine a piece of pottery or porcelain, having a basic understanding of the materials or techniques used in its manufacture can help you identify its origin, date and how much it might be worth. The three main factors to assess are:

- Material
- Glaze
- Decoration

MATERIALS

Pottery
This has a relatively coarse texture, compared with porcelain, and is usually opaque if held to the light; the two main types are earthenware and non-porous stoneware.

Earthenware
Clay fired at a temperature of less than 2200°F/1200°C is classified as earthenware. The body is porous, and may be of a white, buff, brown, red or grey colour, depending on the colour of the clay and on the iron content.

Stoneware
This is made from clay which can withstand firing at a temperature up to 2250°F/1400°C. The high firing temperature makes the

clay fuse into a non-porous body which does not absorb liquids, and may be semi-translucent. Bodies vary in colour.

Porcelain
If the material is slightly translucent the chances are it's porcelain; now you must decide which type – hard-paste or soft-paste. If the body looks smooth, like icing sugar, it's probably hard-paste, if it looks granular, like sand, it's more likely to be soft-paste.

Hard-paste porcelain

A hard-paste porcelain Meissen quatrefoil dish £4,000–5,000

All Chinese and much Continental porcelain is hard-paste, and made from kaolin (china clay) and petuntse (china stone). First the object is fired, then dipped in glaze, then refired. The china stone bonds the particles of clay together and gives translucency. The firing takes place at a very high temperature and so the finished object appears to have the consistency of glass.

The first hard-paste porcelain was made in China in the 9th century AD. In Europe the Meissen factory began producing porcelain in the early 18th century, and before long, factories throughout Europe began making hard-paste porcelain.

Soft-paste porcelain

A Chelsea soft-paste porcelain group depicting Winter and Spring
£4,000–5,000

As the name suggests, soft-paste porcelain is more vulnerable to scratching than hard-paste. There are several types of soft-paste porcelain, each using fine clay combined with different ingredients to give translucency.

Soft-paste can often be identified because the glaze sits on the surface, feeling warmer and softer to the touch

and looking less glittering in appearance than hard-paste. Chips in soft-paste look floury, like fine pastry; chips in hard-paste porcelain look glassy.

Soft-paste porcelain was first produced in Italy during the 16th century. Later factories using soft-paste include St Cloud, Chantilly, Vincennes, Sèvres, Capodimonte and Chelsea.

Bone china

This is a type of English porcelain first made c.1794 using a large proportion of bone ash added to hard-paste ingredients. This body was used by prominent English factories such as Spode, Flight & Barr, Derby, Rockingham, Coalport and Minton.

GLAZES

Glazes are used to make a porous body watertight and also to decorate a piece. They can be translucent, opaque or coloured. Hard-paste porcelain was given a feldspar glaze, which fused with the body when fired. On soft-paste porcelain the glaze tends to pool in the crevices.

A variety of different glazes were used on pottery and porcelain

and each type has its own distinctive characteristics; the main ones are:

A Dutch delftware tin glaze tortoise
£2,000–2,500

Lead glaze

A glaze used on most soft-paste porcelain, and on earthenwares such as creamware.

Tin glaze

A glaze to which tin oxide has been added to give an opaque white finish.

Salt glaze

A glassy looking glaze formed by throwing common salt into the kiln during the firing when the temperature reaches about 1800°F/1000°C.

DECORATIVE TECHNIQUES

Decoration can be added before or after glazing. Underglaze decoration means the colours have been added before glazing.

Underglaze blue

Blue pigment, known as cobalt blue, was used on Chinese blue-and-

white porcelain, European delftware, and soft-paste porcelain.

Overglaze enamels

Overglaze enamels were made by adding metallic oxide to molten glass and reducing the cooled mixture, which, when combined with an oily medium, could be painted over the glaze and fused to it by firing. The range of colours was larger than with underglaze colours

MARKS

Marks are found on the bases of many objects. The most common examples are the factory marks; the Worcester crescent or Meissen's crossed swords. The style of these marks changes periodically and can therefore help with dating. Other marks which appear refer to the individuals involved in the manufacturing. Maker's initials are fairly common, but some designers, decorators modellers and even gilders signed pieces.

● Many marks were copied or faked so marks should not be taken as a guarantee of authenticity.

CHINESE POTTERY & PORCELAIN

Mention Chinese ceramics and many people immediately think of priceless Ming and assume that this collecting area is definitely beyond their reach. In fact, because fine pottery and porcelain have been produced in China for longer than anywhere else in the world, it's not hard to find pieces that are both decorative and inexpensive – although there are of course some extremely highly-priced objects as well.

The Chinese discovered the art of making porcelain in the Tang Dynasty, AD 618–906. When Dutch traders began importing

Chinese porcelain to Europe in the 17th century (the late Ming period), no European maker had yet been able to produce such fine-quality wares and there was a huge demand for Chinese porcelain – as well as a scramble to find out how it was made (see p104). Nearly all porcelain was blue and white until c.1700, when more varied colour schemes such as *famille rose* and *famille verte* appeared. The many objects made for the European market, often using Western shapes but decorated with traditional Chinese designs, are known collectively as "export wares".

LATER CHINESE DYNASTIES

Wei	386–557	Sung	960–1280
Sui	589–617	Chin	1115–1260
Tang	618–906	Yuan	1280–1368
5 Dyn–		Ming	1368–1644
asties	907–960	Qing	1644–1916
Liao	907–1125		

MING
Value depends on quality and condition. Provincial export pieces of lesser quality, or slightly chipped or cracked wares, can be surprisingly affordable. This bowl would be worth over £100,000 but you can find pieces from about £100.

BEWARE
Don't rely on dynasty reign marks alone for dating Chinese porcelain – as many as 80% are retrospective, and were simply used to show respect for earlier classical wares.

MING OR QING?
Ming patterns were often repeated during the Qing period; Ming pieces can be identified by:
- thick bluish glaze, suffused with bubbles
- tendency to reddish oxidization
- knife marks on the tallish foot-rim.

▲ BLUE AND WHITE

Chinese blue and white was made by painting the blue decoration onto the porcelain base, before glazing – a technique known as "underglaze blue". Later wares, such as these Qing export vases (worth £8,000–10,000) can be identified by:

- complicated designs
- harder, more evenly applied blue
- thinner glaze.

▲ FAMILLE VERTE

Famille verte ("green family") porcelain is dominated by a brilliant green colour, overglaze blue and raised enamelling. It was used to decorate export wares from the Kangxi period (1662–1722). £5,000–6,000

▲ FAMILLE ROSE

Wares decorated with opaque pink enamel are termed *famille rose* ("pink family") and appeared c.1718. The style was often copied in the 19th century particularly by the French maker Samson: crackling (a fine network of cracks in the enamel colours) is a good sign the piece is authentic. £500–800

SYMBOLS

The decoration on Chinese ceramics usually has symbolic significance:

Dragons represent authority, strength, wisdom, and the Emperor.

Pairs of ducks symbolize marital bliss.

The peony shows love, beauty, happiness and honour.

The pine, *prunus* and bamboo together denote spiritual harmony.

Cranes show longevity, and were traditionally a form of transport for Immortals.

JAPANESE POTTERY & PORCELAIN

Japanese ceramics have long been among the most sought after of all Oriental works of art. Although their wares often reflect the influence of Chinese styles, Japanese potters developed their own distinctive colour schemes and patterns. According to legend, the first Japanese porcelain was made in 1616, in the town of Arita, some years after it was first made in nearby China. The wares you are most likely to come across are Arita, Imari, Kakiemon and Satsuma. Not all of these cost a fortune – you can still find pieces for a few hundred pounds or less. Decoration can affect value dramatically. The plate below is worth over £12,000 because it is decorated with the cipher of the Dutch East India Company. Without this mark it would only be worth £1,500–2,000.

JAPANESE OR CHINESE?

Japanese blue-and-white wares, such as this c.1690 Arita export dish, have three distinctive features:

- granular porcelain material
- extremely dark (as here) or very soft underglaze blue
- three or possibly more spur marks, on the underside of the piece. £12,000–15,000

◀ ARITA WARES

Arita porcelain is named after the town of Arita, where Japanese porcelain production was concentrated. Although Arita, Imari and Kakiemon were all made in the same kilns, the term "Arita" usually only describes the blue-and-white wares produced.

▲ KAKIEMON WARES

Named after the man who is said to have invented coloured enamelling in Japan, you can identify Kakiemon wares, such as this dish, by their often geometric shape, white ground, high quality, often sparse, asymmetric, painted decoration, and a predominance of reds and sky blues. £10,000–12,000

▶ SATSUMA WARES

Satsuma wares are recognizable by their cream-coloured ground, lavish gold decoration, and finely crazed glaze. Prices vary widely – quality pieces may fetch tens of thousands, but you can sometimes find a single mid-19th century or later piece for as little as £100. This 19th-century vase is one of a signed pair worth £3,000–5,000.

IMARI

Of all the types of Japanese ceramics, Imari (named after the port though which they were shipped to Europe) are the ones you see most frequently. This large late 17th-century vase has many of the features characteristic of Imari wares.
£7,000–10,000

REMEMBER...

Remove loose lids from jars before you pick them up to examine them.

MANUFACTURE

Imari pieces were usually painted with dark underglaze blue decoration (see p105), glazed and fired, then enamelled with colours, gilded and fired again.

DECORATION

Floral designs or landscapes are usually set in shaped panels against the underglaze blue. Some pieces have figural knobs.

COLOURS

Colours typical of Imari are dark blue, iron-red and gilding, with an outline of black. The touches of green on this vase indicate its high quality.

CONDITION

Condition is crucial to value. However, damage can usually be restored and buying a slightly damaged piece can be an affordable starting point if you are on a limited budget.

TYPES

Large display wares such as this vase, which is designed to stand on a mantelpiece, are keenly sought after. Pieces in pairs and sets of three (called garnitures) in particular always command premium prices.

FAKES AND COPIES

Chinese potters made imitation Imari from the early 18th century and, later, European versions were made in Holland, Germany, Venice and Britain. These copies are valuable in their own right. Modern copies, like this Korean vase, may be expensive but have little status as collectables.

CHINESE STONEWARES

Stoneware is made by firing clay at very high temperatures (2,500°F/1,400°C and above) during which process part of the clay melts and hardens creating a robust, water-tight and often slightly translucent body. Stoneware began to be produced in China in the Shang dynasty (1700–1027 BC) and by the Han dynasty (206 BC–AD 220) had become refined enough to be considered more than just a utilitarian material. A range of small objects for the educated élite, such as water-droppers (used in calligraphy), oil lamps and vases, began to be made, often in the form of animals like frogs and rams. These pieces were often decorated using a roulette wheel with incised or carved repeating patterns.

Celadon, the most famous type of Chinese stoneware, was produced in two main centres. A distinctive olive-green coloured celadon was produced in the north-west region of China in Henan and Shaanxi during the Song dynasty (960–1279). After this time the southern celadons of Longquan (in Zhejiang) became the main centres of production and wares were made in a soft blue-green colour.

Among the other important types of stoneware made in China was Cizhou ware, which was produced mainly in the northern provinces of Henan, Hebei and Shaanxi. Pieces are often highly decorative, characteristically adorned with painted, incised or punched designs which proved to be inspirational in the 20th century for modern studio potters such as Bernard Leach. Jun wares are another highly sought-after type of Chinese stoneware. Produced in Linru, central Henan, these pieces were typically heavily potted and thickly glazed in various shades of blue, sometimes with splashes of purple and, more rarely, celadon-like green.

Although larger examples of Chinese stoneware are keenly collected and often attract very high prices, small, less rare items such as teabowls are readily available for modest sums and can form an interesting and visually appealing collection.

◄ YUE WARE
This oval jar dates from AD 265–317 and was probably inspired by metal vessels. It is typically glazed in an olive-green colour; often (as pictured here) the glaze does not cover the entire outer surface and where the base has been left exposed the body has fired to a reddish colour in the kiln. £1,500–2,500

▶ NORTHERN CELADON
Bowls are the most commonly seen examples of northern Chinese celadon, and this one (12thC) is of typical conical form with an olive-green glaze and moulded floral decoration. If the decoration is carved or includes figures the value increases. £1,500–2,000

◄ JUN WARE

This small shallow dish (12th–13thC) is one of the most common Jun shapes. Pieces such as this were fairly robustly potted, with a thick wedge-shaped footrim measuring about ¼in/0.5cm across. Colours range from this pale lavender glaze, to a greener blue and dark blue and purple. The glaze was generously applied and dribbles on the underside are also typical of this type of ware. £1,500–2,000

► BLACKWARE TEABOWLS

This late Song teabowl made in the Fujian province has a typical form with a shallow ridge beneath the rim so it could be easily held. Bowls like this were first used in monasteries by Buddhist monks who introduced tea drinking to China. Glazes on blackware vary from black to this streaked dark brown glaze known as "hare's fur". £1,500–2,000

◄ STEM BOWLS

Stem bowls were used for ritual purposes and the earliest date from the Tang dynasty. This 15th-century Longquan example is typically coated in a thick glaze that softens the contours of the body, although around the rim you can just see the white body where the glaze has run during firing. £1,500–2,000

BEWARE

Celadon has long been coveted by collectors and has never really been out of production. Modern imitations of southern celadon pieces are in most respects, apart from their slightly mechanical and glassy appearance, very similar to the originals.

EARLY ENGLISH POTTERY

Love it or hate it – the naivety of early English pottery leaves few indifferent to its charms and there are enough smitten collectors to make the rarest pieces extremely valuable. During the late 17th and early 18th centuries English pottery underwent a period of rapid development and an enormously varied range of new wares and decorative techniques were developed. Pottery is categorized by the type of material from which the body is made

	SLIPWARE	ENGLISH DELFT	SALT-GLAZED STONEWARE
	c.1720 SLIPWARE BAKING DISH £12,000–15,000	c.1730 BLUE DASH CHARGER £12,000–15,000	18thC TWO-HANDLED CUP £1,500–2,000
HOW, WHEN & WHERE	Made from red or buff earthenware, decorated with white or coloured slip (diluted clay). Zig-zag, feathered and marble designs predominate. Produced in Staffordshire, Wrotham in Kent, Bideford, Barnstaple, Wales, Wiltshire and Sussex. Dates from the 17th to mid-18thC.	Made from tin-glazed earthenware in Southwark, Lambeth, Bristol and Liverpool. Primitive designs of figures, animals and floral subjects mainly painted in blue, white, yellow, green and manganese. Known as "delftware" from Georgian times. Dates from mid-16th to late-18thC.	White Devon clay and powdered flint added to earthenware to make light-weight white wares; salt thrown in kiln during firing formed glaze pitted like an orange skin. After c.1745 more use of *famille rose* type enamel colours to imitate Chinese porcelain. Made in Staffordshire, from mid-18thC.
WHAT TO LOOK FOR	Dishes and mugs. Named or dated wares, especially those of best-known maker Thomas Toft, who occasionally signed his wares on the front – no marks usually. Beware of skilful fakes.	Blue-dash chargers – (plates with blue strokes around the edge as in the illustration; often decorated with monarchs); barbers' bowls, pill slabs, flower bricks. Chips are acceptable. Not marked.	Figures and pew groups (very rare), loving cups, mugs, plates, jugs formed as owls, unusually shaped teapots (camels, houses). Usually no marks.

(such as earthenware, stoneware, creamware) and the type of glaze used (such as tin glaze or salt glaze). If you are thinking of collecting early English pottery it's a good idea to learn the difference between some of the most important, and most common, categories. Below are six types of pottery made before c.1770, as well as pointers on what pieces you can expect to see and which are most sought after.

WHIELDON	AGATEWARE	CREAMWARE	
MID-18thC PUG £3,500–4,500	c.1745 AGATEWARE CAT £2,500–3,500	EARLY CREAMWARE TEAPOT c.1760 £1,500–2,500	
Mid-18thC Staffordshire potter, Thomas Whieldon, developed lead-glazed pottery for tablewares and figures; colours were limited to olive-green, brown, grey and blue.	Layers of differently coloured clays rolled together, sliced to build up mingled layers resembling agate and moulded into wares. Lead and salt glaze were variously used; made in Staffordshire during the 18thC.	Coloured earthenware with transparent lead glaze, developed by Wedgwood in the 1760s, also made in other Staffordshire potteries and in Leeds, Bristol, Liverpool, Swansea and Derby. May be enamelled, plain or pierced.	HOW, WHEN & WHERE
Well-modelled animals like this dog; unusually shaped wares, candlestick figures, cow creamers, cottages with figures. Tablewares are less expensive. Never marked.	Cats, as shown, teawares, jugs, coffee and chocolate pots, shell-shaped wares – inspired by contemporary silver; pieces with more than two differently coloured clays. Never marked.	Red and black enamelling by Robinson & Rhodes; wares marked "Wedgwood"; pierced wares which may be marked "Leeds Pottery". Moulded pieces such as cruets and centrepieces. Few creamwares are marked.	WHAT TO LOOK FOR

SLIPWARE

Slipware is so called because the earthenware body was decorated with "slip": a creamy solution of different coloured clays and water. Pieces were usually dipped into white slip and then extra details were applied by trailing, dotting and combing other slips of varying russet and chocolate colours onto the surface of the body. Decorated pieces were then coated in a thick lead glaze that turned the white clay yellow when the piece was fired.

The overall effect has a primitive charm that collectors in Britain and the United States seem to find highly appealing. Early slipware, which was made from the beginning of the 17th century in Staffordshire and elsewhere in England, can fetch extremely high prices.

▶ **MAKERS**

Rare early pieces marked with the name of their makers are generally the most sought-after slipwares. This armorial charger (c.1685) is marked by William Talor. Other names to keep a lookout for include: Thomas Toft, George Talor, John Wright, John Simpson and Samuel Malkin.
£20,000–30,000

◀ **DECORATION**

This handsome large circular dish (c.1690–1710) is based on silver shapes from Holland and Germany. The simple decoration was created by dipping the piece into cream slip and then trailing and dotting the dark brown, chestnut and cream slip to form this particularly striking decorative effect.
£4,000–5,000

▶ **VALUE**

Makers of slipware did not generally mark their pieces; most names or initials refer to the owner rather than the maker. Because this posset cup, made c.1690, has been inscribed with the name of its original owner, the value is enormously boosted. Even though the piece has fairly serious damage it would still be worth £5,000–8,000

OWL JUGS

AMONG THE MOST DECORATIVE AND VALUABLE PIECES OF SLIPWARE, OWL JUGS SUCH AS THIS ONE (MADE C.1700) WERE MOST PROBABLY USED FOR DRINKING TOASTS TO WELCOME GUESTS. JUGS LIKE THIS HAVE BEEN WIDELY FAKED BUT THIS PARTICULAR EXAMPLE HAS MANY OF THE SIGNS OF AUTHENTICITY YOU SHOULD LOOK FOR ON A GENUINE PIECE.
£15,000–20,000

The glaze is beginning to break and crackle.

There are signs of wear on the studs.

The handle is irregularly shaped and heavy – a fake would probably be more even and finer.

This marbled effect, a favourite technique with slipware potters, was created by dipping the piece into brown and cream slip and then combing the two to mix them slightly.

The base is also thickly potted and uneven – again, fakes tend to be thinner and rather regular in finish.

LATER SLIPWARES

Slipware continued to be made in Britain throughout the 19th century. Affordably priced baking dishes and other utilitarian wares invariably have great charm and can form a highly decorative collection.

▶ WARES

Slipware was also popular for humble domestic wares such as this late 17th-century baluster mug. The robust form is typical of the less elaborate pieces of the time but the date adds value. Such pieces were made to be used and may be damaged – this is slightly cracked and chipped. £5,000–7,000

SALT-GLAZED STONEWARE

Salt-glazed stoneware is made by firing pottery in the kiln to a high temperature (2,500°F/1,400°C) and then throwing in salt. Sodium from the salt combines with silicates in the clay to form a glassy glaze with a distinctive granular surface – often described as looking like the skin of an orange. The technique was developed in Germany and spread to England in the late 17th century, when it was patented by John Dwight of Fulham, London. Throughout the 18th century, salt-glazed wares were made in large quantities in Nottinghamshire and Staffordshire. Teawares and tablewares were the commonest products but various decorative items were also made, including pew groups, cats and other animals. Later pieces were sometimes decorated with transfer prints. Early sculptural pieces tend to attract extremely high prices but you can find moulded plates and other smaller objects from £100. Among the more unusual forms of stoneware is agateware, in which differently coloured clays were rolled together to produce an attractive marbled effect. Popular in the 18th century, agateware was often astonishingly sharply cast and forms often reflect the shapes of silver of the same date. Pieces such as pecten shell teapots and caddies can fetch £1,000.

▶ DECORATION

Most salt glaze was finished with moulded decoration and then covered in a cream-coloured glaze. Pieces decorated with coloured enamels such as this green teapot decorated with large pink roses (c.1760) are much less common and therefore highly collectable. Other typically coloured grounds include blue and aubergine. £2,000–4,000

◀ RARITY

Although made in the 18th century at a similar date to the teapot above, this example is rather more ambitious in form and the raised moulded cartouche or decorative frame around the painted scene is a rare feature. The pink ground colour is also unusual. £4,000–6,000

▶ LOVING CUPS

Two-handled loving cups originally symbolized friendship and trust; later on they became associated with christenings and weddings. It is also possible to find three-handled cups and these are known as "tygs" This typical mid-18th century example is of the two-handled variety and is inscribed with its original owner's initials and is dated 1756. £2,000–3,000

◀ NOTTINGHAM STONEWARE

Brown stoneware was a speciality of potters in the Nottingham region during the 18th century. This pierced tankard has a double shell so it still holds liquid. £1,500–2,000

▶ SGRAFFITO DECORATION

Incised or scratched decoration, known as sgraffito, was used on stoneware from the third quarter of the 18th century. Simple foliate subjects and inscriptions typically painted in blue, as seen on this small tea caddy, are characteristic. £2,000–3,000

▲ STYLES

The influence of contemporary silver design can be seen in the form of this candlestick (c.1750); the heavily scrolled, foliate base reflects the Rococo style and the form of the piece is more ambitious than most. £1,000–1,500

WHIELDON & OTHER COLOURED LEAD-GLAZED WARES

Thomas Whieldon, one of the most famous of the early Staffordshire potters, has given his name to a type of ware decorated with distinctive mottled glazes. The effect was created using coloured lead glazes which mingled together during firing. Whieldon was probably the first potter to develop the coloured lead-glaze technique but numerous other potters in the region also made similar objects; since wares of this type are not generally marked, they are usually called "Whieldon-type". A large proportion of Whieldon ware consists of domestic items such as plates and teawares, or decorative objects such as figurative groups and animals; large hollow wares such as coffee pots are far rarer and therefore tend to command the highest prices. Plates and small jugs will cost under £1,000.

◀ DECORATION
This Whieldon-type cornucopia is typically decorated with applied moulded decoration. Cornucopias (the word means "horn of plenty") were made to attach to a wall and used to hold flowers. You also find salt-glaze versions and both types are highly sought after. £2,500–3,500

WHAT TO LOOK FOR
Several characteristic features can help the collector identify Whieldon ware:
- irregular glaze
- blurred colours that typically run together
- limited palette
- thinly potted body
- slightly iridescent surface covered with regular craquelure, a fine network of cracks running through the glaze.

▲ FRUIT AND VEGETABLES
Naturalistic moulds of cauliflowers, cabbages, lettuces, melons and, as here, pineapples were used by all the Staffordshire potters from the mid-18th century for teapots, coffee pots, tureens and various other objects; this one dates from c.1760. The Victorians later made copies of many of these shapes but they tend to be much more heavily potted and larger, and are far less desirable. £4,000–6,000

► COLOURS

The coloured glazes used for Whieldon ware are restricted to brown, green, grey, yellow and blue. In this case the plate (c.1760) is glazed in brown and green creating a distinctive blotchy "tortoiseshell" effect. £200–300

TOBY JUGS

AMONG THE AMUSING NOVELTY OBJECTS PRODUCED AFTER C.1750 IN THE STAFFORDSHIRE REGION USING COLOURED LEAD GLAZES ARE TOBY JUGS. THESE RESEMBLE A COMICAL MAN WEARING A TRICORN HAT AND WERE BASED ON HARRY ELWES, A WELL-KNOWN CHARACTER NICKNAMED TOBY PHILPOT BECAUSE OF HIS LEGENDARY CAPACITY FOR DRINK.

Toby jugs originally had a cover in the hat. Most are now missing, but an original cover can considerably increase the value of the piece.

Many different forms of toby jug were made and each is known by a special name; this is the most commonly seen "traditional" type. Other forms of the period include: the Thin Man, the Collier, the Sharp Face, Rodney's Sailor, Admiral Lord Howe, the Coachman, the Fiddler and the Stepped. £1,500–2,000

This is one of the most sought-after toby jugs – made by Ralph Wood II, the colours are well controlled and they have not drifted.

LATER TOBY JUGS

During the late 18th and early 19th centuries brightly coloured Prattware toby jugs were made – these are usually worth under £500. Numerous poor-quality copies were also produced in France and elsewhere; these are available for £100 or less.

CREAMWARE & PEARLWARE

During the 1740s a new cream-coloured earthenware with a transparent lead glaze began to make its appearance. Known as creamware, this pottery was refined enough to be considered a substitute for porcelain and from the mid-century was being produced by numerous potters in Staffordshire, Leeds, Liverpool, Bristol and Swansea. Creamware was decorated with moulded decoration, painted enamels or transfer prints and its most successful manufacturer was Josiah Wedgwood who, as a clever marketing ploy, christened his products "Queensware", ostensibly in deference to Queen Charlotte. Pearlware was a variation of creamware with a slightly blue tinge. Developed by Wedgwood in 1779 it remained popular with several manufacturers throughout much of the 19th century. A huge range of highly decorative objects was made in creamware and pearlware and these remain widely available for modest sums, although early rarities can fetch over £1,000.

▶ **PATTERNS**
Chintz patterns, as used to decorate this globular teapot, were popular decoration for creamwares made c.1770; other popular hand-painted designs include bouquets of flowers, ruined castles and picturesque cottages. £1,500–2,000

▲ **TERMINOLOGY**
There is an overlap between pearlware and Prattware. Pearlware figures in high-fired colours are often called Prattware. This figure dates from c.1820. £1,200–1,800

▶ **COMMEMORATIVES**
Creamware and pearlware decorated with transfer prints or decorated in low relief with political personalities of the day were popular from the late 18th to mid-19th century. Value depends largely on the rarity of the subject. This particular example of a commemorative plate depicts Admiral Earl Howe and dates from c.1795; it would be worth £500–700.

◄ BOTANICAL SUBJECTS

Botanical subjects enjoyed a heyday of popularity during the early 19th century; this service dates from c.1810. Most plant and flower specimens were copied from contemporary prints, and pieces such as these were made in both England and Wales. £3,000–4,000 for the set

▶ SERVICES

Vast transfer-printed services were produced in creamware by Wedgwood and other manufacturers. Compared with modern-day equivalents these can offer surprisingly good value. This extensive Wedgwood service (c.1830), transfer-printed in brown in the Indian Temple pattern, contains 93 dinner plates, 20 dessert plates, 23 soup plates and numerous serving dishes. £4,500–6,500

◄ PEARLWARE

Pearlware was used to produce a huge variety of decorative figures and novelty wares, and was left in the white or decorated with coloured enamels. Late 18th- or early 19th-century models of sheep like these were a particular favourite, as were figurative groups. £1,200–1,500 for a pair

LATER ENGLISH POTTERY

Not only is the pottery of the 19th century colourful and decorative, it can often provide you with a fascinating visual record of the major events and personalities of the Victorian age. Firms such as Pratt & Co. perfected colour transfer printing from c.1840 and pot lids, boxes, plates and other wares were decorated with images of the royal family, the Crimean War and the Great Exhibition. Royal events such as Queen Victoria's wedding, the coronation and jubilees inspired a huge number of specially decorated wares. Many of these were originally sold for a few shillings but are now avidly sought after. Other highly popular collectables from this period include Staffordshire figures, blue-and-white transfer printed wares, Wemyss ware and ironstone. If all these are too expensive, look out for 19th-century tiles – you can still find a Victorian printed version for £20–50.

▲ PRINTED BLUE-AND-WHITE POTTERY

Value depends on condition and pattern: because these three meat plates are all slightly damaged, they are moderately priced between £200–400 each. Less sought-after patterns start at around £120; the most valuable may be £2,500 or more.

◀ WEDGWOOD

Coloured objects, such as this 1780s moulded "Jasperware" vase, were made by dipping the object into slip (diluted clay). These wares were also made throughout the 19th century and later. However, the blue used in the 19th century tends to be darker while 20th-century copies are of lesser quality. £500–800.

▲ DINNER SERVICES

This Mason's Ironstone dinner service is made of a heavy earthenware substance first patented in 1813. It is usually easy to identify wares made by this factory as they're nearly always marked. The details of these marks changed over time; If the word "Improved" appears it means the piece was made after c.1840.

● Large dinner services are especially sought after and valuable. £4,000–6,000

WEMYSS WARE

Wemyss pigs such as this were made in Fife, Scotland, from 1880. There is also a wide range of Wemyss mugs, vases, jugs and jam pots, all of which have risen greatly in value recently. This pig is probably worth more than £800.

WHAT TO LOOK FOR

- good-quality painting
- tablewares with red borders – these are early
- figurative subjects – especially cockerels, cats, bees and pigs
- large pieces.

STAFFORDSHIRE FIGURES

Colourful creamware and pearlware figures, such as this spaniel, were produced on a huge scale in the late 18th century and throughout the 19th century. Some were made in Scotland and Wales but the majority came from the Staffordshire Potteries, so all examples of this type are known as Staffordshire figures;

nearly all examples are unmarked so the style of each should be carefully examined.

PAINTING

The detailed painting of the dog's face is a sign of quality and indicates an early date – later figures are more simply painted.

VALUE

Subject matter and rarity affect the price – figures of animals and royal, political and military subjects are particularly desirable. The spaniel would be worth around £1,200.

REPRODUCTION OR FAKE?

Less valuable Staffordshire figures were reproduced throughout the 20th century, often from the same moulds as genuine Victorian pieces. Even though genuine figures are often highly individual, these copies can be identified in several key ways:

Genuine

- crisp modelling
- detailed painting
- colourful decoration
- finger marks inside – from press moulding
- heavy thick walls
- erratic, widely spaced crackling in glaze
- soft gilding
- kiln grit and glaze on foot

Copy or Fake

- soft definition
- little detail
- little colour
- smooth inside – from slip casting
- thin fragile walls
- regular, exaggerated crackling in glaze
- bright gilding
- glaze wiped from foot

MAJOLICA

Inspired loosely by the Italian low reliefs of della Robbia and the old French pottery of Bernard Palissy, which enjoyed huge popularity during the 19th century, majolica ware was produced in England, Europe and America from the mid-19th century. Majolica was modelled in relief and decorated either with pigments added to the body itself or, more usually, to the glaze. Different parts of the design were painted with coloured pigments which when fired melded together with the glaze. The manufacturer's ability to control the glaze during firing was obviously critical and on poor-quality examples the colours bled together with disastrous effect. Until the 1980s majolica ware was a relatively under-valued market but a prominent exhibition brought its decorative charms to the attentions of interior decorators and prices rose dramatically as a result. At present recent market fluctuations appear to have steadied and the market for good-quality pieces seems as strong and buoyant as ever although buyers are becoming increasingly discerning.

▶ **MANUFACTURERS**
Top factories were Minton, George Jones and Wedgwood, but many other large factories turned their hand to majolica including Royal Worcester and Copeland, as did small manufacturers such as Holdcroft and Brownfield. This c.1875 humorous punchbowl supported by Mr Punch is by George Jones, one of the best 19th-century majolica manufacturers.
£3,500–4,500

◀ **DECORATIVE WARES**
Novelty domestic wares such as teapots, game tureens and, as here, strawberry sets were typical of the ornamental tablewares made in the 19th century. This double bird set is by George Jones. Majolica was also used for architectural objects such as fountains and wall tiling, jardinières and garden seats.
£2,500–3,500

▶ **VALUE**
Big names command a premium as do pieces made in America, even though their quality is inferior to English pieces of similar value. Small unusual pieces are also highly coveted by collectors – a very unusual game tureen can make £20,000 or more, although less exceptional pieces fetch under £1,000. This 1880 Minton hare and duck tureen is of a remarkable design and is worth £20,000–24,000.

▶ **FORMS**
This Wedgwood leaf pickle stand
(c.1880) combines plant forms
with majolica glazes. Small
pieces such as this are available
for modest sums. £100–150

CONDITION
Majolica is particularly prone
to chipping and flaking but
because pieces are bought
primarily for their decorative
appeal value is less
dramatically affected by
damage than for other types
of ceramics and restoration is
fairly common.

▲ **SMALLER MAKERS**
Unmarked majolica or pieces by
less well-known makers can still
attract high prices if the design
is strong. This majolica teapot
(c.1878) is by a smaller maker
but the design reflects the
influence of fashionable
Japanesque styles. £600–800

▶ **DECORATION**
High Victorian taste favoured
extraordinarily elaborate
decoration, as seen on this
typical vase of c.1890.
Although rather large it is
unmarked and would therefore
be worth far less than a piece
by Minton. £150–200

REPRODUCTIONS & FAKES
Although fakes are not a major problem some unmarked
pieces have had fake marks added with an etched "Minton"
to boost their value. Modern reproductions are usually
easily identifiable by their lighter potting and their
modelling which is less well-defined.

DOULTON

One of the most prolific and innovative manufacturers of the 19th and 20th centuries, the Doulton factory's success was largely due to the entrepreneurial spirit of Henry Doulton who took over the sole running of the company in 1854. The factory based in Lambeth, London produced utilitarian stonewares such as water filters until 1862 when decorative items, designed by students from the nearby Lambeth School of Art, began to be produced. Over the following decades Doulton established a line in decorated stonewares and employed numerous designers. In 1882

Doulton took over a second factory in Burslem, Staffordshire, where porcelain and earthenware tablewares were produced. The factory became "Royal Doulton" in 1901 and the Burslem factory is still in production although the Lambeth factory closed in 1956. Products are so diverse that collectors often concentrate on wares of a particular type, such as flambé wares, stonewares, faience wares or kingswares. Prices start at around £50 for ornamental wares; the highest prices are commanded by pieces signed by the leading artists of the day, which can fetch over £10,000.

▶ CHINÉ DECORATION
Another popular method of decoration, known as "chiné manner" was patented by Slater for Doulton's. The technique involved pressing lace on to the wet surface of the clay and finishing with hand colouring and gilding. Vast quantities of these wares were made in the late 19th and early 20th century; they remain relatively inexpensive. £50–70

▲ DECORATION
Stonewares were influenced by 16th- and 17th-century designs and often feature incised or applied and hand-carved decoration. Motifs such as beaded borders are typical characteristics as is the restrained palette in shades of blue and brown. This 1879 jug by Florence Barlow and Emma Martin is typically decorated with beaded roundels and paler scrolling foliage. £120–80

◀ HANNAH BARLOW
Deer provide a recurring decorative theme in Hannah Barlow's work, but the *pâte sur pâte* decoration on this vase (made c.1885 at the Lambeth factory) is unusual and was added by William Baron, who later set up his own pottery in Devon (see p130). £300–400

MARKS
Wares are marked with the name of the factory, impressed, printed or painted; they are also marked with the initials of the artist and the date.

DOULTON DESIGNERS

NAME	SPECIALITY	MARKS
George Tinworth	Speciality modelling, religious plaques, frog and mice groups	GT + Doulton
Hannah Barlow	Incised decoration, animal subjects	BHB + Doulton
Florence Barlow	Incised bird subjects	FEB + Doulton
Frank Butler	Bold shapes, decorated with natural forms	FAB + Doulton
Harry Nixon	Song and Chang, flambé wares	H Nixon (on side of piece generally)
Mark V Marshall	Well-modelled stoneware – worked with Martin Brothers	MVM
Eliza Simmance	High-quality Art Nouveau designs	ES

▼ SONG WARE
Inspired by Chinese ceramics Royal Doulton's Song wares came in a choice of subjects and colourways. This "Song" vase (c.1920) by Arthur Charles Eaton is painted with a typically exotic bird. £1,200–1,500

▲ MICE GROUPS
Among the most popular novelties for which George Tinworth is famed are novelty mice groups (c.1890) such as this which shows mice playing instruments. Tinworth also produced frog groups and imp musicians which are equally popular. £700–900

WEDGWOOD I

Josiah Wedgwood occupies a pivotal position in the development of ceramics. His factories at Burslem and Etruria were the first to introduce industrial production techniques to pottery. Wedgwood's name is synonymous with several different types of body such as black basalt, *rosso antico*, caneware, jasper ware, agateware and creamware (see p120), all of which became hugely fashionable and were much copied. A master self-publicist, Wedgwood made high-quality wares that achieved renown throughout England, Europe and America and his fame has endured two centuries. The factory's 20th-century products are of similarly high quality and remain keenly sought after by collectors today (see p140). Wedgwood was also the first potter to commission leading artists to create designs for his products. John Flaxman was responsible for many of the jasper ware designs of the 18th and 19th centuries. The range of Wedgwood available is so enormous that many collectors tend to concentrate on particular objects, on specific types of body or on certain designers. Early marked pieces tend to attract the highest prices.

◀ BLACK BASALT WARE
Basalt ware is among Wedgwood's most popular products, and was produced at the Etruria factory which specialized in ornamental wares. Wedgwood produced a range of library busts of both classical and contemporary figures. This portrait of Sir Walter Scott dates from the 1820s and is quite small (7–8in/18–20cm high). Some busts are of much larger proportions and were made to stand on top of library bookcases. £300–500

BEWARE
Later in the 19th century a rival factory called Wedgewood (note the additional "e") also marked its products with its name. Wares by this manufacturer are generally of inferior quality and therefore far less valuable. Wedgwood wares were also imitated on the Continent by factories such as Sèvres, but few fakes are marked.

MARKS

WEDGWOOD
wedgwood

Although early pieces were unmarked, the vast majority of wares made after 1768 were marked "Wedgwood & Bentley", Wedgwood or with initials. From 1860 a system of date coding was used.

▶ LATER WARES
During the 19th century Wedgwood continued to employ some of the leading decorators and designers of the day. This is one of a set of six plates which were painted by A. Walker. The set of plates features fish, which typifies the late 19th-century predilection for naturalistic themes. £100–200 (for a single plate)

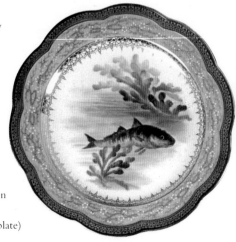

JASPER WARE

INSPIRED BY ANTIQUE CAMEOS AND ROMAN GLASS AND TOMBS, JASPER WARE WAS A FORM OF UNGLAZED STONEWARE INTRODUCED C.1767. IT BECAME ONE OF THE COMPANY'S MOST POPULAR PRODUCTS. THIS PEGASUS VASE WAS MADE IN THE 19TH CENTURY. £5,000-10,000

Many designs were based on drawings by artists of the day such as John Flaxman and inspired by antiquity. These figures illustrate domestic employment and were designed by Elizabeth, Lady Templetown.

The simple cylindrical shape is characteristic of the Neo-classical period.

Jasper ware was made in a variety of colours: green (as here), yellow, lilac, claret, black and white and most commonly blue. Early blue jasper ware was far more distinctive in colour than 20th-century versions: either a very deep purplish blue, or a strong slate blue – not the pale shade nowadays called "Wedgwood" blue.

Cutting of the applied cameo design should be crisp and very refined with a slight translucence in the shallower areas.

QUEENSWARE

Wedgwood's Queensware, a refined type of creamware (see p120), was enormously popular from c.1765 and was generally used for tea and coffee services. Its fame soon spread to Europe, where it proved equally popular and was widely copied. Queensware was named in honour of Queen Charlotte, the wife of King George III. Wares were decorated with moulded designs, transfer prints or hand-painted decoration.

▶ IMITATIONS

Wedgwood's success spawned numerous imitations. Among his copyists the most successful was Turner of Lane End; Adam and Spode also made many Wedgwood imitations. This unmarked belt buckle (late 18th- to early 19thC) may be by Wedgwood but is probably by an imitator such as Turner; if it were marked it would be worth four times as much. £200–300

DEVON POTTERIES

The discovery of deposits of high-quality red clay suitable for making fine terracotta wares together with a burgeoning tourist industry and a growing demand for souvenirs, encouraged a handful of small potteries to set up in Devon in the mid- to late 19th century. In 1869 the Watcombe Terracotta Company began producing painted wares and unglazed pieces decorated with turquoise borders and glazed interiors. The Torquay Terracotta Company made figurative subjects, painted wares and ceramics in the style of the Aesthetic movement. Another South Devon pottery was Aller Vale which made wares decorated with incised mottoes such as jugs

and teapots as well as now obsolete objects such as plaques for resting curling tongs. In North Devon near Fremington, Edwin Beer Fishley produced pottery simply decorated with coloured slips or incised designs. Another important pottery located at Barnstaple was C. H. Brannam, which became well known for its "Royal Barum" ware. The company's reputation grew in the 1880s when it began selling through Liberty & Co, London, and later pieces are in general more elaborately coloured and more varied. Decorators include James Dewdney and William Leonard Baron; the latter eventually set up his own pottery in Barnstaple too.

◀ VASES
Among the most expensive pieces of Devon pottery are those decorated in the style of the Aesthetic movement – such as this pair of vases made c.1878 by the Torquay Terracotta Company.

The vases, designed by Louis F. Day and painted by Alexander Fisher (senior) to represent "morning" and "night", are worth £2,000–3,000 but less spectacular examples sell from £100.

VALUES
Prices vary considerably but these features are desirable:
- pieces in artistic styles
- large sculptural pieces
- large slip-decorated vases.

▶ ALLER VALE
Pixies proved to be a popular motif with tourists; this late 19th-century pixie-adorned jug was made by the Aller Vale pottery, one of the most prolific of the Devon potteries that later merged with Watcombe. £80–120

► **C. H. BRANNAM**
Although the birds and floral roundels that decorate this jug (c.1910) are heavily influenced by Oriental ceramics, the use of incised decoration in conjunction with coloured slips is typical of the Brannam pottery. £150–200

▼ **SOUVENIRS**
Among the less expensive tourist souvenirs produced in the Devon studios some surprising novelty items can be found. This Baron of Barnstaple pottery bell (c.1920) is modelled in the form of a female head. It carries a rather dubious inscription – "The perfect woman speaks only when tolled." £80–120

▲ **TERRACOTTA FIGURES**
Unglazed terracotta figures were a popular product of the Watcombe and Torquay Terracotta companies in the late 19th century. This angel made by the Torquay Terracotta Company is typical of the religious subjects produced there. Portrait busts, classical subjects and figural groups were also produced. £120–180

MARKS
The marks most commonly found on Devon pottery include:
- **"Aller Vale"** impressed name or incised hand-written signature mark
- **"Torquay Terracotta Co"** initials or name in full
- **"Watcombe"** usually a printed mark.

LUSTRE

Lustre or metallic decoration, first used in European pottery probably as early as the 13th century in Spain, enjoyed a revival of interest in Britain in the 19th century. Lustre decoration was applied in a variety of ways: either limited to bands or reserves, applied all over or streaked using a "splash" technique. The Wedgwood factory introduced a mottled range called "Moonlight Lustre". Lustre was often used in combination with stencil-printed decoration and is most commonly seen adorning jugs, teapots, mugs and chamber pots. Such objects were produced in numerous potteries in Staffordshire, Sunderland, Wales and Scotland. Lustre is generally available for modest sums although the price increases if the piece is unusually large or decorated with an unusual print.

▶ COMMEMORATIVE LUSTRE

Pink lustre rims were often applied to the rims of white-bodied commemorative wares in the early 19th century. This plate (c.1816) is decorated with a print showing Princess Charlotte and her husband Prince Leopold with Goody Bewley, to whom they later presented a large copy of the Bible – the Princess's kindness was legendary and this subject was a popular one. £250–300

◀ DECORATION

Wares were frequently adorned with a combination of lustre and enamelling. The body of this 19th-century moulded Staffordshire jug is decorated with a landscape in the background, hounds and a colourful trailing vine motif, all of which are highlighted in lustre. Bands of lustre have also been applied on the inside rim, base and handle of the jug. £100–150

▶ COLOURS

Lustre colours depended on the metal oxides which were used and on the colour of body beneath. Pink or purple lustre, which has been used to decorate this chalice (c.1830), was created using a mixture of gold and copper oxides on top of a white body. If gold lustre was applied to a dark body, however, it created a rich bronze colour, while silver was made from platinum oxides. £100–150

BEWARE

Reproductions and fakes of more elaborate pieces of lustre are occasionally seen – look for signs of genuine age.

MARKS

Lustre was produced in many small potteries and few pieces are marked.

IRONSTONE

Ironstone, a type of robust earthenware still produced today, was patented in 1813 by Charles James Mason, a Staffordshire potter. "Mason's ironstone" was a spectacularly successful material for dinner services because it held the heat well and was particularly hardwearing. Mason's was taken over by Ashworth's in 1859 but continued to produce ironstone. Other factories also produced their own versions of the material to which they gave names such as granite china, opaque china and stone china.

Ironstone can form an attractive theme for a collection since pieces are usually decorated in colourful pseudo-Oriental patterns and shapes are often extremely inventive. Jugs cost from £50 while large services can fetch £1,000 or more, depending on the number of pieces.

▶ SERVICES
Typically decorated in a colourful Oriental style, this sauce tureen (with cover and stand) and side plate is part of a dinner service (c.1820) containing 95 pieces. The value of the service would be £7,000–8,000.

MARKS
Mason's ironstone has an impressed mark; changes in details can help with dating. Spode's impressed mark usually includes the words "New Stone".

◀ WARES
Apart from services, ironstone was also used for a range of items large and small, including ornamental vases, jardinières, wine coolers, jugs, teapots, miniature wares, fireplaces, garden seats and card racks such as this example, made c.1820. Rare shapes command a premium and this rack would fetch £450–550.

▶ SPODE STONE CHINA
Prior to the introduction of Mason's ironstone, Spode produced a similar material called "stone china" (c.1805). This jug (c.1820) is part of a tea and coffee set containing over 35 pieces; it is decorated with an imitation of a Chinese *famille rose* design. Other makers of similar materials are: Davenport, Minton, Wedgwood, Ridgway, E. & C. Challinor. £250–350

COMMEMORATIVE CERAMICS

Commemorative ceramics are a vast collecting area encompassing anything made to mark a particular historical event. Royal weddings and deaths, coronations, jubilees, wars, elections and strikes have all been immortalized in ceramic form and collectors tend to concentrate on a particular theme or character rather than on the subject in general. Any ceramic commemoratives that predate the coronation of Queen Victoria are rare and correspondingly valuable. Most commemoratives date from the mid-19th century onwards, when improved methods of transfer printing allowed potters to make souvenirs inexpensively.

◀ WILLIAM IV CORONATION
Transfer prints on early commemorative wares can contain fascinating historical details. This Staffordshire pottery jug (1830) is unusual in showing William at the Coronation ceremony in Westminster Abbey. £300–400

▼ MAKERS
In the 20th century vast quantities of royal souvenirs were made. Values remain low unless the piece is unusual or by top manufacturers. This Wedgwood tankard by Richard Guyatt marks the marriage of Princess Anne and Captain Mark Phillips in 1973. £30–50

▲ VALUE
Commemoratives of obscure events are less sought after than those celebrating more significant events. Huge numbers of mugs marked the Diamond Jubilee of Queen Victoria in 1897; this mug has more details than most. £60–100

▶ RECENT COMMEMORATIVES
Most commemoratives from recent decades are still available for under £10 but cartoon mugs from the wedding of Prince Charles and Lady Diana Spencer are already increasing in value. This mug was designed by Mark Boxer to commemorate the royal wedding in 1981 and has a comical handle shaped as an ear. £30–45

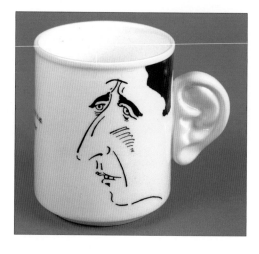

GOSS & CRESTED CHINA

Crested china was made as seaside souvenirs during the late 19th and early 20th centuries when the principal maker was W. H. Goss. Decorated with the coats of arms of the most popular holiday resorts, these pieces provided visitors with souvenirs of their stay and were made in vast quantities until c.1930 when the fashion for Goss abated. Goss pieces were invariably well made and although the Arcadian and Carlton works in England and other factories in Germany made similar crested pieces none could rival Goss for quality. The most sought-after pieces are "Goss cottages" which can fetch upwards of £200.

▶ **COTTAGES**

Goss buildings, representing the homes of national heroes such as Anne Hathaway's cottage (seen here), Lloyd George's home or Charles Dickens' house or other landmarks, can form the theme of a fascinating collection and have become extremely popular. £30–40

▼ **FIGURES**

Apart from heraldic ceramics and model buildings Goss also produced a keenly collected range of decorative figures, some based on famous sculptures such as this late 19th-century bust depicting "The Veiled Bride". £500–700

MARKS
- Genuine Goss china should have a printed mark with a hawk.
- Some crested pieces which were produced in Germany are marked "GEMMA".
- Beware of fake cottages produced with spurious hand-painted Goss marks.

WHAT TO LOOK FOR

World War I pieces from Barmouth, decorated with the flags of Britain's allies, are among the more desirable examples of crested china wares you are likely to come across. Other sought-after pieces include:
- figures
- lighthouses (and other buildings)
- animals.

SUSIE COOPER

Born in 1902, Susan Vera Cooper became one of the most influential ceramic designers of her generation, producing a wide range of commercial wares in a distinctively subtle style. After working for a while for A. E. Gray, Susie Cooper set up her own company in 1929. Early output mainly concentrated on earthenwares, often hand-painted; fine bone china began to be produced after the Second World War. In 1961 the firm of Susie Cooper merged with R. H. & S. L. Plant which in turn was taken over by Wedgwood in 1966. Wedgwood reissued some of Susie Cooper's early designs such as Pink Fern, Polka Dot and Yellow Daisy. The most sought-after pieces tend to be early hand-painted wares and lustrewares; services have also risen enormously in popularity in recent years.

◀ SHAPES
Wares are categorized according to their shape and the pattern with which they are decorated. This part-coffee set (c.1935) is in the Kestrel shape. Other popular forms include Curlew, Jay and Wren. (£350–450 for the pieces shown)

▶ DECORATION
Decoration on Susie Cooper is remarkably wide-ranging: floral designs, transfer prints, incised decoration and geometric patterns were all variously used. This pottery jug (c.1935) is carved with a charging goat, and covered in a moss green glaze. £120–180

MARKS
- Most Susie Cooper pieces are marked with a facsimile signature.
- Pieces can be dated both by mark and by serial number.
- Pieces made while Susie Cooper was working at A. E. Gray's may have both the company name and the designer's own initials.

POOLE POTTERY

Pottery has been made in the region of Poole in Dorset for centuries but the company now known as Poole Pottery was established by Jesse Carter in 1873. Among the earliest pieces it turned out were terracotta jardinières, some designed by Archibald Knox for retail through Liberty & Co, and lustrewares. Other designers who worked for Carter include James Radley Young who designed wares in an ethnic style, and Roger Fry whose designs were retailed through the Omega Workshops. In 1921 the

company took on new partners Harold and Phoebe Stabler and John Adams to form a company known as Carter, Stabler & Adams. Other important designers at Poole are Truda Sharp (later Truda Carter), who produced colourful bold geometric and floral designs, and Olive Bourne, who produced plates decorated with stylized female faces. During the 1960s and 1970s the company continued to produce highly innovative studio wares.

◀ CARTER, STABLER & ADAMS

Under the influence of the new partners a range of sculptural pieces was introduced. Figures include "The Bull" and "Picardy Peasants". This roundel of the "Piping Faun" (1914) was designed by Phoebe Stabler. £1,500–2,000

MARKS

Poole pottery is invariably marked – a wide range of marks were used. They usually include the name of the company together with the decorator's initials or pattern code.

▶ ORNAMENTAL WARES

Among the most sought-after pieces of Poole pottery are the large hand-potted ornamental wares produced in the 1920s and 1930s. This large boldly painted jar and cover is signed by Truda Carter, one of Poole's leading designers. £3,000–4,000.

▶ ARCHITECTURAL CERAMICS

Architectural ceramics are among Poole's large and varied output. This tile advertising panel from the 1920s was made for the bookseller W. H. Smith, with lettering designed by the well-known illustrator Eric Gill. £500–600

DOULTON FIGURES

Doulton figures follow a long tradition of figurative ceramics and, although a few were made at the end of the 19th century by C. J. Noke, the vast majority were produced in the Burslem factory at some time between the 1920s and the present day. Extremely popular with collectors in both Britain and the United States, Doulton figures were produced in an enormously varied range of subjects. Figures are easily identifiable thanks to the marks and names on their bases. Each bears a series number and the prefix "HN" and the factory records are also helpful as they can tell you for how long every design was produced. Pretty ladies in elegant dresses became one of the firm's specialities, as did bathing belles, figures in historic dress, animals, dancers, jesters and street vendors. Value depends on the rarity of the model and on the subject, and rare colour variations also command a premium.

▶ THE PIED PIPER

One of the more elaborately decorated Doulton figures is this "Modern Piper" (1925–38). Based on the Pied Piper of Hamelin, the piece is marked "HN 756". It commands a relatively high value which reflects the decorative appeal of the subject and the fact that the design was made for a relatively short time. £1,000–1,500

▼ RARITY

Lesley Harradine designed this rare and sought-after figure entitled "Scotties" and marked "HN 1281". It was introduced in 1928 and withdrawn in 1938. The Scottish terriers were a fashionable pet at the time; hence the subject's popularity. £1,500–2,000

◀ SUBJECTS

This naked figure entitled "The Bather" was produced in the 1920s and 1930s in several versions. In the 1930s a similar figure was also introduced, dressed in a swimming costume. The clothed figure is rare and therefore slightly more valuable than the naked one. Naked £600–800; clothed £800–1200

CHARACTER JUGS

ANOTHER OF DOULTON'S MOST SUCCESSFUL 20TH-CENTURY PRODUCTS, CHARACTER JUGS CONTINUE THE TRADITION OF THE TOBY JUGS OF THE 18TH AND 19TH CENTURIES, AND WERE PRODUCED IN HUGE QUANTITIES FROM THE LATE 1930s ONWARDS. CHARACTER JUGS WERE OFTEN MADE IN FOUR DIFFERENT SIZES RANGING FROM LARGE, SMALL, MINIATURE AND TINY.

SUBJECTS INCLUDE FAMOUS PERSONALITIES OF THE PAST AND PRESENT. DICK TURPIN, OLD KING COLE, WINSTON CHURCHILL AND FRANCIS DRAKE HAVE BEEN REPRESENTED IN THIS WAY. VALUES ARE HIGHEST FOR RARE VARIATIONS WHICH CAN FETCH £3,000 OR MORE, ALTHOUGH THE MAJORITY FALL INTO THE £100–400 PRICE RANGE AND YOU CAN FIND RECENT EXAMPLES FOR UNDER £50.

MARKS

As with figures, jugs are marked and well documented. They are invariably named on the piece and bear the full factory mark, a date showing when the design was introduced and a "D" series number.

◄ **HANDLES**
The handles of Doulton character jugs are usually modelled to reflect the subject. This "Gondolier" (1964–69) has a handle appropriately modelled as a Venetian gondola. £200–300

► **VALUE**
Rarity rather than date has the biggest impact on value. This Alfred Hitchcock character jug is fairly recent in date (1995), but is a rare variation, because the shower curtain handle (a feature from the film *Psycho*) is pink; later versions, which are far more common, have a blue curtain. £600–800

WEDGWOOD II

The tradition established by Josiah Wedgwood & Company of commissioning leading artists and illustrators to design ceramics for them was one established from the company's earliest days (see p128) and has continued unabated throughout the 20th century. As a result the company is responsible for some of the most distinctive of all British ceramic designs of the modern period. Designers include John Skeaping, Richard Guyatt, Keith Murray, Eric Ravilious, and Daisy Makeig-Jones. Twentieth-century Wedgwood has little uniformity of style and collectors tend to concentrate on the work of particular designers rather than the pottery as a whole. Value depends on the size and elaborateness of the decoration as well as on the reputation of the designer concerned.

◀ DAISY MAKEIG- JONES
One of the chief designers working for Wedgwood in the 1920s, Daisy Makeig-Jones designed the ornamental range known as "Fairyland lustre" – a variegated dark-coloured ground printed with colours and gilding depicting imaginary landscapes and fantastic figures. Although these pieces are in part mechanically produced, some of the rarer designs can attract very high prices. This vase is decorated with Woodland Bridge and Woodland Elves II patterns. Daisy Makeig-Jones also produced less elaborate, more modestly priced ranges of lustreware including "Dragon lustre" and "Butterfly lustre". £3,500–4,500

▶ ERIC RAVILIOUS
The illustrator Eric Ravilious produced a number of designs for Wedgwood in the 1930s including alphabet nursery ware, a zodiac set, a boat race cup and bowl, and a design for a commemorative tankard for the coronation of Edward VIII, which was adapted for the coronations of George VI and Elizabeth II. This nursery plate designed in 1937 is typical of his simple but effective designs. Ravilious himself was killed while working as a war artist in 1942, before many of the wares printed with his designs could be produced. £80–100

◄ **KEITH MURRAY**

Keith Murray was a prominent architect whom Wedgwood commissioned to create a range of more modern designs. Bold geometric shapes in muted shades and simple patterns are typical of his distinctive style. This bowl (c.1935) is a typically strong form with a plain off-white surface, made more stylish by the addition of a silver lustre glazed band inside the rim and on the foot. £250–300

MARKS

Works by designers are usually marked with a printed signature or the words "designed by..." plus the name and the Wedgwood mark. Letter date marks were also used; after 1929 the last two years of the date appear in full.

▶ **OTHER DESIGNERS**

A wide range of designers were employed by Wedgwood in the 20th century, and the value of their work depends on the appeal of the form. This jug (c.1910–30), designed by Alfred and Louise Powell, was made for commercial production and painted by hand. Rarely were ceramics of this type signed by the Powells. £100–120

▲ **JOHN SKEAPING**

Animals in matt glazes were the speciality of John Skeaping who produced designs in 1927 for Wedgwood for a group of ten different animals. Skeaping's subjects include deer, a polar bear, a kangaroo, a bison and monkeys in various glazes and he was paid £10 for each model. Animals are typically marked both with the designer's name and that of Wedgwood. Examples such as this sealion and calf fetch £300–400 each.

CARLTON

Carltonware was produced by the Carlton Works, based in Stoke-on-Trent. The company was founded in 1890 and renamed Carlton Ware Ltd in 1957. The pottery enjoyed a heyday of popularity during the 1920s and 1930s when it produced a huge range of decorative items and tablewares; geometric designs, moulded tablewares, novelty items and lustre decoration are particular specialities. The most desirable pieces tend to be those painted with bold abstract designs or lustre pieces decorated in Oriental style. Tablewares tend to be far less sought after than Carlton's decorative items. Prices range from £50–300 for small vessels to £1,000 and upwards for larger decorative pieces.

▶ GUINNESS ADVERTISING

Objects advertising Guinness have a cult following among collectors. Although estimated at £200–400 for the set, these 1930s toucan wall plaques sold for over £1,000. Beware – there are modern fakes of these.

▼ DESIGNS

Decorative items painted in distinctive abstract designs with bright colours are among the most highly sought after of all Carlton Ware items. This vase typifies the innovative patterns found on pieces of the 1930s; later colours tended to be more subdued. £300–400

▶ ORIENTAL DESIGNS

Lustrewares were produced in large quantities by the Carlton factory. Pieces such as this hexagonal covered vase made c.1930 reflect the influence of Oriental-style design both in their decoration and choice of shape. £200–300

MARKS

- Some early marks have the initials of Wiltshaw & Robinson as well as the name Carlton Ware.
- Designers are not generally named.

SHELLEY

First known as Wileman & Co, then as Foley, the Shelley factory is best known for the highly original Art Deco-style tablewares produced during the 1920s along with nursery wares and pieces based on Mabel Lucie Attwell figures. The most valuable pieces are Art Deco tablewares boldly painted with futuristic designs in very distinctive colour combinations. Less striking designs with floral decoration were produced during the 1930s and 1940s and these tend to be far less sought after. Shelley also produced commemorative pieces and their value depends mainly on the rarity of the design (see p134).

◀ VALUE

The streamlined geometric shape, futuristic design and bold yellow/black colour scheme combine to make this Sunray pattern part-coffee set (c.1930) extremely sought after. Wares are also categorized according to their shape. This form is known as Mode; other shapes are Eve, Vogue, Queen Anne and Regent. £300–500 (for the pieces shown)

▶ FIGURES

Shelley also produced a popular range of figurines and nursery wares, which are keenly sought after, based on the illustrations of Mabel Lucie Attwell. This group (c.1937) is known as "Our Pets" and features children with their pet rabbits. It is rare and therefore more valuable than more common subjects. £800–1,200

MARKS

Pieces are usually marked with a signature in a cartouche and serial number. Marks which include the words "Fine Bone China", date from after 1945. A serial number beginning with a 2 shows the piece was a second.

▶ LATER DESIGNS

The more elaborate designs of the 1930s and later tend to fetch considerably less than those in the Art Deco style and are still available for modest sums. This part-tea service (c.1928), attractively decorated with a landscape design, contains more than 20 individual pieces and would be worth £220–280.

WADE FIGURES

Famous for its range of endearing porcelain and cellulose nursery figures and animals, the Wade factory was founded in 1922 in Burslem, Staffordshire, by George Wade. The company also established a factory in Ireland where it made porcelain for the tourist industry and export market. Price generally depends on the rarity and popularity of the subject. The most sought-after early Disney figures of the 1930s can fetch £1,500. Pieces modelled by Faust Lang, a leading Wade modeller, are also keenly sought after and command a premium, but you will still find animals and other figures for under £1.

MARKS

Figures are not always marked and do not have serial numbers.

◀ DISNEY FIGURES

Disney figures were produced to coincide with new films and are still being produced today. This figure depicts Tramp from the film *Lady and the Tramp* and was produced between 1961 and 1965. £75–100

▼ OTHER SUBJECTS

Apart from animal figures Wade produced a wide range of other small decorative objects including models of Pearly Kings and Queens, the latter (c.1959) shown here, advertising wares, novelty egg cups, vases, money boxes, jugs and trays. Most of these are less valuable than the figures. £40–60

▲ ANIMALS

A vast range of endearing animals such as this seal were produced by Wade in the 1950s. Condition does affect value, however, so look out for small chips and imperfections which will reduce the price quite significantly. £50–100

CELLULOSE FIGURES

A range of inexpensive cellulose figures were produced by Wade in the 1930s. These are especially vulnerable to flaking paint and prices are lower than for ceramic figures from other factories.

BESWICK FIGURES

The pottery-making company founded in the late 19th century by James Beswick was taken over by his son in 1920 and sold to Royal Doulton in 1969. Since the 1920s it has established a reputation for its popular range of decorative china animals. Subjects include figurines depicting animals from Beatrix Potter and Winnie the Pooh. The firm has also produced a range of figures of animals and birds as well as low-relief wall plaques in graduated sets. Horses are a particular favourite with collectors and some figures portray named jockeys with well-known racehorses. The highest prices tend to be paid for rare popular subjects – a series of Beatrix Potter wall plaques made in 1967–69 can fetch over £1,200 each, and even figures produced in the 1980s can make over £100.

◀ DATING
Pieces can be dated from the mark and model by referring to the specialist guides on the subject listed on pp168–9. This Old English sheepdog, "The Dulux dog", was produced between 1964 and 1970. £120–150

▲ HORSES
Model horses are extremely popular with collectors and from the 1950s onwards the firm employed some highly skilled modellers to produce their designs. The Canadian Mountie on a prancing horse shown here is typically finely worked. The group was modelled by Arthur Gredington and produced between 1955 and 1976. £150–160.

▼ VALUE
Among the most sought-after Beswick figures are Beatrix Potter subjects, Alice in Wonderland figures and this set representing Snow White and the Seven Dwarfs, produced 1954–67. £1,000–1,500

EARLY ENGLISH PORCELAIN

When compared with lavishly-decorated Continental wares, early English porcelain may seem relatively unsophisticated – but to many collectors this simplicity is fundamental to its appeal.

English makers tended to be much slower than their Continental counterparts in discovering how to make porcelain. One of the first English porcelain factories – Chelsea – was established by a French silversmith, Nicholas Sprimont in c.1745, nearly half a century after porcelain had first been made in Germany and France. Wares made by Chelsea were mainly intended for the luxury end of the market and are among the most sought after of all English porcelain.

Among the other famous names which were established at the same time as Chelsea, or soon after, are Bow, Bristol, Worcester and Derby. These factories produced many different types of wares and the best way of learning how to recognize the wares of each is to study and handle as much porcelain as possible. This way you will become familiar with the styles, colours, glazes and shapes used. As with almost any type of porcelain, marks are often spurious – they can be a help but should never be relied upon.

MARKS

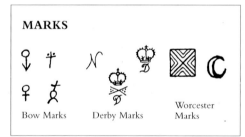

Bow Marks   Derby Marks   Worcester Marks

LOOKING AT PORCELAIN

Never pick up a piece of porcelain by the handle – it might come off. Support the main body firmly with both hands.

▲ BOW
Bow, which was the largest porcelain factory in mid-18th century Britain,

specialized in Oriental-style wares, like this tureen, which has features typical of most Bow pieces:
● white chalky paste
● greenish glassy glaze
● heavy potting.
£4,000–6,000

◀ DERBY
English figures are usually more primitively modelled than those made on the Continent and tend to be less expensive. This Derby figure is worth £800–1,200.

▶ WORCESTER
Hold a piece of Worcester up to the light and you should see a greenish tinge, perhaps with small patches of pinpricks. The moulded cabbage leaf decoration on the handle of this jug is typical of Worcester.
£1,500–2,500

CHELSEA

Chelsea botanical plates of the 1750s are called "Hans Sloane" wares because the designs were based on prints of flowers from Sir Hans Sloane's Chelsea Physic Garden.

A typical feature of Chelsea is the way the specimens are painted on a larger scale than the flowers.

Chelsea wares can be distinguished from most other botanical plates because the flowers take up almost the entire surface of the plate.

The shadows given to the insects are a device copied from Meissen and make them stand out more dramatically.

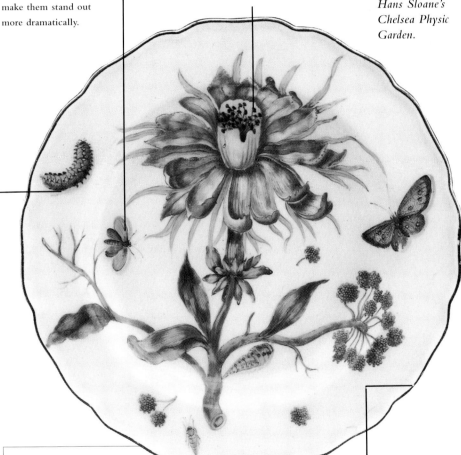

CHELSEA MARKS

Chelsea wares are divided into groups according to the four marks used during the life of the factory. This plate, marked with a red anchor, dates from c.1752–57.

  Triangle period 1745–49
Raised anchor period 1749–52
Red anchor period 1752–57
Gold anchor period 1759–69

Despite a small crack, the high-quality painting makes this one of the most valuable types of botanical plate, worth £8,000–12,000.

BEWARE

Fake red and gold anchor marks are usually much larger than the genuine examples.

OTHER ENGLISH FACTORIES

In general most minor 18th-century English porcelain factories produced useful wares, such as tea and coffee wares and dinner services, rather than purely decorative items. Blue and white was the most popular form of decoration, but some factories also used a polychrome palette based loosely on the *famille rose* of Chinese porcelain. Of the minor factories, Limehouse was the first to be established in 1745 (until 1748), followed by Vauxhall in 1751 (until 1764), Lowestoft 1757 (until 1799) and Caughley (c.1775–99). In Liverpool several factories were established; among the most important were Richard

Chaffers (1754/5–65), Samuel Gilbody (1754–61), Phillip Christian (1765–78) and Seth Pennington (1778–99). Although wares by these small manufacturers are less readily available than those by larger establishments such as Chelsea and Worcester, all are popular with collectors. Recently discovered factories such as Vauxhall and Limehouse have a particularly keen following and command a premium. Caughley, the most prolific of the minor English factories, tends to be less sought after and the factory also produced printed wares which are less valuable than some of its hand-decorated pieces.

▼ LONGTON HALL
Moulded patterns using floral and vegetable motifs were a particular speciality of the Longton Hall factory and this strawberry leaf plate,

made c.1755, is typical of the factory's output. The body is similar to Chelsea Red Anchor porcelain and there are often flaws in the glaze. £600–800

LONGTON HALL WARES
Blue-and-white tablewares, copies of Chinese *famille rose* designs, tureens and pot pourri vases are among the varied output.

▲ CAUGHLEY
A dense chinoiserie pattern is printed on this part-tea set (c.1790), a typical decorative technique for this factory. The use of gilding is also characteristic of Caughley. This is part

of a set which originally would have had tea bowls, a pot stand and possibly a spoon tray too. Caughley porcelain is made using soaprock and may have a greyish tinge. £150–200 (for 6 pieces)

► **LIVERPOOL**
This helmet-shaped sauce boat (1765–76) is attributed to Phillip Christian's factory, which produced cream jugs, sauce boats and a variety of tea and coffee wares. The decoration here is slightly awkward and the painting has overshot the moulded cartouche. The ribbed foot is seen on wares from other Liverpool factories. £500–700

◄ **LOWESTOFT FIGURES**
In general the Lowestoft factory tended to produce very few figures but dogs were more common than other subjects. These examples (1760–70) are inspired by Meissen originals. Lowestoft used a phosphatic body for its figures which often has a slightly greenish tinge. Over time, unfortunately, it suffers from brown rust-like discolouration. £2,000–3,000 each

MARKS
- **Caughley** marked with a "C" (similar to Worcester), or the word "Salopian" or "S"
- **Longton Hall** no marks used
- **Vauxhall** spurious Chinese marks are very occasionally found
- **Lowestoft** crossed swords; a crescent similar to Worcester is also used sometimes

◄ **VAUXHALL**
Vauxhall is a recently discovered factory. These bottle vases (1755) are very similar to Worcester wares but are more vibrantly coloured. Vases of this shape were particularly popular in London and were also made by the Bow factory. The shape has sagged slightly in firing, a defect characteristic of this factory.
£8,000–12,000 for a pair

19TH-CENTURY ENGLISH PORCELAIN

Various exciting new porcelain-making techniques were introduced and perfected in the 19th century. The development of bone china, which was made from the same ingredients as hard-paste porcelain (see p105) with large quantities of animal bone added, meant that less expensive porcelain became widely available.

Practical, relatively inexpensive dinner, dessert and tea services were made in large quantities, many of them embellished with printed decoration, which was also developed at this period.

You can still buy simple transfer-printed flat wares and hollow wares quite inexpensively. Some of the most affordable collectables are those made by the Goss factory during the second half of the 19th century. Statuettes and ornaments with printed decoration made by this factory are available for under £50.

BEWARE

Don't confuse hand-painting, which increases value, with hand-enamelled print (as seen on the left), which is generally less desirable. If it's hand-enamelled you will probably be able to see the transfer print underneath the enamel.

◀ ROCKINGHAM

You may think this is a strange teapot but in fact it's a violeteer – a pot to hold petals and herbs. The highly elaborate moulded and flower encrusted decoration is typical of this factory. £500–800

▲ PRINTED CHINA

Although hand-painted wares are usually more desirable than those with transfer-printed decoration, there are some exceptions. This teapot shows Queen Victoria and Prince Albert – a royal subject always pushes up the price and this would be worth £600–800.

◀ SPODE

Spode was one of the first factories to use bone china. You can recognize earlier (pre-1830) pieces by their mark, which was usually hand painted – later it was printed. Features typical of Spode porcelain are:
- pattern number in red
- very thin potting
- thin, smooth, white glaze.
  £1,200–1,800

At the other end of the spectrum, important factories such as Rockingham, Spode and Minton made a variety of highly ornamental wares, often using lavish gilding, elaborate, high-relief floral decorations and new techniques such as *pâte-sur-pâte*. Value is usually a matter of decorative appeal. Expect to pay more for hand-painted decoration. Any elaborately decorated piece will usually command a premium.

HOW TO DATE 19TH- AND 20TH-CENTURY PORCELAIN

"Royal" in trademark	after 1850
"Limited" or "Ltd" after name	after 1860
"Trade Mark"	after *c*.1870
"England" in trademark	after 1890
"Bone China"	20th century
"Made in England"	20th century

▼ MINTON

One of the most sophisticated innovations introduced by Minton during the 19th century was the technique of *pâte-sur-pâte*. This process was a laborious one which involved applying many layers of white slip (a mixture of clay and water) to a dark body which was then hand carved to expose the dark ground. The pieces were often decorated with lavish gilding and were always expensive; this *pâte-sur-pâte* vase would be worth £3,000–5,000.

◀ COALPORT

French designs of the 18th century became popular again in the 19th century. One of the most famous factories to make porcelain in the style of Sèvres was Coalport, who also copied the styles of Dresden and Meissen. This vase is particularly desirable because of its high-quality hand-painted birds. £1,200+

● Coalport is often marked AD 1750. This is the date the company was founded, not the date of production.

▶ PARIAN

Although this elegant figure looks as if it's carved from marble, it's actually made from Parian, a type of porcelain. Parian figures became popular in the mid-19th century; the best were made (and marked) by factories such as Worcester (as this one is), Copeland, Belleek or Wedgwood and are well detailed. Unmarked figures are much less valuable. £1,000

ROYAL CROWN DERBY

Two different factories flourished in Derby in the later part of the 19th century. The most important was the Derby Crown Porcelain Co Ltd, later to become Royal Crown Derby; second came the Derby King Street factory, headed by Samson Hancock. The two factories were rivals and made similar pieces mainly based on patterns and shapes made in Derby earlier in the century, which in turn were based on designs by Sèvres with coloured grounds and raised gilding. Imari wares were another particular Derby speciality and reached a peak of perfection in the 1890s–1915. After World War I production deteriorated and later pieces from the two factories are far less sought after today. Traditionally considered the poor relation of Worcester and Minton, Derby produced wares which were undervalued until relatively recently. Prices have escalated dramatically over the last few years, particularly for fine cabinet pieces with signed decoration.

◄ DECORATION
Derby porcelain is famed for its high-quality decoration and the finest Derby pieces made after 1895 were signed by the artist. This plate, made for the Duke of York's marriage in 1893, is by Derby's most famous decorator Désiré Leroy. He was a French decorator who had worked at Sèvres and was famed for his painting and gilding. £2,500–3,000

DECORATORS
Pieces by leading decorators are much sought after. Look out for:
- **William Dean** a specialist in yachts and ships
- **Désiré Leroy** the best-known of all Derby painters, who trained at Sèvres
- **Cuthbert Gresley** and **Albert Gregory** well-known flower painters (see p153).

IMARI
One of Royal Crown Derby's most successful specialities was a range of Imari-style patterns. Each pattern has its own name; this toy saucepan (c.1910) is decorated in one of the most popular patterns, the Old Witches'. Cigar pattern and King's pattern are also popular. £350–400 Miniature pieces, such as this saucepan, are among the most valuable of all Imari wares. Rare shapes, such as milk churns, flat irons and casseroles, can fetch £500–800 each.

▼ FIGURES

A wide range of popular figures, many of which were originally made in the 18th century, were produced by the King Street factory. This traditional model of the Tailor on a Goat was reissued c.1900, and is marked "SH" for Samson Hancock. £150–200

▲ FLOWER PAINTERS

This deep blue ground vase made in 1913 is typically based on 18th-century Sèvres porcelain styles; the central panel is filled with a bouquet of roses and other flowers, skillfully painted by Albert Gregory, one of the most famous flower painters at Derby. Cuthbert Gresley is also famed for his floral subjects. £800–1,000

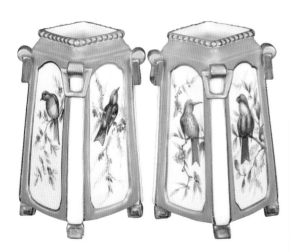

▲ CONDITION

One of these vases (made c.1880 by the Derby Crown Porcelain Co) was cracked and the gilding was slightly worn. In better condition they might fetch twice as much. £250–350

MARKS

Derby pieces are nearly always clearly marked, usually in red, with a printed crown and cipher and normally a year code; these marks are rarely faked. The King Street factory used the original Derby painted mark with the initials "SH" on each side. Sometimes these initials have been ground away in an attempt to make the piece look older than it really is.

ROYAL WORCESTER

The Worcester Royal Porcelain Company was formed in 1862; the kaleidoscopic range of wares produced by this factory spanned from humble domestic goods to the finest cabinet pieces exquisitely decorated by leading painters. Royal Worcester's extraordinary commercial success was largely due to the inspired direction of the factory's artistic director, R. W. Binns, who kept his finger on the pulse of changing fashion and was able to cater to public demand. Worcester excelled in designs of Eastern inspiration; as Japanese art infiltrated the Western world the factory began producing patterns inspired by Japanese ceramics and Indian ivories, Persian ceramics and Oriental metalwork. Worcester is also famed for unusual finishes such as "blush ivory", an effect which was much copied in Germany and Austria. Among the most sought-after pieces of Royal Worcester are signed pieces by leading names such as the Stinton family, Charley Baldwyn and Harry Davis. Figures by Worcester's leading modeller James Hadley are also keenly collected, as are those made in the 20th century by Freda Doughty. Worcester also produced a series of limited-edition figures; these have not held their value as well as figures by Doulton.

◀ DECORATION
Japanese-inspired design was a popular form of decoration on many Royal Worcester pieces; this 1872 vase with frogs, one of a pair, is an amusing example copied exactly from an Oriental prototype. £2,000–2,500 pair

▶ JAMES HADLEY
Hadley was Royal Worcester's most famous modeller. Working in the 19th century, he was responsible for a series of blush ivory figures such as this "piping boy" (1889) which remain particularly popular with collectors today. Value depends on the rarity of the figure; this example would be worth £600–700.

▲THE STINTONS
Harry and his father John Stinton specialized in painting Highland cattle in mountains. James, John's brother, painted game birds rather than cattle. Pieces such as this vase by Harry Stinton, made in 1919, are very popular but value varies greatly according to size. This measures 8in/21cm high and would be worth £1,000–1,400.

▼ FREDA DOUGHTY
Freda Doughty, one
of the most popular
Worcester modellers
working in the 1930s,
produced a series of
children at play, such

as this figure known
as "Dancing Waves".
Royal Worcester also
produced animal
models by Doris
Lindner.
£170–200

**▲ IVORY
DECORATION**
The "blush ivory"
finish provided a
background for
formal floral
decoration which
proved to be very
popular in the late

19th/early 20th
century. It is seen to
great effect on this
pot pourri vase. Many
other makers both in
England and abroad
copied this unusal
Royal Worcester
colouring. £250–350

▶ VALUE
Most blush ivory vases
such as this one (c.1910)
were decorated by
hand, applying colour
to a black printed
etched outline of the
design. The best
designs are by Edward
Raby who sometimes
signed his work
with his initials
somewhere in the
printed design.
The blush ivory
ground was sometimes
painted entirely by
hand and this adds to
value. £250–300

MARKS
Standard Royal Worcester
marks are date-coded with
a series of letters and dots. By
looking in a specialist mark
book you can work
out the year of manufacture.
- From 1862 "Worcester Royal Porcelain
  Works", within a circle surmounted by
  a crown enclosing a cipher and crescent
  with the date code beneath were used.
- After 1891 "Royal Worcester England"
  was used (as above).
- From 1938 the words "Bone China"
  appear in addition to the standard mark.

NANTGARW & SWANSEA

The fortunes of Wales' two most famous porcelain factories were inextricably linked. William Billingsley, England's foremost flower painter on porcelain, opened the Nantgarw works in 1813, and shortly after moved to the Cambrian pottery, Swansea, where true porcelain had not hitherto been produced. A few years later he returned to Nantgarw, but such large quantities of porcelain were lost in firing that the company was soon in financial distress and closed down four years later. Billingsley is famed for producing fine white highly translucent porcelain of unrivalled quality

and products were aimed at the upper echelons of the London market. Many pieces were sold in the white and decorated in London. Not surprisingly, considering its short-lived existence, Welsh porcelain is scarcer than that from other factories – and for this reason commands a premium. Many unmarked pieces are misascribed and identification is a matter of expert opinion. Pieces painted in Wales are more sought after than those decorated elsewhere – the most famous decorators were Thomas Baxter, Thomas Pardoe, David Evans and William Pollard as well as Billingsley himself.

▶ **DECORATION**

Decoration on much Welsh porcelain was inspired by French taste of the late Regency period, with Neo-Rococo flowers on a white ground a typical form. This Swansea plate (c.1815) is typically decorated with delicately painted flowers on a white ground. £500–700

◀ **LONDON**
DECORATED WARES

Although as a general rule pieces decorated in London tend to be less valuable than those decorated in Wales, decorative examples such as this made c.1820 with its detailed bird border are still popular with collectors. £700–1,000

BODY

On Swansea porcelain the body may be one of three different types and this can affect value. Early pieces were made from "glassy" paste; the most sought-after pieces are made from "duck egg" paste – with a slight greyish tinge; later pieces were made from what is known as "trident" paste and are considered somewhat less desirable.

▼ WARES

Nantgarw mainly produced plates, cups, saucers and a range of small ornaments. Swansea was famed for tea and dessert services, cabinet pieces and decorative objects such as taper sticks and inkwells. This tureen, made c.1815, is unmarked but the roses and shape are characteristic of Swansea. £500–600

◄ NANTGARW

Beautifully painted floral subjects were produced at both Nantgarw and Swansea and the marks are often the only way to tell the two apart. This Nantgarw plate (c.1817–20), stylistically very similar to the one opposite, is typically painted with a bouquet of irises, tulips and other flowers. £500–700

MARKS

NANT-GARW C.W.

Nantgarw wares were usually marked with an impressed "NANTGARW CW" (for china works). Many Swansea pieces were marked in red with a painted, stencilled or impressed "SWANSEA".

BEWARE

Many French porcelain blanks, especially vases, were also decorated in London with identical decoration to that used on Welsh plates. Fake Swansea marks are also known to have been added to English porcelain to make it more valuable.

MINTON

The Minton factory, founded by Thomas Minton in 1798, was one of the 19th century's biggest and most varied producers of every type of ceramic, ranging from architectural fittings such as tiles and majolica, to humble earthenware and fine bone china. Minton's greatest period spans from the mid- to late 19th century, although the company is still in production today. Among its finest wares were pieces made using the *pâte sur pâte* technique, which had been developed on the Continent. *Pâte sur pâte* was introduced to Minton, and the English market, by Marc-Louis Solon, a former employee of Sèvres. Japanese styles also influenced the factory c.1870–80; many patterns were based on Japanese porcelain, including cloisonné, using brilliant turquoise enamels. The Art Nouveau style was reflected in Secessionist wares designed for Minton by John Wadsworth and Leon Solon. Prices for Minton not surprisingly reflect the variety of objects made by the factory. Top examples of the sophisticated *pâte sur pâte* technique were expensive when made and similarly rank among the factory's most valuable products today; even plates cost around £1,000. Printed tiles designed by leading artists such as John Moyr Smith can be bought for £25, however, and many other less elaborate pieces can be found for similarly modest sums.

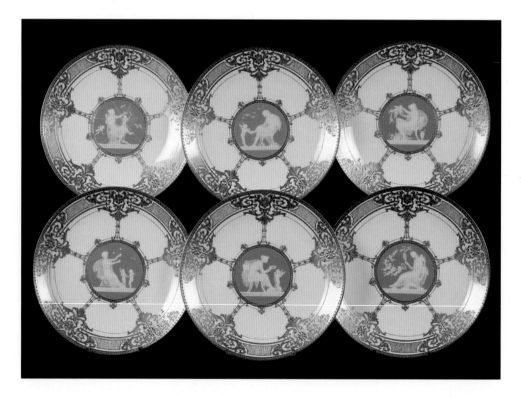

▲ *PÂTE SUR PÂTE*

Pâte sur pâte was one of Minton's most sophisticated and expensive products. The technique involved building up decorative cameos by applying layers of white slip to a darker base. Many of these pieces were also adorned with lavish raised gilding. These plates (1911) are by Alboin Birks, one of the finest exponents of the technique. Vases from the Minton factory decorated using the *pâte sur pâte* technique are also highly sought after by collectors.
£1,000–1,400 each.

▲ SERVICES

As well as ornamental pieces Minton also produced dinner, dessert and tea services, many of which are still available at very reasonable prices. These plates,

from an eight-piece part-dessert service date-marked 1870, are decorated with rich turquoise borders and sprays of wild flowers. £150–200 (for the part-set)

▶ SECESSIONIST STYLE

Minton was highly original in its use of innovative design in the late 19th century. Its "Secessionist" wares are identifiable by their unusual shapes and simple decoration. This vase is probably by John Wadsworth, a leading designer of the day; it is decorated using a slip-trailed technique and reflects the influence of Continental Art Nouveau. Another leading designer in this style was Marc-Louis Solon. £200–300

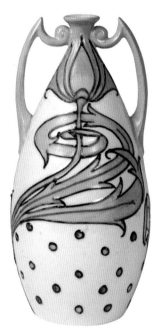

▲ ORIENTAL DECORATION

Japanese cloisonné provided the inspiration behind a range of brilliantly decorated ornamental pieces such as this vase (c.1876) in which gilding was used to

simulate the effect of the copper wires used in true cloisonné to divide the panels of differently coloured enamels. Pieces similar to this were designed by Dr Christopher Dresser but this example is unsigned. £350–500

MARKS

Nearly all Minton is marked, either with the name "MINTON" or "MINTONS". Pieces made before c.1914 usually have an additional date code mark.

COALPORT

Founded in the last decade of the 18th century, the Coalport factory made fine ornamental wares alongside domestic pieces such as tea and dinner services, and the factory is still in production today. The varied tastes of the day are mirrored in the changing styles of the factory's output. Coalport mimicked styles first made by Meissen, Dresden and Sèvres with coloured grounds, eccentric shapes and generous helpings of decoration. The factory is also famous for flower-encrusted pieces made in the 1830s; these were known as "Coalbrookdale" but were in fact produced by the same company. Confusingly for collectors Coalport was also a major supplier of white porcelain to independent china painters and many wares carry decoration which was not done at the Coalport factory.

◀ "COALBROOKDALE"
Elaborate floral decoration and scrolls were hallmarks of the "English Dresden style" fashionable in the 1830s. Pieces in this style made at Coalport are popularly known as "Coalbrookdale"; this typical clock case is lavishly decorated in the Rococo style. £800–1,200

▼ JEWELLED COALPORT
At the turn of the century until the 1920s the Coalport works achieved huge success with jewelled porcelain, a distinctive decorative technique made by placing beads of turquoise enamel on a gilded or coloured ground. These pieces are much collected and even tiny cups and saucers can cost £400–500 or more.

▲ DECORATORS
Coalport allowed artists to sign pieces in the late 19th and 20th centuries. Among the best-known decorators are Edward Ball and Percy Simpson who painted landscapes. John Randall, a specialist in exotic bird subjects, and Frederick Chivers, a specialist in still life, decorated this elaborate vase (c.1905), one of a pair. £1,000–1,500 for the pair

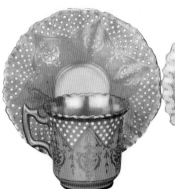

ROCKINGHAM

Perhaps better known than it deserves to be, this short-lived factory is famous for its rather unconventional output. Founded in Yorkshire in 1826 by the Brameld family, the company took its name and mark from its financial backer, the Earl Fitzwilliam, Marquis of Rockingham. The company concentrated on ambitious decoration and in 1830 began making a service for King William IV, which ultimately led to its financial ruin; 12 years later, in 1842, the firm finally closed. Despite the limited output Rockingham is extremely popular with collectors and pieces command a premium compared with other more prolific factories. Simple cups and saucers fetch from £100 and more; small vases start at around £500–800. Most Rockingham was marked but many unmarked pieces by Minton and Coalport have been wrongly attributed over the years to Rockingham.

◀ QUALITY
Lavish gilding and accomplished painted decoration are typical of Rockingham. This plate is of particularly fine quality since it was a specimen design for the celebrated service produced by the factory for the coronation of William IV and first used for Queen Victoria's coronation.
£3,000–5,000

▶ ANIMALS
Rockingham produced an assortment of animals including cats, dogs and rabbits. Rockingham animals, are invariably marked unlike those of other factories. This cat was made c.1830.
£800–1,000

▲ PLAQUES
Plaques are rare among Rockingham's output and this example is particularly unusual and valuable because it is signed and dated by Thomas Steel, a leading artist who is known to have worked at the firm in 1830.
£4,000–5,000

MARKS
A griffin taken from Earl Fitzwilliam's arms was first printed in red, then purple after c.1830 when "Manufacturer to the King" was added.

Rockingham Works Brameld

SPODE

This large Staffordshire factory was founded by Josiah Spode in 1776, and from the end of the 18th century throughout the 19th century produced a vast range of domestic earthenwares and Parian, as well as grander bone china services and ornamental pieces reflecting the prevailing taste for Classical or Rococo style (see p164). The company was bought out by Copeland & Garrett in 1833 and is still in production. Spode's most distinctive products include the Imari patterns popular c.1815–25; pieces with coloured grounds; and pieces with hand-painted decoration by leading decorators such as C. F. Hürten. Lavish gilding is also a feature of many of the best pieces. This is a vast and diverse collecting field and although less distinctive than those of some other factories, products range from highly elaborate ornamental wares to humble bat-printed wares.

◀ PRINTED WARES
Among the least expensive Spode pieces are bat-printed wares such as this milk jug of c.1815, which is decorated with a picturesque landscape. Bat printing was a method that relied on soft glue rather than paper to transfer printed designs.
£90–120

MARKS   **SPODE**

Before 1830 Spode usually hand-painted this name on porcelain (or impressed on pottery). After 1833 the names "Copeland & Garrett" usually appear with "Late Spode" in the middle. The word "Copeland" is used alone after 1847.

▶ PATTERNS
Patterns are identified by numbers and this vase (c.1825), decorated in a floral design on a blue and gilt scale ground, is an example of pattern number 1166, one of the most popular of all Spode patterns with today's collectors.
£500–800

◀ DECORATORS
Decorators at Spode did not usually sign their work; their names are not generally known but their high-quality decoration can attract high prices none the less. This straight-sided chocolate cup and stand (c.1815) is skilfully painted with loose sprays of flowers within rectangular gilt panels but the low value reflects the damage it has suffered.
£200–300

DAVENPORT

Another successful Staffordshire factory, Davenport was established in 1794 by John Davenport and produced earthenware, basalt, creamware, bone china and even glass throughout the 19th century, until its closure in 1887. Davenport has no particularly distinctive style but is recognized for decoration of high quality. Pieces were usually marked with name and pattern number which, along with their style, are helpful clues for dating. Davenport patented a technique for making thinly potted porcelain plaques, many of which were sold to independent decorators. Although popular with collectors, Davenport tends to fetch lower prices than pieces by Worcester, Swansea or Rockingham, even though it is often of equally fine quality and can provide excellent value. Among the most affordable pieces to look out for are blue-and-white printed plates from £30–70.

◄ **DECORATION**
This is an early Davenport plate (c.1810–15), heavily decorated with chinoiserie inspired by Meissen. The highly detailed form of decoration seen here is unique to the Davenport factory.
£140–180

MARKS
Davenport was marked with a crown between c.1870 and 1886; the words "Davenport Longport" also appear in some early and later marks.

SERVICES
Davenport produced some very extensive dinner services using porcelain and various other less expensive materials. This part-dessert service (c.1815) is made from pearlware; other large services were made from ironstone (see p133). £1,000–1,500 (for 17 pieces, allowing for some damage).

PARIAN

Named after Roman marble quarries at Paros, Parian was a hugely popular 19th-century material used to make inexpensive imitations of marble sculpture. Copeland and Minton both claim to have invented Parian in the 1840s and by the mid-century many other factories were also producing it. Copeland called the substance "statuary porcelain" in the early days, while Wedgwood termed its version "Carrara ware" after another famous Italian marble quarry. Parian's advantage was that it contained a high proportion of glass crystals and its vitreous nature meant that dirt did not adhere to it. Many of the leading 19th-century sculptors designed models to be reproduced in Parian; copies of famous antique works were also made, as well as busts of literary and historical personalities.

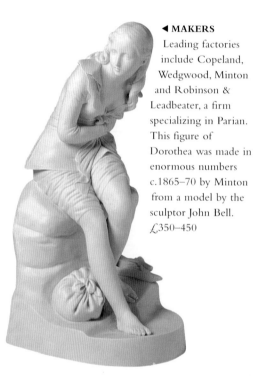

◀ MAKERS
Leading factories include Copeland, Wedgwood, Minton and Robinson & Leadbeater, a firm specializing in Parian. This figure of Dorothea was made in enormous numbers c.1865–70 by Minton from a model by the sculptor John Bell.
£350–450

MARKS
Parian figures are usually marked by their maker on the base or on the back of the model. Some pieces may also be titled and have a date code.

VALUE
Value depends on a piece's maker, its decorative appeal and its size. Prices range from under £40 for small busts to over £1,000 for larger subjects.

◀ SUBJECTS
Parian figures depicting famous royal, political and literary figures were also popular. This figure of the Duke of Wellington is by Samuel Alcock & Co after a sculpture by G. Abbott, and dates from 1852.
£350–500

ART UNIONS
Parian figures are often stamped with names such as "The Crystal Palace Union" or "Art Union of London". To raise funds for the Arts, "art unions" ran lotteries where art lovers could buy tickets in the hope that they might win an original work such as a specially commissioned Parian figure. Copeland was one of numerous firms who made figures for art unions.

BELLEEK

Established in 1863 by David McBirney and Robert Williams Armstrong in County Fermanagh, Northern Ireland, Belleek specialized in producing an incredibly thin high-quality white porcelain using a glazed Parian body. Warm and creamy in appearance, Belleek resembled the texture and translucence of sea shells and before long the factory began making wares in the forms of shells decorated with iridescent glaze, as well as finely woven baskets. Belleek has always been popular in the United States, and in fact workers from the Irish factory emigrated and set up rival establishments there; their products are termed "American Belleek". The factory is still in production and the same designs have been produced throughout its existence. Small pieces of Belleek cost from £30 while larger more elaborate pieces such as baskets can fetch between £4,000 and 5,000.

<table>
<tr><td>

▲ DATING
Baskets can be dated from the number of strands from which the centres are woven. Baskets such as this

</td><td>

from the 19th century are three-stranded; after c.1900, as potting became even finer, four strands were used.
£250–350 (damaged)

</td></tr>
</table>

▲ DESIGNS
The fine lustrous body perfected at Belleek looked like mother-of-pearl and shells provide a recurring theme for many ornamental pieces. This pair of oval shell jelly dishes (c.1870–90) are moulded with shells among coral branches enriched with pink and turquoise. £150–200

MARKS
The first mark with the word "BELLEEK" in black was used only until 1891 after which the second mark was used, adding the word "IRELAND" to the name. More modern marks are in green or gold.

▲ TEAWARES
Belleek's unusual teawares are also popular with collectors. The value of teasets depends on the number of pieces they have. This delicately green-tinged jug, made in the late 19th early 20th century in the Neptune pattern, is worth £70–80.

CONDITION
The fineness of Belleek makes it vulnerable to damage and even hairline cracks can devastate value. The basket top left has had some restoration; in perfect condition it might be worth £1,000–2,000.

CONTINENTAL POTTERY

Most Continental pottery was made from an earthenware base, covered with a glaze to which tin oxide has been added, and is known as tin glaze. Tin-glazed pottery is given different names according to its country of origin. In Italy and Spain it is called *maiolica*, in France and Germany it is known as *faïence*, and in the Netherlands as Delft.

The richly coloured designs and motifs found on Continental pottery of the 17th and 18th centuries provided a popular source of inspiration for makers of the 19th century and later. Most of these later copies are highly decorative and collectable in their own right.

▼ SPANISH MAIOLICA
Shiny metallic lustre decoration, as on this rare 15th-century dish, is a characteristic of Spanish pottery. Similar pieces were reproduced in Italy in the late 19th century by the Cantagalli factory – these copies were originally marked on the base with a singing cockerel. £10,000–15,000

▲ DRUG JARS
Maiolica apothecaries' drug jars were made both for display and for storage – hence their colourful decoration. Shapes vary according to the jar's original contents. Wet drugs were stored in bulbous jars with spouts like this, dry drugs were usually stored in straight cylindrical ones called *albarelli*. £8,000–12,000

▲ FRENCH FAÏENCE
This beautifully painted 18th-century plate was made by one of the most prominent French factories – that of the Veuve (widow) Perrin. Many wares from this factory are marked "VP", but the mark is also seen on copies, so always check the quality of the painting – painters from the factory were sent to the French drawing academies. £800–1,200

◀ DUTCH DELFT
Tulips were a Dutch obsession and Delft tulip vases were made in simple cushion shapes like this. Others resembled elaborate pagodas, standing several feet tall. £5,000–7,000

BEWARE

Some genuine pieces of *maiolica*, *faïence* and Delft have fake inscriptions to make them seem more valuable: be suspicious if the calligraphy seems to lack fluidity and if you see any grey specks in unglazed areas – a sign the piece has been refired.

COPIES

Many honest copies were made in the 19th century, marked by makers such as Doccia, Molaroni, Maiolica Artistica Pesarese and Bruno Buratti – these are collectable but considerably less valuable.

CONDITION

Don't expect to find early *maiolica* in perfect condition, chips and cracks are commonplace and pieces are still valuable despite damage. The rim of this tazza has been replaced in parts but is still worth over £12,000 because the painting is of such high quality. However, you can still find smaller, less finely painted examples from as little as £800.

ITALIAN MAIOLICA

The surfaces of valuable Istoriato (story) dishes, such as this 16th-century Urbino tazza, are used like the canvas of a painting to show a mythological or religious subject – this picture of Rebecca and Isaac is from a Raphael drawing.

COLOURS

As in most Italian *maiolica*, the colours that predominate are blue, yellow, orange, black and green. If a wider range of colours is used it may indicate the piece is of higher quality or later date.

CONTINENTAL PORCELAIN FIGURES

Ask a collector to name a European porcelain factory and the chances are the first one they'll think of will be Meissen. This factory is famous because it was the first in Europe to discover the secret of making hard-paste porcelain (in the early 18th century) and because of the high quality of its products.

Meissen began to concentrate on producing figures from c.1730, following the arrival of a young sculptor named Johann Joachim Kandler. Before long, Kandler's figures became even more popular than Meissen tablewares. As other porcelain factories sprang up throughout Europe, they too began producing

figures in the style of Meissen – some of them even using the Meissen crossed swords mark to make their pieces even more tempting.

If you're a new collector you may find the differences between the figures made by the various factories are often so small as to be easily overlooked, but as you become more experienced, details such as the modelling, the shape of a base, the colours and the glaze can tell you by whom and when a piece was made. Don't be afraid to pick the figures up and look underneath for marks – but always remember to support them well in your hand when you do.

◀ **MEISSEN**
You may think this twisting figure of Harlequin, made c.1740, looks as if it's about to topple over – but the turning pose is typical of the best Meissen figures which are always full of movement.
£15,000–20,000

REMEMBER . . .
Crossed swords alone don't mean you have a piece of Meissen – this is the most commonly faked mark and was copied by Worcester, Minton, Bow and Derby – among others.

▶ **VIENNA**
The different colours on a figure can tell you where it was made. The combination of strong green, pale mauve, puce and yellow used on this group is typical of many Vienna figures produced c.1760–70.
£3,000–5,000

▲ **FRANKENTHAL**
Frankenthal figures, such as this one, are often high quality despite their rather stiff poses. Features typically found on Frankenthal pieces are:
- large hands
- doll-like faces
- arched edge to bases
- tufts of green moss.
£2,500–3,500

IS IT MEISSEN?

Is the figure made from white paste, perhaps with a slight grey tinge?

NO → • If it is slightly blue and smoky it might be made by Vienna.

→ • If it has a distinct grey tone it may be modern Meissen.

YES ↓

Is it obviously separately modelled from the base?

NO → • If it looks as if it is growing out of its base it could be Nymphenburg.

→ A c.1660 Nymphenburg figure of Summer

YES ↓

Is the base covered with flowers and leaves?

NO → • If it has patches of moss it could be Frankenthal.
• If it has a rough base or triangular gilt patterns it might be Vienna.

→ • If it has an undulating base with gilt or puce scrolls it might be Frankenthal.

YES ↓

Is the face severely modelled but subtly coloured?

NO → • If the features are very childlike it could be by Hochst.

A Hochst group c.1700
£3,000–5,000

YES ↓

Is the painting very detailed, using either bold or pastel shades?

NO → • The colours on 19thC Meissen are often washed out and lack the fine details of the best 18thC pieces.

YES ↓

Is it marked with crossed swords on the base, the back or the side?

NO → • If there is no mark it could be an early figure by Vienna.

IF ALL THE ANSWERS ARE YES, THEN YOU MAY HAVE A PIECE OF MEISSEN.

MARKS OF OTHER MAKERS

▲ Hochst
◀ Frankenthal

▲ Nymphenburg

COMMEDIA DELL'ARTE

1   2

3   4

1 Scaramouch
2 Harlequin
3 L'Avvocato
4 Columbine

One popular subject for porcelain figures were characters from the famous *Commedia dell' Arte* (Italian Comedy). These were modelled by many factories and appear in a wide variety of poses. Their value depends on the quality and their condition, rather than the subject. Prices range from under £300 to over £20,000.

CONTINENTAL TABLEWARES

There are many different ways to build up an interesting and attractive collection of Continental porcelain. You might decide to concentrate on the wares of one particular factory, or a particular type of ware, coffee cups for example, which can still be bought singly and affordably. Alternatively, you may want to concentrate on pieces with a common style of decoration, perhaps painted with landscapes or flowers.

Whatever aspect you choose, you will find Continental porcelain in a huge range of styles, shapes, colours – and prices. Value is largely a matter of four key factors: maker or factory, style, quality of workmanship and condition. Identification is usually a matter of recognizing the characteristic features of each factory's wares such as the shapes, colours and type of paste and glaze they used. It is the combination of these factors, together with the mark (if there is one), which can tell you whether a piece is genuine or not.

► **CONDITION**
All these unusual Meissen vegetables have had some restoration, and this has reduced their value (to about £600 for the artichoke or the pair of peas). In perfect condition they would be worth about twice as much.

▲ **DECORATION**
Decoration can give away the maker's identity – Middle

Eastern figures, as seen on this plate, are typical of the Paris factory. £1,200–1,800

► **STYLES**
Dating some types of Continental porcelain can be confusing because during the 19th century factories like Sèvres often repeated earlier shapes and decorative styles. This Sèvres tea service uses shapes which were first fashionable in c.1790, but it was in fact made in 1837. £7,000–10,000

COPIES

Some copies are very skilful and are collectable in their own right. One of the most famous 19th-century copyists, Edmé Samson of Paris, made this copy (left) of a Meissen original (right). You can tell it's a copy by the greyish colour of the porcelain, the heavier weight, and less lavish gilding. Copy £400–600; original £8,000–12,000

BEWARE

It's a great mistake to attach too much importance to marks, because many were copied – more than 90% of the Vincennes/early Sèvres linked Ls appear on later copies. One way of detecting fakes is by looking at the paste from which the piece is made – most copies are on hard-paste, but the original mark was used only for soft-paste (see p104 for how to tell the difference).

▶ SÈVRES

This Sèvres jug can be dated by the distinctive pink known as "*Rose Pompadour*" (after King Louis XV's mistress, Madame Pompadour). This colour was introduced c.1757 and was probably discontinued shortly after Madame Pompadour's death in 1764. £3,000–4,000.

COLOURS

Certain colours are associated with particular factories or periods. Some rare colours increase value.

1   Greyish turquoise: Meissen, c.1770
2   *Bleu Celeste*, Sèvres
3   Apple Green, Sèvres
4   Böttger Green, early Meissen
5   Lemon yellow, Meissen c.1730–50
6   Egg Yolk, Meissen c.1730–40
7   Tan, German and Swiss factories
8   Russet, Fürstenberg, Ludwigsburg
9   Dark brown, German factories
10 Iron red, all factories
11 Purple, Meissen
12 Claret, Vienna
13 Puce, German factories, c.1750
14 *Rose Pompadour*, Sèvres, 1760s
15 Lilac, Meissen, c.1740–55

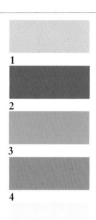

BERLIN & LATER GERMAN FACTORIES

Berlin's first factory, founded in 1752 by W. K. Wegely, closed only five years later. In 1761 King Frederick the Great, together with a financier, established a second factory which the King later took sole charge of, succeeded by the State; this factory survives to the present day. Berlin porcelain of the 18th century is extremely rare and you are far more likely to come across 19th-century pieces, exquisitely decorated with detailed panels on solid coloured grounds, which are easily confused

with porcelain made around the same time in Vienna and Paris. The Berlin factory also produced quantities of porcelain plaques, many of which were independently decorated with copies of well-known paintings. During the 19th and early 20th centuries the area near Meissen surrounding the city of Dresden became a major German centre of porcelain production with numerous factories producing ornamental and tea and dinner services in the style of Meissen and Sèvres.

◀ **VALUE**
Berlin and Dresden porcelain is widely available at a range of prices depending on the usual criteria of size, subject and decorative appeal. Pieces such as this Berlin *solitaire* (c.1775), beautifully painted in puce with Watteauesque figures in landscape vignettes, reflect the Rococo taste for monochrome decoration and no frames. £7,000–9,000

▶ **TOPOGRAPHICAL & CITY VIEWS**
Topographical and city views were a speciality of Berlin and Viennese porcelain decorators from the early 19th century. Scenes such as the one of the Gross Schloss decorating this egg are often named and among the most finely detailed of those produced anywhere in Europe. Earlier examples have either rectilinear or formal borders. The Neo-Rococo gilt borders here indicate a date c.1880. Small decorative items like the egg shown here are rather unusual; plates and cabinet cups and saucers are much more readily available to collectors at lower prices. £1,000–2,000

FIGURES
A range of figures based on Meissen models was made by Wegely. The second factory made a series called "The Cries of Berlin", modelled by the Meyer brothers.

MARKS
Berlin marks include a sceptre on early pieces; **KPM** from 1832 an orb appears; sometimes the letters "KPM" either in underglaze blue or red or impressed are also found.

▶ PORCELAIN PLAQUES
Popular paintings by artists such as Watteau, Murillo and Richter provided the subjects for huge numbers of porcelain plaques manufactured in Berlin. Ladies were favourite subjects too; this plaque shows a copy of a portrait of Beatrice Cenci by Guido Reni (c.1880). £2,000–3,000

▶ DECORATION
Snowball vases or *Schneeballen*, decorated with May blossom, were first made by Meissen in the 18th century, but several 19th-century factories continued the tradition by covering the entire surface of objects with tiny florets. This large unmarked vase could be made by a number of factories in the Dresden area. £1,000–1,200

◀ CARL THIEME
A brilliant example of the 19th-century love of excessive ornament, this baluster vase was made by Carl Thieme, one of the major manufacturers in the Dresden area. Pieces such as this are obviously extremely vulnerable to damage and small chips are acceptable. £2,000–3,000

VIENNA

Vienna was the second European factory to begin producing hard-paste porcelain. The factory was founded by Claudius Innocentius du Pacquier, who bribed and cajoled the secret from various disgruntled Meissen employees. Until the 1780s Vienna produced a similar range of wares to those made by Meissen, but figures were rarer and more stiffly modelled. In 1744 the company was taken over by the State and the hitherto limited production increased in quantity. In 1784 a new director was appointed and the factory began producing wares in the Neo-classical style, with elaborate painted scenes and heavy gilding of very similar appearance to wares from centres such as Berlin and St Petersburg. The Vienna factory closed in 1864 but many imitations of its more elaborate wares were produced in the late 19th century.

Porcelain from the du Pacquier period is rare, and consequently prices start at around £1,500. Also highly desirable are pieces from later periods decorated by sought-after painters such as Joseph Nigg, a famous flower painter. Prices for other late pieces are chiefly dependent on their decorative appeal.

◀ DECORATION
The use of solid gilt grounds became more prevalent at the turn of the 18th century and was used by all leading factories from Paris to St Petersburg. This coffee cup is decorated with a combination of Classical key border and informal Rococo scattered flowers.
£400–600

DU PACQUIER PORCELAIN
Porcelain from the du Pacquier period (1719–44) is rarer than Meissen and few pieces have survived. It is similar in composition to early Meissen and often has a greenish tone. Wares are usually decorated with chinoiserie and very formal Baroque strapwork borders. Dominant colours are puce, iron red and monochromes. Compared with Meissen the manner of painting is naïve. Figures are rare and idiosyncratic.

▲ WARES
Although tablewares made up the bulk of the factory's output it also made some enchanting accessories such as this exquisite travelling casket (c.1785), decorated in French style with a dotted green ground.
£3,000–5,000

▲ LATER "VIENNA-STYLE" WARES
After 1864 other European factories continued to produce wares in similar style. This vase and cover, one of a pair decorated with scenes of Galatea, and Europa and the Bull within seeded gilt lines, are late 19th-century pastiches of Vienna wares of the early 19th century. Less sensitively painted than the genuine article, they are worth a fraction of the price. £600–700 for the pair

▼ STYLES
The landscape subject within formal borders shows the transition between the decorative Rococo and the nascent Neo-classical styles. *Tête à têtes* (small teasets or cabarets) containing enough pieces for two became fashionable in the mid-18th century as part of the trend for boudoir intimacy. £12,000–18,000 for 8 pieces

▲ TOPOGRAPHICAL SCENES
Topographical scenes were one of the specialities of Viennese decorators and the scenes were often named on the base. This cabinet cup and saucer (c.1830) is decorated with a named view of Schönbrunn palace. £1,200–1,500

ITALY

Italy was the first European country to try to produce porcelain and began experimenting in the 16th century. In 1575 Duke Francesco de Medici opened a short-lived factory in Florence but the first successful porcelain factory, Vezzi, was not established until 1720, when a former Meissen employee, Christoph Hunger, stole the formula and took it to Venice. Other leading factories at Doccia and Cozzi soon followed suit and the most famous Italian porcelain of all was made from 1743 at Capodimonte, Naples. When Naples fell under Spanish rule the Capodimonte factory moved to Buen Retiro in Spain, but returned to Naples in the late 18th century. Some Italian porcelain is characterized by its greyish granular appearance and is easily confused with pieces from minor German factories. Prices tend to be comparatively high and there is a strong home market. The most readily available pieces tend to be from Doccia, mostly in the quasi-Oriental or Neo-classical style.

MARKS

- The most common mark is the red or gold anchor of Cozzi – this is much bigger than the similar Chelsea mark.
- Capodimonte use a fleur-de-lis mark, usually in underglaze blue or gold.
- After 1757 Doccia marked with this star; a red, blue or gold "F" is used 1792–1815.

▼ IDENTIFICATION
The rather delicate but primitive brushwork decorating this teacup and saucer is similar to Kakiemon styles of the 1740s. The angular scrolled handle is characteristic of the Capodimonte factory and can be found on coffee pots and other similar wares.
£1,500–2,000

▲ CAPODIMONTE
This figure of a pug (c.1750) is a copy of a Meissen original by J. J. Kaendler of c.1740. Reinterpreted in the soft-paste porcelain of Capodimonte, the crisp details are to a great extent lost but this would still be worth more than the Meissen original.
£4,000–6,000

FIGURES
Italian factories made a range of figures dressed in a variety of ways. A classical subject is less desirable than a group in contemporary dress, and pieces should always be in good condition.

◀ SHAPES
The forms used by Italian porcelain-makers are often idiosyncratic and distinctive from those used by factories elsewhere in Europe. This Doccia coffee pot (made c.1775) combines an early baluster form, an oddly shaped spout and a shallow domed cover with Neo-classical decoration. The tentative, fussy gilding is also characteristic of much Italian porcelain. £5,000–8,000

▶ DECORATION
One feature of late 18th- and 19th-century decoration is the use of relief-moulded decoration. This small covered beaker, made by the Cozzi factory c.1780, is decorated with the low-relief lion of Venice. £800–1,200

◀ NAPLES
Neo-classical decoration was very popular on Neapolitan porcelain of the late 18th century and this coffee can and saucer (c.1790) are no exception. Fashionably decorated with Classical figures on a black ground panel, they boast borders of palmettes and swags which are also derived from antiquity. These ornaments are most probably inspired by the local archeological excavations at Herculaneum and Pompeii on the Bay of Naples. £2,500–3,500

VINCENNES & SÈVRES

France's most famous porcelain factory, Sèvres, started life at Vincennes near Fontainebleau, where in 1738 a new factory began to produce soft-paste porcelain. In 1756 the factory moved to Sèvres, near the home of one of its keenest patrons, Louis XV's mistress Madame de Pompadour; soon after, the King became the owner of the factory. After 1769 Sèvres began making hard-paste porcelain (as well as soft paste) and after c.1803 stopped making soft paste completely.

Sèvres porcelain is famed for its lavish gilding and brilliantly coloured grounds,

which formed a framework for panels decorated with flowers, figure subjects or landscapes. Its illustrious reputation has however attracted numerous imitators. Marks and styles were copied throughout Europe and confusion also arises because at the time of the French Revolution the factory was taken over by the state and numerous pieces were sold in the white to independent decorators in France and England. Coloured grounds are prone to faking; probably about 90 percent of all *bleu céleste* pieces, in the delicate sky blue for which Sèvres is known, are imitations.

MARKS

The interlaced Sèvres "Ls" were centred with a date letter from 1753. This is one of the most commonly faked of all porcelain marks. Look for strong definition on genuine pieces – a weak and attenuated mark is usually suspect.

▶ **VINCENNES**
All Vincennes and Sèvres forms are known by special names; this double-handled vase, made c.1755, is called a vase *Duplessis à fleurs* – after the celebrated sculptor employed by the factory to create interesting shapes. This colour, called *bleu céleste*, was the most popular of all coloured grounds – and also the most commonly faked. Pieces from the

Vincennes period are rare and therefore command a premium. £5,000–8,000

▲ **COLOURS**
The brilliant shade of green used for this tea caddy (c.1780) was another of Sèvres' most distinctive colours. The range of coloured grounds was gradually introduced in the 18th century. Knowledge of these colours can help with dating and spotting fakes, since some pastiches

combine late colours with early date marks. Green was introduced in 1756. Other Sèvres colours include: *bleu lapis* (lapis blue), 1749; *bleu céleste* (sky blue), 1752; *jaune jonquille* (pastel yellow), 1753; *violette* (violet), 1757; *rose* (pink), 1758; *bleu royal* (royal blue), 1763. £2,000– 3,000

◀ **GILDING**
Sèvres gilding is invariably soft and richly applied and the factory developed a wide range of distinctive techniques. This coffee can and saucer (made 1768) are decorated with the popular *œil-de-* *perdrix* (partridge eye) gilded decoration; *caillouté* (pebble) decoration was another favourite pattern; while on some pieces gilding was raised and tooled to create detailed bouquets of flowers and foliage.
£800–1,200

▼ **DECORATION & FORM**
Monochrome decoration as on this tea service was less commonly used at Sèvres than in German factories but the shapes of the pear-shaped jug with tripod feet and ovoid teapot with ear-shaped handle are absolutely typical of 18th-century Sèvres forms. £5,000–7,000

BISCUIT FIGURES

The Vincennes and Sèvres factories also produced a range of unglazed porcelain figures modelled by E. M. Falconet, often after the designs of François Boucher. This type of porcelain is known as biscuit. Until recently these figures remained relatively inexpensive although they have risen considerably in value in the last few years.

◀ **LATER SÈVRES**
Like other leading European factories in the early 19th century Sèvres began producing more formally decorated pieces using semi-mechanical methods of gilding. This pale blue (*bleu agate*) tea service is made from hard-paste porcelain and looks much harder and sharper than the earlier pieces illustrated on these pages.
£1,500–2,000

LATER FRENCH PORCELAIN

From the late 18th century and throughout the first half of the 19th, Paris blossomed as a centre of porcelain manufacture as dozens of factories and enamelling shops began producing dinner services, tewares and ornamental pieces for the newly affluent population. As the 19th century progressed, the rising costs of running a commercial factory in the capital encouraged many manufacturers to move to the countryside near Limoges, where labour was cheaper and raw materials were readily available. Most French factories of this time have little individual style, relying heavily on earlier designs from Sèvres and elsewhere for inspiration. All factories produced only hard-paste porcelain (although some also made pottery) and marked their wares erratically. Many unmarked pieces and pieces with spurious Sèvres marks also survive; these are often catalogued either as "Paris" or as "Sèvres style". Prices depend heavily on the size and decorative appeal of the subject. Small plates are available for under £300, while large decorative vases can cost £1,000 or more.

◀ DECORATIVE WARES
Metal-mounted vases and covers are typical of the decorative items produced from the mid-19th century. The figurative panel, probably copied from a painting by Boucher or Watteau, is set against a dark blue ground – probably the most popular of all coloured grounds at this time.
£2,000–3,000

IMPORTANT 19TH-CENTURY FRENCH FACTORIES
Sèvres continued to be France's best-known porcelain factory, but other leading names included:
- **Paris** Jacob Petit, Dagoty & Honoré, Darte Frères, Discry, Talmour, Pouyat, Nast, Clignancourt
- **Limoges** Denuelle, Michel & Valin, Alluaud, Ardant, Gibus & Cie, Jouhanneaud & Dubois, Haviland, Ruaud

MARKS
As with many pieces of this type the vase above is marked only with imitation Sèvres marks; few pieces are marked by their manufacturer, and some are not even porcelain. If genuine marks do appear they are usually of the overglaze, stencilled or printed varieties.

▲ PICTORIAL SUBJECTS
Scale and ostentation were typical of many of the decorative items produced at this time and pictorial plates featuring Louis XVI and Marie Antoinette were especially popular after c.1850. Many of the portraits on plates such as these were transfer-printed and then enamelled over. Their value lies chiefly in their decorative appeal. £300–500

◀ **THEMES**

The fashion for Egyptian subjects, a hallmark of French Empire style in the early decades of the 19th century, was fuelled by Napoleon's campaigns in North Africa. This elaborate centrepiece is adorned with characteristic sphinxes supporting a basket bordered with lotus petals. Both stylish and large (measuring 18in/46cm high) this piece would command a high price in the market. Smaller pieces would cost a fraction of the price. £4,000–5,000

▶ **TEA SETS**

Among the wide range of tea sets produced at this time were cabarets – small tea sets usually for two also known as *tête à têtes* (see below) and *solitaires* for one.

This late 19th-century cabaret is painted with 18th-century court beauties and includes a teapot, large sugar bowl, jug, cup and saucer and matching tray. £600–800

◀ **VALUE**

Quality and an illustrious provenance can dramatically affect the value of porcelain. Painted in a tasteful *grisaille* (grey monochrome), the decoration of this *tête à tête* made c.1785 by the Paris factory of the Duc d'Angoulême is highly refined, and the set has a royal history: it was a gift from Marie Antoinette to a Swedish count. £2,500–3,000

OTHER PORCELAIN CENTRES – DENMARK & LOW COUNTRIES

The first porcelain factory was established in Copenhagen in 1760 with the help of German craftsmen from Meissen and Fürstenberg. The factory produced soft-paste porcelain in its early years (these pieces are very rare) and began making hard paste after 1783. Royal Copenhagen is perhaps most famous for the massive service made for the Russian Empress Catherine the Great in c.1780–1805. Known as Flora Danica, each piece was adorned with a different botanical study, and the pattern is still produced today. Among Royal Copenhagen's other successes are Art Nouveau-style pieces produced in pale grey shades, small figures in regional costumes and animals. The second most famous Danish factory is that of Bing & Grondahl; founded in 1853, this company produced high-quality wares in similar styles to Royal Copenhagen.

Porcelain was also produced in various centres in the Low Countries. In Belgium the most famous centre was at Tournai; in the Netherlands Amstel, Weesp and Oude Loosdrecht all produced porcelain from 1757–1820. In general although wares from these factories are easily available in their native countries comparatively few examples are seen for sale on the international market.

▲ OTHER PATTERNS

Royal Copenhagen also produced a wide range of tablewares in styles derived from Meissen and other European centres, and its more recent products are still available for modest sums. This conventional service, made in the early 20th century and based on French Rococo patterns, contains over 125 pieces including: tureens; platters; sauceboats; leaf-shaped dishes; serving, dinner, dessert and hors d'oeuvres plates; salt, pepper and mustard pots; butter dishes; bowls; cups and saucers; jugs and many more items. Perhaps surprisingly it would be cheaper to buy than a modern equivalent. £3,000–5,000

▲ FLORA DANICA

Versions of this exquisitely painted service have been produced ever since the first one was made (late 18th century) for Catherine the Great. Modern services are less valuable than those made pre-1900. Early painted decoration looks lively and robust; modern decoration may seem flatter. The porcelain on modern versions is finer and more glassy in appearance. This service made c.1900 contains 55 pieces. £14,000–16,000

▶ FIGURES

Royal Copenhagen figures have enjoyed huge popularity with collectors and are among the most popular pieces. Groups such as this in historical dress provided a favourite theme, as did figures in regional dress. These 20th-century groups of elegant couples are typically well modelled and painted in detail with subtle shades. £200–300 each

◀ TOURNAI

Figures were one of the specialities of the Belgian Tournai factory, which was the largest manufacturer of porcelain in the Low Countries. Many figures were unglazed and these, made c.1765 and part of a group depicting the Four Seasons, are also typical in their idyllic pastoral theme. They are probably based on a Boucher subject and are easily confused with Sèvres biscuit groups and later Derby wares. £1,500–2,500

OTHER PORCELAIN CENTRES – RUSSIA

Russia's foremost factory was established in St Petersburg c.1748 and became the Imperial Porcelain Factory in 1763. Early wares reflected the style of Meissen but under imperial patronage the factory began making more ambitious pieces. Wares of the early 19th century are particularly distinctive, and characteristically have detailed pictorial decoration and extravagant gilding. After the 1917 Revolution the factory was taken over by the State and went on to produce some interesting Constructivist designs which are much sought after. The factory is still in production. Russia's second most famous factory was established by Francis Gardner in 1776 and flourished until the 1880s when it was taken over by the rival Kuznetsov factory. Gardner was famed for figures in regional costumes and often used matt unglazed surfaces in sombre colours, especially Prussian blue.

▶ KUZNETSOV PORCELAIN

The Kuznetsov factory became Russia's biggest porcelain manufacturer at the turn of the 19th century, producing a wide range of wares for the home and export market. This Kuznetsov beaker (c.1900) is decorated with a portrait of the Tsar's son surrounded by typical Russian designs. Similar commemorative beakers were also produced in enamel. £400–600

▲ ST PETERSBURG

Painted with a scene showing a military encampment set against a solid blue ground with a formal ribbon border this sucrier (c.1780) reflects the early Neo-classical fashions popular in England, France and Austria. £700–900

▶ TOPOGRAPHICAL SUBJECTS

The scene of St Petersburg which decorates the centre of this Imperial Porcelain Factory plate (c.1820) is typically detailed and pictorial. The elaborately moulded rim is however unusual at this time and the gilded wreath decoration is unique to St Petersburg. £1,000–1,500

VALUE

THIS PLATE REFLECTS THE
EARLY 19TH-CENTURY FASHION
FOR LAVISH GILDING AND
DETAILED DECORATION, AND
IT HAS SEVERAL ADDITIONAL
DESIRABLE FEATURES
WHICH ADD SIGNIFICANTLY
TO ITS VALUE.
£3,000–5,000

A signature by a leading
artist – S. Daladugin.

The soldiers' regiment,
rank and the date are
also inscribed on the
reverse of the plate.

Exceptionally high-
quality painting. Similar
pieces were made in
Meissen and Berlin and
often identification relies
on marks and differences
in the palette.

MARKS

St Petersburg porcelain is marked with
a crown and also with the initials of the
emperor or empress of that particular
period in Roman letters. Other factories
often used Cyrillic letters and marks can
be the cause of confusion.

◀ **POST-
REVOLUTIONARY
DESIGNS**
Porcelain made
after the 1917
Revolution was
decorated with
interesting and
innovative angular
designs which were
inspired by the new
styles developed by
Russia's Constructivist
designers. Subject
matter typically
reflected the country's
new political ideals,
and this cup and saucer
designed by Maria V.
Lebedeva in 1923 is
decorated with factory
scenes and workers in
a typical Constructivist
palette of various reds,
black and grey.
£1,500–2,000

The production of silver has a long and distinguished history, encompassing all the major decorative art styles. As a result, collectable silver is available internationally in a wide variety of forms. It is therefore perhaps unsurprising that, despite the vagaries of fashion, old silver has remained one of the most enduringly popular collecting areas. Although silver is not cheap, small 19th-century objects are still available for £100 or less, and old Sheffield plate and electroplate also offer excellent value.

From the earliest times silversmiths realized that pure silver was unworkably soft, and had to be mixed with other more resilient base metals before it could be made into objects.

A silver standard was introduced in Britain in 1300 and all silver objects made after this date had to be tested and marked to show they contained more than 92.5% pure silver. This marking system has survived in Britain and Ireland with few modifications to the present day. Marks provide the collector of such silver with an invaluable aid. You may come across silver with fake or altered marks, or unmarked pieces, but these are relatively scarce, and once you have learnt to "read" the marks, you will be able to identify where, when, and often who made most pieces of silver. Nonetheless, you should always take into account the style of a piece to make sure it is consistent with the date of the marks. Much Continental and American silver was also marked in some way, although in many countries the system was less rigorously applied.

BASICS

HALLMARKS

There are four main marks:

- The sterling guarantee
- The town mark
- The date letter
- The maker's mark

Sterling guarantee mark

1. Leopard's head
2. Leopard's head crowned
3. Lion passant

Silver that is at least 92.5% silver is termed "sterling" silver. All silver objects of sterling quality were stamped with a leopard's head from 1300. By 1478 the leopard had a crown; from 1544 the sterling mark changed to a lion passant, shown walking to the left (after this date the leopard's head was used as London's town mark).

4. Britannia mark
5. Lion's head

Between 1697 and 1720, a higher standard of silver, known as the Britannia standard, was introduced. During this period the sterling mark was replaced by a figure of Britannia, and a lion's head in profile.

Town marks

Marks showing the town of assay were introduced by the end of the 15th century. Common marks are:

6. London
7. Birmingham
8. Chester
9. Dublin
10. Exeter
11. Edinburgh
12. Glasgow
13. Sheffield
14. York

Date letters

$\boxed{F}$ $\boxed{f}$ $\boxed{f}$ $\boxed{F}$

15   16   17   18

15 1721 16 1781
17 1741 18 1801

Marking with a date letter, which changed each year, was introduced in 1478 in London, and later in other parts of the country. The letters usually follow an alphabetical sequence, but the dates they indicate are unique to each assay office. The letters are contained within a shield of variable outline.

Maker's marks

 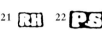

19 Matthew Boulton
20 John Café
21 Robert Hennell
22 Paul Storr

Marks to show the identity of the maker were used from the 14th century. The earliest were pictorial symbols, but from the late 17th century marks increasingly incorporated the silversmith's initials.

ALTERED AND FAKE MARKS

Forged marks

Fake marks which have been added or "let in" to a piece are often incorrectly placed and may look distorted; if they have been made by recasting a genuine piece there may be small granulations visible in the outline.

Transposed marks

Marks are sometimes taken from a low-value object and inserted in a larger, potentially more valuable one. If you breathe on transposed marks you should be able to see a faint outline around the marks where they were soldered in.

Illegal alterations

An Act of 1844 made it illegal to alter any piece of silver without hallmarking the additions. However, many pieces were updated to make them more useful, or more fashionable, rather than to deliberately deceive.

PATINA

Over years of use, silver develops a soft glow, or patina, caused by accumulated scratching and knocks and bruises. This patina is important to value. Repolishing old silver on a buffing wheel can destroy the patina of a piece and is always considered undesirable.

WEIGHT

Although an item which is heavier than average may not appear much larger or heavier, any extra weight is usually synonymous with quality, and heavier pieces tend to be more valuable.

STYLES OF DECORATION

Silver styles reflect the taste of the period, and can often provide a good indication of date. Decoration may be applied to the surface or the border of a piece and usually adds to value (see pp188–191 and p203 for some of the different types).

CONDITION

Restoration work is usually detrimental to the value of a piece of silver. If lead has been used in the repair it can be especially unsightly. Always find a specialist silversmith if you decide a piece needs to be repaired. Areas particularly vulnerable to damage are:

- **Feet:** these can be pushed up through the base with time.
- **Handles:** the metal of the body may be pulled away by the handle.
- **Hinges:** can be broken and are often difficult to repair.
- **Pierced decoration:** may be relatively fragile and prone to damage.

SHEFFIELD PLATE

Sheffield plate, made from a fusion of copper and silver, was introduced in c.1740. Most Sheffield plate is unmarked, although some late 18th century pieces had marks very similar to those found on silver.

- A piece with "Sheffield plate" stamped on it is most likely to be electroplate made in Sheffield in the 19th century, and not genuine Sheffield plate.
- Sheffield plate tends to be much less expensive than solid silver, but the best pieces are still keenly collected.

ELECTROPLATE

This method, involving covering a base metal with a thin layer of silver by electro-deposition, was used from c.1840. The base metal was initially copper, but later nickel was used, hence the term EPNS (electro-plated nickel silver). Electroplate has a harsher, whiter appearance than sterling silver or Sheffield plate and is usually marked by its maker, or bears indications of quality.

- Apart from pieces by an eminent maker like Elkington & Co. who pioneered the process, electroplate is less collectable than other types of silver.

DECORATION

The decorative style of a piece of silver gives a valuable clue to its date and, occasionally, its origin, particularly when the hallmarks are indistinct or absent. With the exceptions of early 18th-century English silver and American silver produced throughout the 18th century, which were generally plain and unembellished, various forms of decoration were usually applied to the surface of the metal according to contemporary popular taste. New decoration was often added to an old piece of plain silver to accommodate changing trends, and engraved armorials and initials were often removed and replaced with new ones. The ability to identify contemporary decoration is extremely useful, as decoration added at a later date can reduce the value of a piece of silver considerably. Traditional designs have been reproduced by machine from the 19th century.

ENGRAVING

The technique of engraving involves cutting a decorative pattern by removing metal from the surface with a sharp tool called a "burin" or "graver". The style of the work frequently provides a valuable clue as to whether the engraving was done at the time of manufacture or added later. Some of the finest engraving was produced in continental Europe, particularly in the 17th and early 18th century in The Netherlands and Germany where engravers were inspired by fashionable prints.

An extremely versatile technique, engraving was most commonly used for crests, arm orials, initials and inscriptions and was especially suited to such large items as the salver (1940) shown left and wine coolers with generous surface areas; on many items the engraving is featured within a decorative cartouche. In armorials the form of the shield and the design of the cartouche can provide important evidence for determining the date of a piece that has not been fully hallmarked, and occasionally it is possible to trace the arms to a particular individual, which adds to the interest and may also add to the value.

An engraved coat-of-arms was sometimes removed (polished out or erased) and replaced with a new one when silver changed hands, leaving the metal thin and weak. Coats-of-arms that have been re-engraved or added at a later date to an earlier cartouche will be more sharply defined than earlier engraving.

BRIGHT-CUT ENGRAVING

Bright-cut engraving as seen on this tea-caddy of 1796 was a popular form of decoration at the end of the 18th century, especially for Neo-classical ornament. It is identical in execution to engraving, but the design is carved at an angle with a burnished steel chisel, creating facets on the surface of the metal that reflect the light at different angles and add a sparkle to the decoration. The facets are easily worn away by polishing, and such wear is detrimental to the value – bright-cut engraving adds to the value only if it is still crisp.

CHASING

Popular at the end of the
17th century and again in the
mid–18th century, chasing, as
featured on the salver shown
above, is the highly skilled art
of hammering metal to create
a form of relief. The metal is
displaced (but not removed)
into the decorative pattern
with a chasing tool – a blunt
or ball-pointed chisel or
punch. The impression of
the chased pattern can often
be seen on the reverse or
underside of the piece.
Chasing is often referred to
as "flat-chasing".

The most common
decorative motifs included
flowers, foliage and scrolls of
various types, and during the
Victorian period the plain
surfaces of earlier silver items
were frequently lavishly chased
to satisfy the prevailing taste

for excessive ornament. With
silver chased at the time of
manufacture, hallmarks were
added after the piece had
been decorated, and any
later decoration was generally
superimposed on the
hallmarks. Paul de Lamerie
and Aymé Videau are among
the 18th-century silversmiths
celebrated for the exceptional
quality of their chasing.

EMBOSSING

The technique of embossing,
also known as "repoussé"
work, involves hammering a
piece of silver from the back
with decorative punches or dies
to create a relief pattern. Detail
and definition are added by
chasing on the front of the relief
design. The embossed decoration
is visible on the reverse of the
Victorian rosebowl (1890)
shown above. European
17th-century Baroque silver was
often decorated with embossed
flower and fruit motifs. By the
19th century, embossing had
fallen out of fashion, in favour
of faster, more cost-effective
die-stamping.

MATTING

For a matt effect to be achieved,
silver is worked with small
hammers to create a compact
pattern of tiny dots and render a
surface dull. Matting was
especially popular in England
and Germany in the mid-17th
century. It was used to great
effect on beakers to simulate
sharkskin, as in the above
example (c.1800). Matting
was also used in producing
background decoration to
give an impression of depth.

ENAMELLING

This clock (c.1895) by Liberty
& Co. is typical of the enamelled
silver favoured by devotees
of the Arts and Crafts style.
The process of enamelling

involves applying a paste or oil-based mixture of metallic oxides to make a glaze. When fired, the glaze fuses onto the surface of the object, creating a colourful decorative effect. In the Victorian and Edwardian periods the technique was popular for decorating small silver objects, such as vesta, card and cigarette cases, clocks and perfume bottles, which were often embellished with inlaid enamel plaques painted with hunting scenes, stories from Classical mythology, erotic images and landscapes. Enamelling is easily chipped, which will lower the value.

PLIQUE-A-JOUR ENAMELLING

Rarely found on English silver, *plique-à-jour* is a form of enamelling that was particularly popular for small objects such as spoons and ladles, notably in Scandinavia, France and Russia. The enamel is contained in an unbacked metal framework, creating the effect of a stained-glass window. This technique was used especially on items decorated in the delicate, sinuous Art Nouveau style, such as the case shown above (c.1900).

GUILLOCHE ENAMELLING

In *guilloché* enamelling the silver is engraved or engine-turned and then covered with a layer of translucent enamel, which allows the decorative design to shine through to shimmering effect, as on this pill box of 1934.

ENGINE-TURNING

In engine-turning, introduced at the end of the 18th century, machine-driven lathes are used to carve lines into the surface of the silver, creating a textured effect. The most common designs are waves, rosettes and braids.

NIELLO

The niello technique seen on this spoon (Moscow, 1875) was originally used by the Romans. A black compound consisting of

silver, lead, copper and sulphur is first heated and then reduced to a powder. A design is cut out of the silver, filled with the black compound and heated until the powder granules fuse together. The object is polished down after firing, leaving the carved decoration filled with niello and the surface smooth. As niello is a metallic alloy, it is stronger than enamel and less prone to damage. Most examples of niello found today have been made outside Britain and the USA – many are from France, Russia and the former Austro-Hungarian Empire – and date from the 18th to the early 20th centuries.

APPLIED WORK

Applied decoration describes ornament that is not part of the basic form of an object. One technique is Celtic strapwork, featured on the cream jug above (1932). Another is the "cut-card" technique, developed in the late 17th century and perfected in the early 18th century by Huguenot craftsmen. Cut-card work involves cutting a decorative shape from a thin sheet or card of silver, and then soldering it to the body of the vessel. Cast ornament may also be applied, as may beaded or reeded wires, soldered around the body or applied to the rim, foot and edges for decoration and strength.

PIERCED WORK

The technique of piercing entails making tiny cuts through the silver either to create a purely decorative design, as on this basket of 1789, or for a more practical purpose such as to make holes in the top of a sugar caster. The tedious and time-consuming process, which was carried out by hand until the late 18th century, initially involved using a chisel to punch out the patterns. From the 1770s this was done with a fretsaw. Hand piercing was eventually replaced by mechanical piercing, which dramatically reduced the time and cost of producing objects with pierced decoration. In the

18th century, pierced decoration was favoured for decorative tableware, including épergnes, mustard pots, salt-cellars with colourful glass liners, dish rings and cake baskets. Hand-pierced decoration tends to be slightly rough, while machine-piercing is usually more precise and consistent. The thin-gauge silver used from the late 18th century is vulnerable to damage if pierced.

PARCEL GILDING

Silver has frequently been gilded to make it resemble gold, as well as to protect it from tarnishing. The term "parcel gilt" is used to refer to an object made of silver that has been partially covered with a gold deposit, such as this jug made in 1842. When restricted to specific areas of an object, this technique is often used to great effect for highlighting decoration and distinguishing it from the background. The dangerous early method of mercury gilding had been replaced by the safer technique of electrogilding by the mid-19th century. Silver drinking vessels were often gilded on the inside to preserve the metal from corrosion caused by the acid present in wine.

DIE STAMPING

Die-stamped silver objects such as this caddy spoon, made in 1789, are created by pressing sheet silver into a mould and forcing it into the desired shape of the mould by means of punches or drop hammers. The dies were originally made by skilled craftsmen known as "die sinkers". With the advent of machine production in the late 18th century, the process became an especially fast and efficient method of reproducing a design or object. It was also a relatively inexpensive technique, encouraging manufacturers to mass produce whole objects, such as spoons and forks, cost effectively, as well as elaborate decorative surfaces. Used extensively throughout the 19th century, die-stamping was also a favoured method for manufacturing handles and feet in Sheffield plate. These components were stamped in halves, filled with lead and then applied to the object. As the metal is stretched through the die-stamping technique, it may be very thin and vulnerable to wear. Sometimes holes may be present, especially on objects featuring relief decoration.

TEAPOTS, COFFEE & CHOCOLATE POTS

Tea, coffee and chocolate became fashionable in the late 17th century, and over the next two centuries large numbers of pots for serving these drinks were made.

The shapes of tea and coffee pots can help with dating them, but because many 18th-century styles were repeated in the 19th and 20th centuries you need to check the marks on the base as well to tell whether the piece is a later reproduction. There is nothing wrong with buying, say, a 19th-century coffee pot in an 18th-century style, provided the marks are correct for the date it was made and the pot is priced as a reproduction. Bear in mind that coffee and teapots were made to be used and many have become well worn as a result – before you buy one examine it carefully for damage, which can be expensive to restore.

MARKINGS

Teapots are usually marked on the base – it's less common to find marks on the side. The maker's mark on a handle may be different from that on the body, as handles are nearly always later replacements, particularly if they are made of silver. Lids should also be marked.

▲ TEAPOTS

The "bullet" teapot has a lid with a concealed hinge, which was attached before the base was soldered on. Check lids carefully before buying – if the hinge is weak it may be impossible to restore. £4,000+

◀ DECORATION
Decoration can help with dating. This piece shows a technique known as bright-cutting, which was popular in the late 18th century. £1,500–2,000

WHAT TO LOOK FOR

- Check the point where the handle joins the body to make sure it's secure.
- Examine the hinge on the lid – check it is not weak or restored
- Make sure the spout isn't split.
- Breathe on the finial and around the spout and hinges – this helps to show repairs.

◀ STYLES
Some 19th-century teapots were so elaborately decorated it is hard to imagine they were ever used! This one, made in 1814, is covered with undulating foliage and has a handle made to look like bark. £1,500–2,000

COFFEE POTS

This 1734 coffee pot could have been used either for coffee or chocolate, but pots which have a removable finial, with a hole in the lid to insert a swizzle stick for stirring the sediment are usually termed "chocolate pots.". Some examples were even produced with matching stands and burners, all of which should bear the same marks.

PAUL DE LAMERIE

One of the most acclaimed silversmiths of the 18th century, Paul de Lamerie, was a Huguenot (a French Protestant) and a political refugee who built up a prosperous London business. De Lamerie's clients included royalty and his most famous pieces were very lavishly decorated.

MARKS

These should be in a line by the handle, or in a group, or scattered on the base. Lids should also be marked.

MAKERS

The mark of a well-known maker can add enormously to the value of any piece of silver – this pot was made by Paul de Lamerie, so it would be worth over £30,000; a similar pot from a lesser known maker would cost £5,000–7,000.

● Other famous and collectable names to look out for are: the Batemans, the Barnards, the Fox family, Robert Garrard & Co. and Paul Storr.

ALTERATIONS

During the 19th century, covered tankards, such as the one on the left, became unfashionable and were sometimes converted into the much more popular coffee pots. Converted pots, such as that on the right, are illegal unless the additions are marked.

MUGS & JUGS

A huge variety of cups, tankards and jugs have been made over the centuries. They remain highly popular with today's collectors. The vast majority of those you are likely to come across today date from the 18th century or later. Although silver is relatively robust, jugs and mugs have often been well used and condition is important to value – so examine pieces carefully before buying them.

Other factors which affect the value of mugs and jugs are common to any type of silver – namely quality, date and maker. You will find that a mug marked by a known maker will invariably cost more than an unmarked one. Elaborate decoration will also raise the price – although take care because many once plain 18th-century tankards (lidded mugs) were elaborately decorated in the Victorian period and these are less desirable than a plain piece in original condition.

MUGS	TANKARDS
BALUSTER MUG c.1740 £1,500–3,000	**EARLY 18TH-CENTURY TANKARD** £4,000–5,000
WHEN AND WHY Made from the late 17thC, early mugs mirror the shapes of pottery – with bulbous bases and slender necks. Those made in the early 18thC had straight tapered sides; later the baluster shape became popular. Mugs became fashionable as christening gifts in the 19thC.	Most date from c.1600–1780. Made for drinking ale, they became less prevalent as wine and spirits became more popular. Georgian tankards are usually plain; some have armorials. Tankards made in the 19thC (often for presentation) were usually very elaborate.
WHAT TO LOOK FOR **Marks:** until the end of the 18thC, in a group under the base; later pieces are marked in a line by the handle. • Check handles and rims for signs of weakening or splitting. • Examine sides for signs of erased armorials (see p197).	**Marks:** on one side of body or base and on lid; earlier tankards have marks in a line on top of the lid; later they are in a group inside. • Check handle sockets; they may have become weak. • Examine the thickness of cover – if it's domed, and thin, it may have been reworked from a flat lid.
OTHER STYLES	

BEWARE

Tankards were often converted into more useful jugs during the 19th century. To be legal the conversion must have later marks on any parts which were added – such as the spout. This jug was once an 18th-century tankard but it was converted and decorated in the Victorian period. Pieces which have been converted from other forms usually have less elegant proportions than originals. £1,500–2,000

JUGS

CREAM JUG, 1730
£1,500–3,000

Made from the 16thC for shaving or for serving liquids such as beer, wine, water, milk or cream. Earlier jugs occasionally had hinged lids, but by the mid-18thC many small open jugs on three legs were made for serving milk or cream.

Marks: should be on the base or on body, near handle, or under spout. Lidded jugs should have a full set of marks on the body and a maker's mark and lion passant only on the lid – a full set of marks on the lid means it was probably once a tankard!
- Beware of soldering around the spout – it could indicate a less valuable conversion.

SAUCEBOATS

GEORGE III SAUCEBOAT, 1761
£3,500–4,500

Earliest date from c.1710 and have a spout at each end and two handles on either side of the centre. Later, shallow jug-like sauce boats with central pedestal feet were popular. Three small feet were used in mid-18thC, after which central bases returned to favour.

Marks: usually underneath in a straight line; those made in the 1770s sometimes have marks under the lip.
- Check legs aren't bent or pushed through the body.
- Examine handles (they can be vulnerable).
- Look at rims – these can be split.
- Pairs – they are worth at least three times the value of singles.

WHEN AND WHY

WHAT TO LOOK FOR

OTHER STYLES

CADDIES & CASTERS

Don't be shocked by the extravagance and the cost of the caddies on this page – tea was once so expensive that it was drunk only in the wealthiest homes, and the caddies for storing this precious commodity were intended as objects for display as much as for storage. Caddies were usually kept in the drawing room; some had detachable caps for measuring the tea, while others were even fitted with a lock and key to protect their precious contents from dishonest servants! Nowadays,

caddies are keenly collected – and the finest examples can be expensive.

Casters also played an essential role in fashionable dining rooms as liberal quantities of spices and seasonings were essential to disguise the flavour of stale food. Early casters had straight sides; baluster casters were made from c.1705, becoming taller during the century. Most were originally made in pairs or sets and today these are always particularly sought after.

▶ CADDIES
Sets of caddies always command a premium. This set of two caddies and a sugar box would be particularly valuable because each piece has its original arms and it comes complete with its fitted box.
£10,000–15,000

▲ CASTERS
Sugar casters first appeared in sets of three; one large caster for sugar, and two smaller ones for dry mustard and pepper. The shape of casters changed little from c.1705. Better quality ones, such as this, have elaborately pierced covers. This is one of a set made by David Tanqueray in 1713 and is worth over £5,000.

▲ MARKS
The bodies and lids of caddies should have a full set of matching hallmarks, although early 18th-century pieces with detachable lids, such as this one, are often unmarked on the cap.
£2,500–3,500

WHAT TO LOOK FOR
This caddy has three key features you should look out for on other pieces:
- high-quality decoration
- unworn condition
- date marks of the 18th century – 19th-century caddies are usually less valuable. This particular one is worth about £2,500–3,500.

SALVERS & TRAYS

The difference between salvers and trays is that trays have handles while salvers do not. Both were used as presentation pieces as well as for practical purposes, and good examples are always popular with collectors. Many salvers survive from c.1700 onwards, but trays were not made until the end of the 18th century. Those that are decorated with elaborate borders will probably cost more than simpler ones.

Salvers and trays often had the armorials of their owner engraved in the centre – if the crest belongs to a well-known family it can increase the item's value – as well as providing an interesting insight into the previous owner of your tray.

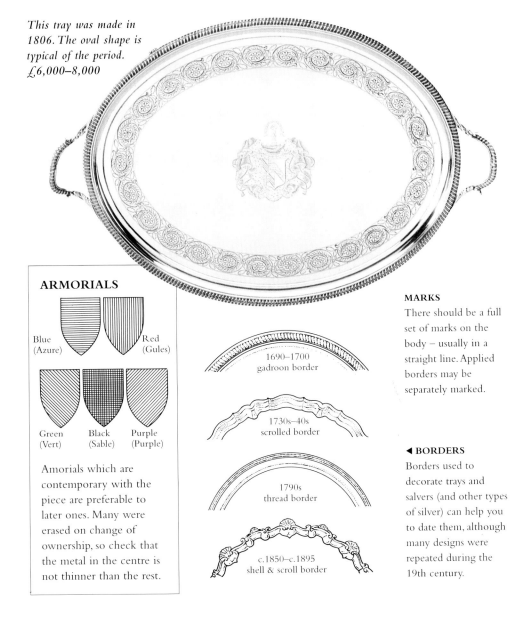

This tray was made in 1806. The oval shape is typical of the period.
£6,000–8,000

ARMORIALS

Blue (Azure)   Red (Gules)

Green (Vert)   Black (Sable)   Purple (Purple)

Amorials which are contemporary with the piece are preferable to later ones. Many were erased on change of ownership, so check that the metal in the centre is not thinner than the rest.

1690–1700
gadroon border

1730s–40s
scrolled border

1790s
thread border

c.1850–c.1895
shell & scroll border

MARKS

There should be a full set of marks on the body – usually in a straight line. Applied borders may be separately marked.

◀ BORDERS

Borders used to decorate trays and salvers (and other types of silver) can help you to date them, although many designs were repeated during the 19th century.

FLATWARE

Knives, forks and spoons are usually termed "flatware" by silver collectors. Depending on your budget there are a number of different ways to collect flatware. Complete services, which usually comprise settings for 12, are rare and so may seem prohibitively expensive, but odd numbers of spoons and forks in the most common patterns, such as

Old English, Fiddle, or Hanoverian are relatively easy to find, and it's often far less costly to build up a service piecemeal. Flatware services do not usually include knives. These often had thin metal blades which can quickly become worn; as a result most collectors prefer reproductions, which are more robust.

▶ APOSTLE SPOONS

Produced from the mid-15th century, Apostle spoons (so-called because the handle is decorated with the figure of an Apostle) are among the most valuable of spoons. These are sometimes faked by reshaping ordinary 18th-century spoons – you can spot these by the stiffness of the figure and the later marks, if they remain. £1,000+

▼ PATTERNS

Different patterns are easily identifiable by their names; below are some examples of the most popular ones which have been repeated continually since they were first made and are still in use today. The date of a piece of flatware can affect its price even more dramatically than other types of silver.

1 Rat-tail **2** Old English **3** Fiddle end
4 Beaded **5** Albany

▲ OLD ENGLISH PATTERN

The most desirable flatware services contain a dozen tablespoons, table forks, dessert spoons, dessert forks and teaspoons. This 77-piece Old English pattern service has the added bonus of a basting spoon and other serving pieces and this will increase its value.
£6,000–8,000

BEWARE

Badly worn flatware is virtually impossible to restore and is worth only scrap value. Only the fork on the left is in good condition. The one in the centre is badly worn, the other has been trimmed to disguise the damage.

CANDLESTICKS

Even though we no longer depend upon candlelight for illumination, nothing graces the dining table more elegantly than a pair of silver candlesticks. Most candlesticks and candelabra were originally made in pairs or larger sets. Expect to pay more than double for a pair of candlesticks than you would for two singles – even if they're the same design and size! To be a true "pair" candlesticks must be the work of one maker and of more or less the same date.

This typical mid-18th century candlestick was made by casting the separate sections – base, stem (or column), sconce (or capital) and nozzle – in moulds. Cast candlesticks are usually more desirable than "loaded" ones,

which were made from thin sheets of silver with an iron rod down the inside, and filled with pitch to give weight. A pair of cast candlesticks like this would cost £3,000+.

NOZZLES

Nozzles – which hold the candle and stop wax dripping down the stem – should have the maker's mark and a lion passant.

SCONCES

If the seam on the stem and sconce is not in alignment, the candlestick has been heavily repaired. Here you can see the lion passant mark on the sconce.

STEMS

During the 18th century, stems became progressively taller; early candlesticks rarely measure more than 7in/13cm; this mid-18th century one is 10in/25cm.

BASES

Sheet candlesticks are marked in a line above the base, cast ones are marked in the well, or under each corner.

◀ CHAMBER CANDLESTICKS

These were used to light the way to bed and, unlike other candlesticks, are usually sold singly. This one was made in the 1780s and, like many of its kind, is fitted with its own snuffer.
£1,000–1,500

▲ CANDELABRA

The separate parts of a candelabra are frequently replaced – four nozzles on this pair are replacements, but these examples were made by John Scofield, an eminent 18th-century maker, so the price would still be £15,000+.

DRESSING-TABLE SETS

Dressing-table sets, sometimes fitted in wooden travelling cases, were made throughout the 19th and early 20th centuries. They succeed the earlier lavish toilet sets that, from the late 17th century, were essential luxuries for noblewomen and very often given to them by their husbands to commemorate their marriage or the birth of an heir. The essential accessories of a dressing-table set were a hand mirror and hairbrushes, backed with silver; perfume bottles or flasks with silver mounts, clothes brushes, combs and shoehorns were often also included. Larger sets may also have contained eye-baths, jewel caskets, pomade jars and even drinking cups, and some elaborate examples featured secret compartments. Made of silver or silver gilt, these items were often either embossed or enamelled, and then engraved with initials or a monogram. It is important to check that all the pieces in a set are by the same maker and match exactly. Prices vary according to the number of items in a set, the extent of the decoration and the condition.

▶ **19TH-CENTURY TRAVELLING SETS**
This parcel-gilt, velvet-lined set, made in 1844 by R. & S. Garrard & Co., is a fine example of the portable sets in vogue in the 19th century. By the 1830s such sets were no longer confined to the dressing table of a lady's chamber and range from the simple to the highly sumptuous.
£7,000–10,000

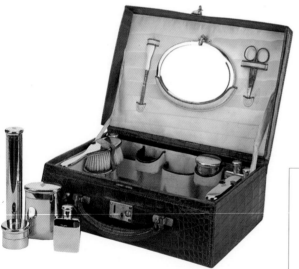

▲ **EARLY 20TH-CENTURY TRAVELLING SETS**
Ladies' travelling sets such as this one from the 1920s, fitted in an elegant crocodile-skin case, are more popular among today's collectors than larger, more lavish examples. Travelling boxes usually came with outer canvas covers to protect the exotic wood or leather from wear and tear. £1,500-1,800

MARKS
Garrard has been a key name in the silver trade since the 18th century, with Robert Garrard I and his son Robert Garrard II particularly influential. Due mainly to the direction of the latter, the family firm was appointed Goldsmith to the Crown in 1830 and, in 1843, Crown Jewellers. This mark was used from 1822 until 1900, but wares made since 1900 bear the initials "RG" only. In 1963 Garrard & Co. merged with Mappin & Webb Ltd and Elkington & Co. to form British Silverware Ltd.

▶ **SETS FOR MEN**
From the 19th century, silver toilet sets for gentlemen were not uncommon, although they were always smaller and not as elaborate as those for women, and for personal use rather than show. They were usually housed in fitted cases and were essential accessories when travelling by the newly popular motor car. The scent bottles are generally plain, with very simple decoration, as shown by the three cologne bottles in the leather travelling box featured right. Made c.1920, these bottles have glass stoppers fitted within silver screw tops. £400–450

◀ **POPULAR GIFTS**
Small silver sets for the dressing table such as this one decorated with gold-coloured enamel (1940) were popular presents for young women coming of age. Many found today are of fine quality and good value for money, although those that have been used extensively may be quite worn. Watch out for damage to the enamel and check that an engraved monogram has not been removed, which leaves the silver very thin. Sets in good condition, fitted in a pretty, lined box, will be most highly priced. £250–500

WELL-KNOWN NAMES
Dressing-table silver by a celebrated maker such as Bernard Instone is extremely collectable and commands a high price today. These sets are made of very high-quality, heavy-gauge silver and typically show close attention to detail, for example through the use of exotic materials or elaborate decoration such as hand-hammering seen on the mirror handle (1925) shown here. £2,200–2,500

MISCELLANEOUS SILVER

If you want to collect on a modest budget, the vast array of small novel objects made from silver can provide an ideal collecting area. Look carefully in the display cabinets of a general antiques shop, or at a silver auction, and among the pieces you are likely to find individual items such as pincushions, card cases, nutmeg graters, vinaigrettes, snuff boxes, sewing cases, glove stretchers, letter openers, vestas and sovereign cases – to name but a few! When you examine the marks you'll find Birmingham's anchor mark appears again and again, because from the late 18th century, silversmiths in this area produced small silver items in their thousands. Usually, the less expensive pieces tend to be those produced during the 19th century; earlier objects are scarcer and can be highly priced.

▶ SNUFF BOXES

The decoration of small boxes has a huge bearing on their price; hunting scenes are particularly sought after – this silver gilt snuff box, made in 1828, would be worth over £1,500+.

▶ VINAIGRETTES

Vinaigrettes such as these were used to contain aromatic salts, vinegar or perfume and are smaller than snuff boxes, although equally in demand. £1,500–2,000

▶ DECORATION

A piece of silver decorated with a recognizable scene is especially desirable. This Victorian pin tray shows Windsor Castle – one of the most popular views; St Paul's Cathedral or scenes of Edinburgh are also keenly collected. £800–1,200

WHAT TO LOOK FOR:

Silver boxes
- Check the hinge isn't damaged.
- Make sure the marks on the base are the same as those on the lid – if they don't match, the box may have been altered.

BEWARE

Sometimes snuff boxes are turned into vinaigrettes by adding grilles – just as vinaigrettes are sometimes turned into pill boxes by removing their grilles! £200

▶ **MIRRORS**
Like most silver-framed
mirrors, this one is part
of a set of dressing
table silver. Its
unusually fine quality
is reflected in the high
price it commands –
over £100,000 for the
set! During the late
19th and early 20th
century other less
expensive mirrors
were made from
wooden frames
covered with velvet
and decorated with
die-stamped silver.
These are often
badly worn and
can be very difficult
to clean but are still
sought after.

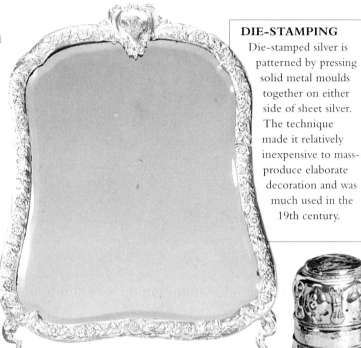

DIE-STAMPING
Die-stamped silver is
patterned by pressing
solid metal moulds
together on either
side of sheet silver.
The technique
made it relatively
inexpensive to mass-
produce elaborate
decoration and was
much used in the
19th century.

▲ **SILVER AND
GLASS**
Glass and silver are
often combined to
produce some highly
decorative objects;
particularly dressing
table accessories, but
before you decide to
buy a silver and glass
object remember to
check that the glass
is not broken because
it can be costly to
replace, especially if
shaped. This 1911
Ramsden & Carr silver
and enamel case still
contains its original
glass bottle. £2,000+

▲ **ART NOUVEAU
SILVER**
Silver items reflecting
the Art Nouveau style,
marked by well known
makers or retailers, are
becoming increasingly
collectable. This box,
with its typical Art
Nouveau motif on
the lid, was made for
Liberty & Co. and
would be worth
£800–1,200.

SILVER DECORATION
Small silver is decorated in a wide
variety of ways. Some of the most
common terms used to describe the
techniques are:
Bright-cutting: a type of faceted
engraving.
Chasing or Embossing: patterns
made by hammering or punching tiny
marks onto the silver.
Card-cut decoration: flat shapes
added to handle mounts, etc.
Filigree: open wire panels decorated
with little silver beads.

CIGAR & CIGARETTE CASES

As a result of the increased popularity of smoking in the late 19th century, cigar and cigarette cases were produced in great numbers. They were made in two forms: either as boxes for storing cigars and cigarettes at home or as portable carrying cases. Early cigarette cases are small, as cigarettes made before c.1900 did not have filters and were consequently shorter than those manufactured today. Many portable examples are oblong, with rounded sides and corners, and are characteristically slim or curved to fit comfortably inside a pocket. Enamelled cigarette cases featuring battle scenes, aircraft and animals are among the most sought after by collectors, although in general those decorated with naughty erotic scenes tend to achieve the highest prices.

◀ CIGAR CASES
This Russian case with a pull-off cap was designed to hold a small bundle of cheroots or cigars and would fit comfortably inside a pocket. These cigar cases were made in great numbers in the mid-19th century, and were embellished in a variety of decorative techniques, from embossed hunting scenes to enamelled and elegant engraved designs. The ancient technique of niello, revived in the 19th century, has been used to decorate this example. £400–600

▶ CIGARETTE CASES
This cigarette case (1925), which has been enamelled with *trompe l'oeil* decoration to simulate a packet of cigarettes, is typical of early 20th-century designs. It comes with a matching vesta case. £600–800

▼ EXCLUSIVE DESIGNS
After World War I cigarette smoking became fashionable among the wealthy, and elaborate silver cigarette cases, such as this spectacular tube-shaped example (1915) set with a rose-diamond thumb-piece, were made for ladies to carry on special occasions. This example was designed by the Russian goldsmith and jeweller Carl Fabergé and is extremely desirable. £2,000–3,000

FABERGÉ MARK
Under the direction of Carl Fabergé (1846–1920) the Fabergé firm in St Petersburg became one of the world's most renowned jewellers. As shown, designs are marked "KF" or "K. Fabergé" in Cyrillic letters.

◀ ART DECO

This fine-quality cigarette case, decorated in the Art Deco style with bold, bright colours and a stark geometric design, typifies the exuberant examples produced in the 1920s and 1930s. This case was possibly made in continental Europe and would originally have been fairly expensive. £300–400

COLLECTING

Late 19th- and early 20th-century cigarette cases do not fit modern cigarettes, and unless the cases are jewelled or made of an especially valuable material, in general – as with vesta cases – they are not especially popular among today's collectors.

▶ SINGLE CIGAR CASES

This unusual Birmingham torpedo-shaped case (1902) was intended to hold a single cigar and fit neatly into a jacket pocket. Holders for two or three cigars were also made. Cases such as this, with elegant decoration, are highly prized. £200–300

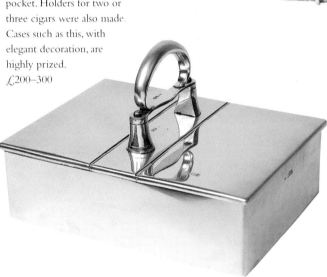

◀ CIGARETTE BOX

Fine-quality silver cigar and cigarette boxes for the table or desk, such as this very handsome London-made example (1928) with a sprung handle, had wooden or solid-silver bases, whereas less-valuable examples are usually lined in the base with pieces of leather that are "loaded" and lined with cedar wood to keep the contents fresh. Today these boxes are often converted for use as jewellery boxes, lined with velvet. £900–1,000

▶ FAMOUS SMOKERS

This late 1970s parcel-gilt cigar box by Stuart Devlin has a flat base, wooden liner and flat silver top. It has been embossed with scenes depicting the life of Sir Winston Churchill, whose celebrated fondness for cigars makes him an appropriate subject. £600–800

VESTA CASES

Vesta cases were made to hold friction matches, invented c.1840 and known from the late 19th century as "vestas" after the Roman goddess of the hearth. These small cases were initally adapted from snuff boxes, with the addition of serrated strikers. As smoking became more fashionable from the late 19th century, small rectangular boxes with rounded corners and closely fitting hinged lids – vital to prevent matches from combusting – were popularly made for vestas. They were produced in a wide variety of shapes, with engraved, chased or enamelled decoration. From c.1890 Birmingham was the major centre of production of these in Britain, although the very highest-quality workmanship is usually found on London-made cases. Some vesta cases have double compartments for matches, or were combined with other objects such as pen knives, cigar cutters or stamp holders. From the late 19th century, novelty cases were produced in great numbers. With the introduction of the more durable petrol lighter, the production of vesta cases stopped after World War I.

▶ EROTICA
Many vesta cases made in the late Victorian and Edwardian periods were enamelled with nudes seated or reclining in erotic poses, as on this example of 1904. Providing a welcome diversion for a naughty gentleman while lighting his pipe, these risqué designs adorn some of the most highly treasured vestas. £300–500

▲ ▶ ANIMAL FORMS
Some of the most common novelty vesta cases are in the form of birds and animals such as the "fish" (1900) and plated "owl" with glass inset eyes (1890s) shown here. The head of the "owl" tilts back on a hinge. It is a high-quality London-made vesta case and would be sought after among collectors.
Fish: £200–250; owl: £100–150

▼ SPORTING THEMES
This vesta case (1920s) in the form of a golf ball would no doubt appeal to golfing enthusiasts as well as to collectors of vesta cases. The lid is hinged at the top for easy closure, and has a loop for suspension from a silver chain. The flattened round shape means that this case would neatly slip into the pocket. £200–400

**▶ NOVELTY
VESTA CASES**
Novelty vesta cases
such as this *trompe l'oeil*
example (c.1900) in the
form of a rolled-up
newspaper with an
enamelled "stamp"
were produced in the
USA in great numbers
between 1890 and
1910. The interiors
were often gilded
to prevent the
phosphorous
match heads
from reacting with
the silver. £400–500

**◀ PICTORIAL
VESTA CASES**
Pictorial cases such as
this example featuring
the popular characters
Mr Punch and his dog
Toby are great rarities
and extremely valuable.
The finest examples are
usually enamelled (as
here), although others
are chased or engraved.
Fine pictorial vesta
cases were a speciality
of makers such as
Sampson Mordan
& Co. and Henry
William Dee.
£5,000–7,000

◀ SETS
This unusually large
(3in/7.5cm) vesta case
(1903) was made in
London by Sampson
Mordan & Co. This
popular design, made
as part of a series with
each enamelled soldier
representing a different
regiment, was first
produced in the late
19th century. Cases
from this series feature
very fine enamelling
and are highly prized
and valuable.
£2,000–3,000

◀ ART NOUVEAU
The major exponent of
the Art Nouveau style in
the USA was Tiffany &
Co., who inspired the
mass-production of such
designs as this stamped
example of c.1900. The
sensuous nymph and
naturalistic imagery are
typical Art Nouveau
motifs. The serrated edge
at the base is for striking
matches. £60–80

**SAMPSON
MORDAN & CO.**
This London firm –
famed for its pens,
pencils and novelty
and character wares –
entered its first mark
in the 1820s.

OTHER METALS

Pewter, brass, copper, Sheffield plate and electroplate are just a selection of the most commonly seen metals that have been used to make a wide variety of decorative and utilitarian objects throughout the centuries. Dating unmarked metal objects can be a potential minefield if you're not sure what to look out for. The style of a metal object rarely provides a reliable way of deciding when it was made because many early designs were copied in the 19th and 20th centuries.

Before you make a purchase don't be afraid to pick up different pieces to compare their weight: most modern copies are noticeably lighter in weight than genuinely old ones. Look for signs of wear and tear consistent with age: the undersides of objects should be covered with a fine patina of scratches and edges of plates and hollow wares should be worn smooth. Treat anything with sharp edges or which looks as though it's in perfect condition with suspicion.

◀ **PEWTER**

Pewter, or "poor man's silver" as it is sometimes known, is an alloy mainly made of tin and lead, in varying proportions. Prices range from around £800, although pieces in poor condition are less desirable. This c.1780 flagon has an attractive acorn finial and domed cover typical of the period, as well as "wriggle-work" decoration, and is worth £2,000–3,000.

HOW OLD IS IT?

- Pewter more than 50 years old develops a characteristic dull glowing patina through polishing and continual use.
- Fine-quality pieces made before c.1826 are usually marked with a maker's stamp and a crowned X mark showing the purity of the metal.
- Tavern pewter made after c.1826 should bear capacity marks.

▲ **BRASS**

Old brass objects, such as this George III candlestick, often reflect the decorative styles of silver objects from the same period. Pieces marked with maker's stamps are especially desirable and command a premium; this candlestick is marked by the famous maker E. Berry, and so a pair would be worth £1,000–2,000.

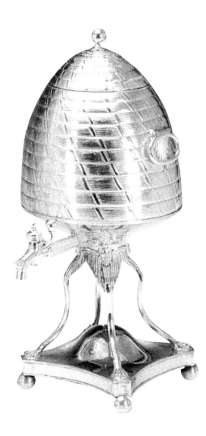

◀ **SHEFFIELD PLATE**
Old Sheffield plate was made from a thin layer of silver fused onto a sheet of copper. This type of plate was used from c.1760 as a less expensive alternative to silver. Although highly collectable, Sheffield plate remains good value; this c.1810 novelty tea urn is worth £800–1,200.

● You can usually identify old Sheffield plate by its slightly pinkish tinge caused by areas of silver wearing thin and revealing the copper body beneath.

▶ **COPPER**
If you find a piece of metalware marked with a twisted rope symbol you're in luck because this is factory mark of leading 19th-century manufacturers Perry, Son & Co. This unusually-shaped Perry jug is doubly desirable as it was also designed by Dr Christopher Dresser, one of the most influential designers of the Victorian period. £1,500–2,500

▲ **ELECTROPLATE**
● The technique of applying a thin layer of silver over a nickel or alloy base was developed in the mid-19th century.

● Electroplate is very susceptible to wear – you can see how the silver has worn thin on parts of this corkscrew. £300–500

● You can have pieces replated but this gives an unnaturally bright appearance which is considered less desirable.

Antique glass is a fascinating and accessible collecting area. Despite the fragility of the substance, glass from the 18th century and later is relatively easy to find, and plain objects can still be inexpensive.

Although the precise origins of glass production are unknown it was certainly made in ancient Egypt, Syria and Rome. The method by which the basic material is made is very simple: A silica (usually sand) is heated with a flux (potash or soda) and a stabiliser (usually lime) until it fuses together.

One of the most obvious objects to collect are antique drinking glasses. Made in large numbers throughout the 18th century, these have long been popular with collectors. Value depends on the rarity of the decoration, as well as the shape of the bowl, stem and foot. Many of the more valuable types of 18th-century glass have been faked so always try to buy from a reputable source and take expert advice when in doubt about a purchase.

The colourful glass produced in the 19th century is also becoming increasingly popular with some collectors. Many new glass-making techniques were introduced during this period as were a number of new colour variations. Two of the most attractive 19th-century types to look out for are cameo glass and overlay glass, although the best examples, those marked by famous makers, can be expensive. Despite this growing popularity, unmarked glass from the 19th century is still available at reasonable prices, and 19th-century table glass can sometimes be less expensive than modern equivalents.

BASICS

The body of a glass item is known as the metal. The colour and texture of the metal change according to the ingredients used. There are three main types of glass:

SODA GLASS

Also known as *cristallo*. Made in Venice from the 13th century. The soda was derived from the ashes of burnt seaweed, and gave the molten glass a malleable quality which allowed glassmakers to create very elaborate shapes.

POTASH GLASS

Called *waldglas* in German. Potash glass was first made in Bohemia in Northern Europe. The potash was derived from burnt wood and bracken. Potash glass is particularly hard and is well suited to cutting and engraving.

LEAD GLASS

Made from potash with the addition of lead oxide (instead of lime), this glass, developed by George Ravenscroft, was used in England and Ireland from the late 17th century, and in Europe from the late 18th century. Lead glass is characterized by its weight and clarity and is well suited to cutting.

DECORATION

Decoration which has been added onto glass can add substantially to its value. The main decorative techniques used are:

- Cutting
- Enamelling
- Gilding
- Engraving

CUTTING

Cut facets in glass emphasize its refractive (light-transmitting) qualities. Cut decoration can help with dating. The earliest patterns were shallow surface cuts. Patterns became increasingly elaborate in the late 18th and early 19th centuries (see p214–215).

An 18th-century enamelled wine-glass attributed to William Beilby £4,000–6,000

ENAMELLING

Painting in coloured enamels was popular on Venetian glass from the late 15th century and became fashionable in England in the mid–18th century. The best-known English enamellers were the Beilby family. There are two types of enamelling:

- **Fire enamelling:** the enamel was painted on the surface of the glass, and the glass fired to fix the decoration. This is the most permanent and usual form of enamelling.
- **Cold enamelling:** also known as cold painting, involved painting the glass without firing. This technique has the disadvantage that the enamelling wears off easily, and was mainly used on inexpensive items.

GILDING

Gold decoration can be applied to the surface of glass in a number of different ways. The most permanent method of gilding is by firing the gold onto the surface of the glass. An alternative method was oil gilding, which involved applying a gold powder or leaf onto an oil base and then burnishing. Gilding applied using this method is easily rubbed off.

ENGRAVING

Engraving was first introduced by Roman glassmakers It is used to add both patterns and scenes. There are four types of engraving:

A diamond-etched wine glass. Dutch, 17th century. £1,400–3,200

Diamond point engraving: the design was scratched onto the surface of the glass using a tool with a diamond nib. This technique was used in the 16th century in Venice, and in Britain in the late 16th century.

Wheel engraving: the design was engraved using small copper wheels of varying diameter, which rotated against the surface of the glass, and an abrasive. The method was widely used in Germany in the 17th century, and became the most common

form of engraving in Britain from the 18th century.

A stipple-engraved glass, Dutch, c.1745. £2,500–3,500

Stipple engraving: a fine diamond needle was tapped and drawn on the surface to form a design built up from dots and small lines. This technique was popular in the Netherlands during the 18th century and is also found on English glasses.

Acid etching: this technique involved covering the surface of the glass with varnish or grease, and scratching the design with a needle or sharp tool. The surface was then exposed to hydrofluoric acid which etched the design on the glass.

This method was popular in the 19th century.

AUTHENTICITY

Fakes of many of the more expensive types of antique glass abound. Victorian glassmakers made imitations of 18th-century glass and many fakes have also been produced in the 20th century. These are often discernible in four key ways:

- **Colour:** the distinctive tint caused by impurities may not be present in reproductions.
- **Manufacturing method:** hand-blown glass usually has a pontil mark – a rough bump under the stem – where it was cut from the pontil rod. It may have striations of ripples in the glass and the rim may be of uneven thickness. Later machine-made glass does not have these imperfections.
- **Proportions:** glass has varied in style and proportions throughout the centuries. On old glasses the foot is usually as wide as the bowl, or slightly wider. The wrong proportions may indicate a fake.

DRINKING GLASSES & DECANTERS

When compared with antique ceramics of the same date, the majority of antique glass remains relatively inexpensive. You can still find sets of 19th-century glasses for under £150 at antiques shops and general auctions, and incredibly, an antique decanter will often cost less than a modern one.

During the 18th century, large numbers of drinking glasses were made in many different styles. The variety still available means that there are lots of possibilities for collecting glass. You may decide to focus your collection on, say, glasses with air twist stems, Jacobite glass, cordials, or gilded glass, or you may prefer to simply collect single examples of each type as they catch your interest. Simpler 18th-century glasses may cost as little as £80–120, but very elegant examples, or those with elaborate or particularly unusual decoration can be much more valuable.

SIGNS OF AGE
- a conical or funnel bowl
- a foot that is wider than the rim
- flaws in the glass and a slightly irregular body indicating it was handmade
- a bumpy "pontil mark" under the foot
- a greenish or greyish tinge in the glass
- signs of wear on the foot – fine and irregular scratches.

JACOBITE GLASSES
Glasses engraved with roses, doves and oak leaves were made in the 18th century to show furtive allegiance to the Old Pretender (James Edward Stuart) and the Young Pretender (Charles Edward Stuart). Jacobite glasses are particularly collectable but can be expensive – an especially rare one was sold in 1992 for £66,000.

◀ COLOUR TWISTS
Stems with threads of coloured glass are keenly sought after; value depends on the number of colours. This one has blue and opaque white twists, and would be worth about £1,800.

▶ GILDED GLASS
Glasses with original, soft 18th-century gilding, such as this one, are very desirable, but are rarely seen in perfect condition. £600+

BEWARE
You can spot less desirable later gilding by its harder, brighter appearance.

Collectors categorize and assign value to drinking glasses according to the shape and decoration of the bowl, stem and foot. This one is of medium quality – it has a plain round funnel bowl and a relatively simple knopped stem, but because it is larger than most 18th-century glasses (measuring 9in/22cm tall) it is worth slightly more than usual. £600.

The bowl of this 1720 glass is a round funnel shape; other bowl shapes are show below.

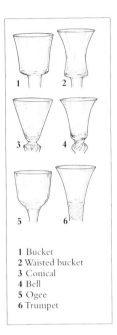

1 Bucket
2 Waisted bucket
3 Conical
4 Bell
5 Ogee
6 Trumpet

This is a multi-knopped stem, so-called because of the series of projections with which it is decorated; some stems have only one knop, which may contain a tear drop of air, other stems are decorated with air twists.

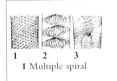

1   2   3

1 Multiple spiral

2 Single series

3 Double series.

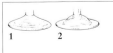

1   2

1 Conical foot

2 Domed foot

This glass has a domed foot, a feature which is characteristic of many early glasses; others have conical feet. Check the edge of the rim for unevenness, as this may mean a chip has been ground down.

▶ **DECANTERS**
Decanters were often decorated with engraved or gilded labels describing their contents. This one is made from "Bristol" blue glass – an area associated with coloured decanters, although not all were made there. £250–350

CUT & PRESSED GLASS

Nothing makes glass sparkle more brightly in candlelight than cut decoration, and this is one reason why cutting has long been one of the most popular ways of embellishing all types of glass objects. Early glass was simply cut by hand, in fairly shallow patterns, but gradually patterns became deeper and designs more elaborate, and by c.1830 mechanized wheel cutting had become the norm. In the 19th century production increased as new techniques for machine-made, press-moulded glass – which looked like cut glass but was much quicker to produce – were developed in America.

Although 18th-century cut glass has increased in popularity and price; it can still be good value. If you want to collect cut glass to use on the dining table rather than simply for display look out for sweetmeat dishes, jellies, custards, fruit bowls and candlesticks; many of these are still relatively inexpensive, especially if you buy them singly.

▶ **IRISH GLASS**
If you see a piece of glass which looks rather lopsided the chances are it's Irish! Glass made in Ireland, such as this bowl, can also often be identified by its greyish tinge and the typical shallow diamond cutting of the decoration. £800

CUT OR PRESSED?
Cut glass is usually far more desirable and valuable than pressed glass, and there are several ways of identifying it:
- sharply faceted decoration
- no mould lines along the inside
- irregular thickness.

CUT GLASS PATTERNS
These are some of the most common cut glass patterns used during the 18th and 19th centuries. However, because they have been repeated in the 20th century, the pattern alone is not a reliable guarantee of authenticity – you should also look at the colour of the glass, and for flaws in the metal and slight irregularities in shape that show it is handmade.

Plain sharp diamonds

Pillar flutes

Star cutting

Strawberry diamonds

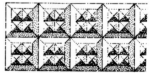

Cross-cut diamonds

Fine diamonds

THE HANDKERCHIEF TEST

Plain early glass has sometimes been decorated with later engraving to make it seem more valuable. To check the decoration is authentic, drop a white handkerchief in the glass – old engraving will look dark and grey, new engraving white and powdery.

- A handkerchief is also useful to reveal the colour of the glass.

▲ PRESSED GLASS
During the Victorian period clean and coloured pressed glass plates were often made to commemorate important events; this one celebrates Queen Victoria's Golden Jubilee. £30–40

▼ LATER CUT GLASS
Extensive sets of less elaborate turn of the century cut glass can still be very affordable. This is a selection from a set of 89 items made c.1900; the whole set would cost about £400–600.

◀ ROCK CRYSTAL
Engraved lead glass, cut and polished to simulate the natural facets of rock crystal, is known as "Rock Crystal" and became popular during the 19th century. £300–400

COLOURED GLASS

Coloured drinking glasses and decanters were produced in relatively small quantities in England during the 18th century. However, many 18th-century styles were copied in the late 19th/early 20th century and some later versions are so convincing that even more experienced collectors can be confused.

Most of the coloured glass you are likely to come across dates from after c.1800, when many lavishly decorated glass objects were made in Britain, on the Continent and in the United States.

WHAT TO LOOK FOR

● Pieces marked by the workshops of Thomas Webb, W. H. B. & J. Richardson and Stevens & Williams (now Brierley)
● larger pieces
● unusual shapes – particularly for ornamental pieces
● multiple layers of glass
● high-quality design – Neo-classical figures are especially desirable.

◀ OPALINE GLASS
Although at first glance this goblet looks as though it's made from porcelain, it's actually an example of English opaline glass made c.1850. Much opaline glass was also made in France; quality can vary – the best pieces are made from lead crystal and are very heavy.
£400+

▶ CAMEO GLASS
Cameo glass – made by overlaying the base colour with a layer of contrasting glass which was then carved to reveal the colour underneath – is one of the more expensive types of 19th-century coloured glass. This large bottle is nicely carved and has a silver lid, so it is worth £1,500–2,000; but even miniature bottles would be worth £200.

▲ RUBY GLASS
Ruby glass, sometimes made from tinted glass or from clear glass with a ruby stain on the surface, was produced in both Bohemia and England. These pieces were made in England in the mid-19th century. The value of the piece on the left is high (£2,500–3,000) because of the elaborate silver gilt handles; the jug on the right is worth £500–700.

PAPERWEIGHTS

The most sought-after antique paperweights are those made by famous French factories such as Baccarat, Clichy and St Louis during the mid-19th century. Patterns were built up from tiny slices of different coloured rods or canes of glass, set in a mould and covered in clear glass. Sizes vary from under 2in/5cm to over 4in/10cm; unusual sizes, especially miniatures, are highly collectable.

BACCARAT

You can often identify the maker of a paperweight by the type of rods it contains and the way they are arranged. The rods in this example include silhouettes of a dog, a horse and a deer, all designs typical of the Baccarat factory. Other common Baccarat silhouettes include arrowheads and shamrocks. £6,500–7,000

BEWARE
Reproductions of antique paper-weights abound, but can be identified by their lighter weight.

IDENTIFYING MARKS
Baccarat paperweights often include signed and dated canes – this one is marked *B 1848*. St Louis and Clichy paperweights are also sometimes marked with initials.

MILLEFIORI
Millefiori (meaning "thousand flowers") paperweights are so-called because their canes resemble a carpet of flowers.

▲ ST LOUIS
Large single flower heads were much used by the St Louis factory. Sometimes flowers were laid on a criss-cross lattice ground, usually in white or pink, known as *latticinio*. £500–600

▲ CLICHY
Clichy weights can often be identified by the characteristic rose they contain. This one would be worth over £2,000 but more common types fetch from around £400.

▲ OVERLAY WEIGHTS
Some rare weights, such as this one made by Baccarat, contain a layer of opaque glass through which windows are cut to reveal the design beneath. This particular example would be worth £3,000 or more.

Clocks have been appreciated and treasured from at least the 17th century to the present day. Unlike other types of antiques, clocks are unique in that they are "working" pieces. Sometimes described as "mechanical pictures", clocks can be appreciated both for their visual appeal and for their technical mastery. They also serve a more practical purpose in telling you the time.

If you're a novice collector thinking of investing in a clock, it's probably best to buy one that's in working order. Most clocks can be repaired, but restoring a "bargain" can be a laborious and expensive business, and unless the problem is very straightforward it's often cheaper in the long run to buy a clock which has been properly overhauled and restored to working order by a skilled clockmaker.

Most clocks are relatively easy to date and identify because the vast majority were signed by their maker on the dial and movement, and records of most makers have survived thanks to the tight control of the governing body, the Clockmakers Company, which was founded in 1631. Value depends on the maker, movement, case and condition, but a clock's visual appeal lies largely in its case, which usually reflects the furniture style of the period, but these are rarely signed and little is known about this aspect of the trade.

Despite their popularity, clocks are available at a wide range of prices. Plain carriage clocks are available from about £800, a simple bracket clock might cost £4,000, and a late 19th-century longcase from £4,000.

BASICS

There are three key elements which you should assess before buying a clock;
- the mechanism, or movement
- the dial
- the case.

MOVEMENTS

The movement consists of a system of brass and steel wheels and gears, known as the train. It is usually housed between two brass plates.

The escapement: this part of the movement controls the speed at which a clock runs.

Verge or balance wheel escapement: the balanced wheel was used on lantern clocks until c.1670. The oscillating balance wheel releases the two pallets or "flags" on the vertical bar, which engage the toothed wheel. The verge escapement is similar but has a short pendulum.

Anchor escapement: this was first used in longcases from c.1670, and became standard for longcases and brackets. The anchor engages with the teeth of the escape wheel. Clocks with an anchor may have a long or short pendulum.

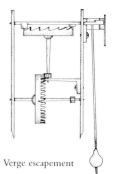

Verge escapement

Balance wheel

PENDULUM

Weight-driven and spring-driven clocks usually have a pendulum to control the clock's speed, which swings in a regular arc. The pendulum is a brass or steel rod with a metal disk, or bob, at the bottom (usually lead cased in brass). On a verge escapement the bob is usually on a threaded rod. On an anchor escapement, the bob slides on the rod and can be locked in place tightening a nut. Adjusting the position of the bob on the rod alters the timekeeping of the clock.

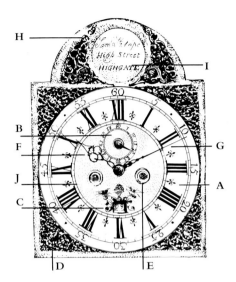

DIALS

A chapter ring
B subsidiary dial
C calendar aperture
D applied corner
　　spandrels
E winding holes
F hour hand
G minute hand
H dial arch
I engraved boss
J "matted" centre

The dial is the face
of the clock and is
attached to the
movement by a
number of brass "feet".
A dial has an important
bearing on price.
Clocks with replaced
dials are much less
desirable. There are
four main types of dial:

Brass dials: this is the
earliest type of dial,
used on lanterns,
brackets and longcases.

Each one has the hours
engraved on a separate
chapter ring.

Painted metal dials:
found on most clocks
after c.1800. These
became increasingly
elaborate in the 19th
century.

**Painted wooden
dials:** found on British
dial clocks, tavern
clocks and Continental
clocks. If authentic, the
wood should show
some signs of cracking
caused by changes in
temperature.

**Enamelled metal
dials:** common on
carriage clocks and
other types of French
clock. They are made
out of enamel which
hase been fired on top
of a thin copper sheet.

HANDS

Early clocks only have
one hand (for hours),
but from c.1660 most
have a minute and an
hour hand. Second
hands are usually
shown on a subsidiary
dial. Hands are usually
made from blued steel,
although gilded brass is
found from c.1790.
Until c.1740 the hour
hand was elaborate; the
minute hand was
longer and simpler.

● Replacement hands
　are acceptable if they
　are in the right style.

CASES

The case houses the
dial and movement.
Knowledge of materials
and styles is useful in
dating a clock and in
assessing its value.In
Britain and the United
States, wooden cases
were popular. Metal
cases, or those
combining materials
are more likely to be
Continental.

Wooden cases: these
were introduced in the
17th century. Many
cases are covered with
thin veneers of wood.
The most common
woods are ebony,
walnut, mahogany
and rosewood. Wooden
cases are sometimes
decorated with inlaid
marquetry (patterns
made by using different

woods, see p74),
lacquer, applied metal
mounts, brass inlay
(particularly on
rosewood cases), or
a combination of
tortoiseshell and brass
(known as boulle
work).

Metal cases: brass is
the most common
metal; all carriage
clocks are brass-cased.
Old brass is uneven
and shows marks left
by the casting process;
modern rolled brass is
of uniform thickness.
Brass cases may be
elaborately engraved
or decorated with
enamel colours.

SIGNATURES

Most clocks are signed,
although a signature is
not always a guarantee
that the clock was
made by the maker
whose signature it
bears; 19th-century
clocks may be signed
by the retailer rather
than the maker.
Genuine signatures
are usually found in
the following places:

● until 1690: along
　the bottom of the
　dial plate.
● from 1690–1720:
　on the chapter ring.
● after 1720: on the
　chapter ring; or on
　the boss in the arch
　or on a separately
　applied plaque.

BRACKET CLOCKS

Not all "bracket" clocks stood on wall brackets. Clocks of this type were also used for tables and mantlepieces. Nowadays the term is used to describe all clocks with short pendulums and spring-driven mechanisms. These clocks are also sometimes called "mantel clocks" or "table clocks".

Bracket clocks were made from c.1660, the earliest with square brass dials; by the beginning of the 18th century, arched dials became more common. Among the most often seen British bracket clocks are those with mahogany veneered cases. Large numbers were produced from the late 18th and early 19th century, mainly in London, and you can still find clocks of this type for around £6,000-12,000. Also frequently seen are French 19th-century clocks, which were made in a wide variety of shapes. Many of these incorporate such lavish decoration that you may need to take a second look before you realize they're clocks at all.

▼ EARLY BRACKETS
Early (pre-1700) bracket clocks, such as this c.1695 one, are usually the most valuable. You can generally identify them by their ebony, walnut or even olivewood veneered cases and elaborately decorated square dials.

▶ REGENCY CLOCKS
You can recognize a bracket clock made in the Regency period, as it will usually have a convex dial signed by its maker, simple hands made from brass or blued steel, and a mahogany or rosewood case.
£6,000–10,000

MAKERS
The value of a clock is greatly increased if it's signed by a famous maker. The dial and backplate of this clock (above and right) are signed by Thomas Tompion, one of the most famous English clockmakers, known as the "father of English clockmaking", making it worth over £100,000+! Other famous names include the Knibb brothers and Edward East.

▲ FRENCH BRACKET CLOCKS
Depending on the degree of elaboration, prices for French clocks start at around £1,500. This one is decorated with a bronze figure of a Negress (representing Africa), a gilt panther and tortoises. It is therefore worth £8,000 or more.

MOVEMENTS

Most mahogany bracket clockss originally had a verge escapement (see p218–219); many of these were later converted to an anchor escapement but this should not put you off buying.

STRIKE/SILENT LEVER

The strike/silent lever controls the striking mechanism of the clock and can be used to turn it off without affecting its running.

MAHOGANY BRACKETS

Most mahogany clocks are larger than earlier ebony or walnut examples. This one, which was made c.1783, is of a standard size and measures 20in/51cm. £12,500

CLOCK CARE

- Carefully dust and wax wooden cases.
- Never attempt to clean brass or silvered dials.
- Ask an expert to oil and clean the clock's mechanism.
- Hold clocks upright if you are moving them from one room to another.
- Secure or remove the pendulum before a long journey.

BEWARE

Check the finials all match. On many clocks some have been replaced – this is less desirable.

CASES

Both elaborate and simple cases were made from mahogany. This example is fairly simple, but the six illustrations below show some of the more elaborate varieties.

Lacquer	Mahogany	Mahogany	Mahogany	Ebonized	Mahogany
c.1770	c.1780	c.1780	c.1795	c.1810	c.1827
ht 25in/63.5cm	ht 19½in/49.5cm	ht 20½in/52cm	ht 15¾in/40cm	ht 19in/48cm	ht 26in/66cm

LONGCASE CLOCKS

Perhaps because of their homely appearance and reassuring "tick-tock" sound, longcases, popularly known as "grandfather" clocks, are among the most appealing of all antique clocks. Most longcases were made in Britain from the late 17th–19th centuries, although lesser numbers were also produced in Europe and the United States. The standard longcase runs for 8 days and has an anchor escapement. Like most types of clock, value is dependent on the quality of the case, movement and dial, and on the identity of the maker. If a clock has an unusual or attractively painted dial, or an elaborate marquetry or lacquered case, it will cost more than a run-of-the-mill version. Size can also have a bearing on price. Smaller longcases are usually more expensive than larger ones – and for good reason – taller ones were built to fit in rooms with much higher ceilings than are found in many homes today. So before you buy a tall longcase remember to check that it will fit!

DIALS

Originally only square, dial faces developed arches in c.1720. Most longcases have brass dials, as shown here, or painted ones, like the clock opposite. Brass dials are usually about 12in/30cm in diameter and have

an applied chapter ring (the band showing the numbers) and applied decorative spandrels (corners).

QUICK DIAL CHECK

| Square (17thC) | Arched (c.1700–19thC) | Circular (c.1800) |

▲ WALNUT LONGCASES

Some of the earliest longcase clocks were decorated with walnut veneers over an oak carcass. Cross-banded veneers (short strips applied so that the grain lies at right angles to the main veneer) add to the value. £35,000+

▲ MARQUETRY

Floral marquetry was a popular decoration on longcases between 1680 and 1710. Earlier examples have small panels of marquetry inset in the veneer but are otherwise similar to walnut longcases; later ones, such as this, are much more lavishly decorated. £25,000+

Finials are easily damaged and replacements, though acceptable, are less desirable.

The small dials measure the seconds and the calendar months.

The hands on most longcases are made from "blued" steel – the metal was heated to create the dark colour.

The trunk – centre section of the case – has a door which opens to allow you to adjust the pendulum and fit the weights. Longcases were designed to stand against a wall, so the backs are usually made from unpolished wood.

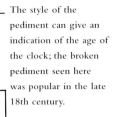

The style of the pediment can give an indication of the age of the clock; the broken pediment seen here was popular in the late 18th century.

The painted dial has attractive figures in the spandrels and a moon disc, showing the phases of the moon, in the arch. Look for crazing (a fine network of cracks) on painted dials as this is a sign of authenticity.

NAMES TO LOOK OUT FOR

This clock is signed by a Birmingham clock-maker named Edward White. London makers of longcases are usually particularly sought after, especially Thomas Mudge Sr., William Dutton and John Holmes.

MAHOGANY LONGCASES

Mahogany was used to make longcases from the mid-18th century until the early 19th century. This example, which was made in 1785, has a fairly elaborate case and it is worth around £6,000. However, you can still find simpler 19th-century versions from about £4,000.

The wood used for the base and plinth should match the rest of the case. Variations in the colour and overall appearance may mean that parts have been replaced and this will reduce the clock's value.

CARRIAGE CLOCKS

Few people today would think of packing a carriage clock when they go on a journey, even though, as one of the earliest types of travelling clock, this is what they were made for. Carriage clocks usually have brass cases and were fitted with handles so they could be more easily carried – hence their name. Many also came with a leather travelling case. Nearly all carriage clocks were made in France during the 19th century and the early years of the 20th century; a few were also produced in England. Carriage clocks are among the least expensive types of antique clocks available. You can still buy less elaborate models for around £800–1,200 although good-quality ones may cost over £3,000.

CHECKLIST OF TYPICAL FRENCH CARRIAGE CLOCK FEATURES

- white enamel dial
- black numerals
- stamped mark or signature on the backplate
- 8-day duration spring-driven movement with going barrel
- bevelled glass panels
- blued steel hands.

QUALITY FEATURES

- engraved metal case
- panelled *cloisonné* (floral enamelled decoration) case
- porcelain case
- subsidiary dials.

FIRMS & MAKERS TO LOOK OUT FOR

Auguste (active from 1840), French
Abraham-Louis Breguet (1747–1823), French
Achille and Louis Brocot (active 19thC), French
Dejardin (active 19thC), French
Pierre and Alfred Drocourt (1860–89), French
Frodsham family (19th/20thC), English
Paul Garnier (b.1801–d.1869), French
Japy (1772(early 20thC), French
F. A. Margaine (c.1870–1912), French
E. Maurice (active 1880s), French
James McCabe (19thC), English
Soldano (c.1855–80), French

◀ REPEAT BUTTONS

Some carriage clocks have a repeat button on the top of the case: when the button is pressed the clock repeats the last hour struck. This one was made by Henri Jacot c.1890. £2,000–2,600

◀ ENGRAVED CASES

Engraved-case carriage clocks are more valuable than plain ones. Look for elaborate, detailed decoration which covers as much of the case as possible. This one was made by Le Roy & Fils c.1865. £5,000–6,000

◀ SUBSIDIARY DIALS

Clocks with smaller subsidiary dials are especially desirable. This English carriage has a seconds dial; some clocks have dials showing the days of the week, but the most common subsidiary dial is an alarm. £2,000

NOVELTY CLOCKS

Novelty clocks, which tell the time in a particularly unusual or intriguing way, are among the most fascinating of all clocks. The earliest novelty clocks date back to the 17th century, but most of those seen today come from the 19th century when they were produced by several French, Swiss and British makers. The value of a novelty clock is dependent on its rarity, appearance and the complexity of any moving features, rather than the clock mechanism itself. Condition is also particularly important, as broken novelty clocks can be extremely complex and expensive to repair.

▶ **MYSTERY CLOCKS**

This is one of the most common types of novelty clock. The movement, concealed in the base, rotates the figure slightly from left to right, and this motion makes the pendulum swing, even though the figure holding it seems unconnected to the mechanism. £4,000

◀ **AUTOMATON CLOCKS**

Automaton clocks are among the most varied and valuable of novelty clocks. This one is relatively simple – it contains a bird which every hour sings a melodic nightingale song, while flapping its wings, turning its head and opening its beak. £6,000–8,000

▶ **SKELETON CLOCKS**

The basic principle of the skeleton clock is to display as much of the working mechanism as possible. The origins of skeleton clocks lies on the Continent, but the most complex and elaborate pieces are English. This typically elaborate example (with protective glass dome removed) dates from c.1870, and was made by J. Smith & Sons. £9,000–15,000

Rugs & Carpets

Contrary to general belief, the only difference between a rug and a carpet is size. Rugs are usually small enough to hang on the wall – up to 6ft/2m long – anything larger is usually referred to as a carpet. Broadly speaking, rugs and carpets fall into two main groups: serious collector's rugs and decorative rugs. Older rugs (over 100 years old) are usually only of interest to the specialist collector. More recently-made rugs and carpets are chiefly of interest to the decorative buyer.

Weaving and carpet-making are among the most ancient crafts and probably originated in central Asia. The oldest surviving fragment, called the Pazyryk Rug, was found in Siberia and dates from the 5th century BC.

Most rugs are categorized by their place of origin or the tribe who made them. To be able to identify the difference between, say, a Kazak and a Kuba, you need to familiarize yourself with the various distinctive colours, patterns, motifs and weaves characteristic of each type.

The size, richness of the colours, fineness of the knots, intricacy of design and condition are all important when valuing an antique rug. Collectable rugs should be handmade. To check, look on the reverse – you should be able to see the design on the back as well as on the front. Next, part the pile and look at the knots; if there are loops rather than knots this indicates a machine-made rug of very little interest to collectors. Many types of antique rug cost little more than modern replicas. Woven Kelims and Soumacs can be found for upwards of £300.

BASICS

MATERIALS

The foundation material of a rug (the warp and weft) is usually wool, cotton or silk. The best-quality wool is fine, soft and shiny. Inferior-quality wool is coarse and lacks lustre.

COLOURS

Colour is one of the most important factors in assessing old rugs. The best colours are those made from natural vegetable and insect dyes.

Natural dyes

Blues and reds predominate in most old rugs. Warm red colours are usually derived from the plant, madder. Blue comes from indigo.

● Sometimes crimson comes from insect dyes such as cochineal. This indicates a date after c.1850 when cochineal was first imported to the East.

Chemical (aniline) dyes

These were introduced c.1890; they tend to be harsher in tone, and are not colourfast.

Chromatic dyes

These were first used in the early 20th century. They can be difficult to distinguish from natural dyes as they are colourfast, but they lack the subtlety of natural dyes, and come in a wider colour range.

KNOTS

The type of knot used to attach the pile to the warp and weft can help to identify where it was made. The quality of a rug is reflected by the fineness of the knots, which are measured according to their number per 15 square in/square decimetre. A coarse rug may have only 400 knots per 15 square in whereas a fine one may have many thousands. The knots are tied over the warps of the rug by hand and then cut to the correct length. Each row of knots is separated by one or more lines of weft beaten into place with a metal comb. Two main types of knot are used:

● Turkish, symmetric or Ghiordes; this was used in Turkey and by many tribal groups in Persia and central Asia.
● Persian, asymmetric or Senneh; used in Iran and by some central Asian groups. The threads can be open to the left or right.

PERSIAN RUGS

Richly coloured and exotic, Persian rugs have long been highly sought after; the finest are made from silk and are among the most expensive of all Oriental carpets. Most Persian carpets seen today date from the 19th and 20th centuries and can be either tribal village pieces woven both for trade and for use, or town-made factory woven pieces, produced specifically for the Western market.

CARPET CARE

Carpets can be washed with plain warm or cold water and a mild detergent. Snow is a good way of removing dust – cover the rug with snow and brush it off and it will take the dust with it!

◀ PRAYER RUGS
Garden motifs recur in many Persian rugs and are inspired by the Islamic notion of the garden of Paradise. Prayer rugs – small carpets used to kneel on during prayer – such as this late 19th-century one, show the garden through a *mihrab* or arch. £800–1,800

▶ KELIMS
Unlike other types of carpets, Kelims are flat-woven which means they have no knots and no pile. Traditionally made entirely from wool there are many modern reproduction kelims on the market, identifiable by their bright colours and coarse weave. Old or antique rugs like this Qashqai kelim from the late 19th century, are finely woven and softly coloured. £800+

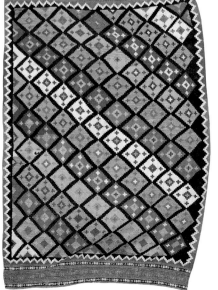

▲ CONDITION
The town of Heriz in northwest Iran was a prolific centre of carpet production. This Heriz carpet has areas of repiling, and the outermost borders at each end have been cut and bound; even so, because of its attractive pattern, unusual and sought-after ivory coloured field and good size – 168in x 114in/4.35m x 2.97m – it would still cost over £6,000.

CAUCASIAN & TURKISH RUGS

Distinctive geometric designs are a keynote of many types of Oriental rug made in the region between the Black and Caspian Seas. In this rugged mountainous area, known as the Caucasus, carpets were made by villagers using small looms. Each different region has its own distinctive characteristics. Among the most famous and frequently seen Caucasian rugs are Kazaks, Shirvans and Soumacs.

Turkish carpets fall into two distinct groups: those made by nomadic tribal weavers and those made in urban or Imperial factories. Rugs cover a wide spectrum of prices, from expensive silk rugs to cheaper Anatolian kelims, which are still available for a relatively modest outlay.

▼ SOUMACS
Soumacs are a type of kelim and are one of the easiest of the Caucasian rugs to identify because they are flat-woven rather than knotted, but, unlike other kelims, are patterned on one side only, with the weft left uncut for warmth. This is a Soumac bag-face – trappings such as bags, saddle covers and tent hangings are always popular with collectors and can be surprisingly expensive. £400+

▲ KAZAKS
Large, bold geometric patterns and long, fine-quality wool are features of Kazak rugs.

They are usually relatively small – this one is 5ft x 3ft 9in/ 150 x 113cm and is worth £1,500–5,000.

KAZAK MOTIFS

Pinwheel   Karachov   Fachralo   Bordjalou

Kazaks are often named according to their distinctive designs. These are some of the most commonly seen motifs.

WHAT TO LOOK FOR
- bright vibrant colours – preferably coloured with vegetable dyes (see p226)
- finely textured weaving
- good condition, unless very early
- complete rugs – cut down ones are less desirable
- a natural patina.

IS IT OLD?

- Check the pile with a magnifying glass. If the fading is soft and gradual it's old; if you can see three distinct bands of colour the rug may be artificially aged.

- Lick a handkerchief and rub it on the carpet – dyes which come off copiously may be chemical – an indication that the carpet is not of great age.

WHAT DO COLOURS MEAN?

RED	happiness
BLACK	rebellion and devastation
BROWN	plentitude, fruitfulness
WHITE	cleanliness, serenity, purity
GREEN	rejuvenation
GOLD	prosperity

► LADIKS

The central Anatolian village of Ladik is renowned for its fine-quality prayer rugs (see p227). This one contains a poetic inscription at the base of the niche. £5,000+

◄ SHIRVANS

Shirvans typically have fine knots, short pile and small geometric patterns, in which dark blues and strong reds predominate. £1,500–3,500

MODERN RUGS

Modern rugs, such as this Shirvan, are coloured with synthetic dyes which look harsh compared to naturally dyed rugs. Modern Shirvans can also be identified by their longer pile and cotton warp and weft. Although they are still of interest to the decorative buyer they are far less valuable. This one is worth £300–500.

INDIAN & CHINESE RUGS

A prison may seem an unlikely setting for valuable carpet-making, but during the 19th century large numbers of woven and pile carpets were made in Indian jails such as Agra, Amritsar and Hyderabad and today these are extremely sought after. Indian piled carpets, first made in the 16th century for the Mongol rulers, often reflect the influence of Persian rugs which were used as a source for some designs. India is also famed for its flat-woven *dhurries* – the Indian equivalent of kelims.

The real and imaginary beasts and symbols of power, wealth and good luck which pepper the surface of many Chinese rugs make them highly distinctive – and easy to recognize. Most of those you are likely to come across date from the 19th century or later and were specially made for the Western market.

VALUE POINTS

- Pile Agras are among the most valuable of Indian carpets – prices range from £20,000-70,000.
- In Indian carpets, white or yellow grounds are usually more valuable than red or blue, which are more common.
- *Dhurries* are the least expensive of Indian carpets; prices range from £500-2,000 for a large one.
- Chinese carpets are also fashionable at the moment. Those made in the 19th century usually fall in the £3,000–15,000 price range.
- Post-World War II Chinese carpets that drew on French designs and look less "Chinese" are not as valuable as traditionally patterned ones.

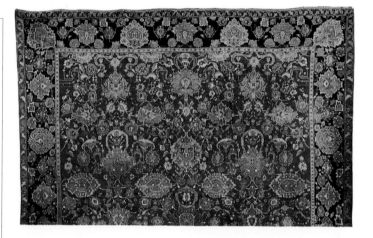

▲ INDIAN CARPETS
Carpets made in India for the European market were often extremely big. Large rectangular carpets are usually more sought after than square ones. This Agra measures 19ft 8in x 13ft 11in/ 600 x 424cm. £30,000–50,000

▼ CHINESE CARPETS
Traditional motifs seen in Chinese art provided the inspiration for patterns on rugs made in China. The design of this Ninghsia rug was probably adapted from contemporary brocade. £5,000–10,000

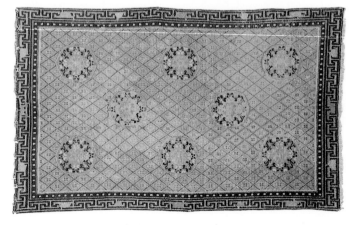

EUROPEAN RUGS

If you visit a sale of Oriental rugs or a specialist carpet dealer, you may be surprised at the large number of European-made carpets on offer. Carpet-making was introduced to Europe by Moorish invaders in the 8th century. Among the most popular and abundant Western rugs are needlework rugs. Many were made by ladies of the leisured classes from the 16th century onwards, but some were commercially produced during the 19th century. Designs are colourful and extremely varied; some patterns were adapted from Oriental rugs, others were derived from printed textiles.

Flower-filled rugs from the Aubusson region of France have also enjoyed a huge upsurge in popularity. If the price of an Aubusson is out of your reach, you may be able to find slightly worn small rugs or fragments for more modest sums.

AUBUSSON RUGS
The most sought after Aubussons, such as this example, made c.1890, were flat-woven on a loom (although some piled examples are known). £15,000

PATTERN
The design was built up one colour at a time, each colour woven back and forth only in the area required. When a new colour was added a vertical split was left between the wefts, which was stitched up by hand afterwards.

BORDERS
The border of this Aubusson has been cut or folded back and the design along one edge has been distorted as a result. Aubussons were originally made with very wide plain borders and were intended to fit right up to the walls and to be cut to fit around fireplaces.

NEEDLEWORK RUGS
The pleasant floral design, good condition and gentle, yet unfaded, colours are all signs of a good-quality rug. Such traits add to the desirability of this mid-19th century needlework rug and mean that it is worth around £5,000–10,000.

Art Nouveau & Art Deco

Art Nouveau and Art Deco are two of the most significant movements to emerge in the last years of the 19th and early 20th centuries. The appearance of furniture and applied arts of this period was dramatically altered by these new styles which swept through Europe, Britain and the United States.

"Art Nouveau" derives its name from a shop in Paris, *La Maison de l'Art Nouveau*, which retailed glass and furniture designed by such innovatory figures as René Lalique, Emile Gallé and Louis C. Tiffany. The style first appeared in Belgium c.1892 before spreading to France at the end of the 19th century. Most Art Nouveau objects are characterized either by sinuous fluid forms derived from nature or, particularly in Britain, by simple straight-lined designs with a heavy vertical emphasis.

"Art Deco", named after the 1925 Paris *Exposition Internationale des Arts Décoratifs et Industriels Modernes*, embraces two very different approaches to the applied arts. On the one hand, French designers made luxurious objects of the highest quality in exotic woods. On the other, modernists like the Bauhaus in Germany developed clean simple shapes suitable for mass production using the "new" materials like tubular steel and chrome that were becoming available.

In the middle years of the 20th century Art Nouveau and Art Deco became rather unfashionable but today almost any type of object reflecting these styles is highly collectable, although prices for many small mass-produced objects are still relatively low.

FURNITURE

Art Nouveau and Art Deco furniture covers a wide spectrum of quality and prices. The most sought-after and valuable pieces are large, commissioned handmade items, by known designers. Smaller functional objects, such as writing desks, chairs and original mass-produced furniture, are widely available and relatively inexpensive.

► **CHARLES RENNIE MACKINTOSH**
One of the most influential British Art Nouveau designers, Charles Rennie Mackintosh, usually designed his furniture to commission. The clean simple lines of this chair are in stark contrast to the fluid forms of most French Art Nouveau furniture.
£100,000

◄ **LIBERTY**
Furniture made for the influential firm of Liberty & Co. is usually marked with a Liberty label and despite being highly collectable it can still be affordable. This dressing table is part of a set which also includes a pair of wardrobes; the whole suite would be worth about £3,000.

▼ EMILE GALLÉ

This small table, designed by Emile Gallé, one of the leading French exponents of the Art Nouveau style, has five features characteristic of most furniture made by Gallé:

- strong sculptural quality
- inventive design
- fruitwood marquetry inlay
- stylized floral decorative motifs
- a signature.

It is worth £7,000–10,000.

BEWARE

Pieces marked GALLÉ which lack the originality of earlier designs and are less inventive in their use of inlay may have been made by Gallé's firm after his death. Although collectable, these are less valuable than pieces made in Gallé's lifetime.

WHAT TO LOOK FOR

Much unsigned furniture of the 1920s and 30s, such as this cocktail cabinet, remains relatively inexpensive. Quality can vary; you should look for:

- uncracked veneers
- original upholstery
- pale woods
- simple but dramatic geometric forms.

£1,500+

▶ LUDWIG MIES VAN DER ROHE

One of van der Rohe's most popular Art Deco designs, Barcelona chairs such as this were first made in 1929 and have been mass-produced continuously since World War II. Pre-mass-production chairs are worth around £10,000 – ten times more than later versions – and can be recognized by:

- a bent chrome steel top rail with separate sections joined by lap joints and screwed with chrome-headed bolts
- a welded stainless steel rail along the top.

GLASS

Unlike most earlier glass (see p212–217), the value of a piece of Art Nouveau or Art Deco glassware is dependent largely on its maker or designer. This was the heyday of influential glass makers such as Emile Gallé, Daum and Lalique in France, and Louis Comfort Tiffany in America. Designers no longer tailor-made their output of glassware primarily for the dining table. Glass was increasingly used to make a plethora of decorative vases and new electric lamps and, spurred on by the new requirements of "modern" life, designers produced objects as diverse as car mascots, jewellery and scent bottles. All named glass of this period is widely collected, and the best pieces are very expensive, but you can still find some unmarked pieces or smaller objects for relatively modest prices.

◀ DAUM FRÈRES
Daum glass, such as this vase, is often very similar to that made by Gallé but can usually be identified by a gilt signature *DAUM NANCY* on the black enamel on the underside. £3,000

◀ GALLÉ GLASS
The best pieces, such as this lamp, are made from hand-carved cameo glass (formed by fusing two or more layers of coloured glass, the top layer carved to reveal the colours underneath). Later machine-made versions are less valuable and are identifiable because the carving is not so deeply cut. £15,000+

FAKES
Fake Art Nouveau glassware abounds. The commonest items likely to deceive are:
● "Tiffany" lamps – with fake marks identifiable because they do not usually have the marked pad on the shade.
● Cameo glass marked "Gallé" recognizable by its stiff, lifeless decoration.

MARKS
Gallé pieces are usually marked with a cameo or incise-carved signature. If you see a star after the signature, the piece was made during the first three years after Gallé's death, between 1904 and 1907.

▶ TIFFANY
Tiffany lamps have bronze or gilt bronze bases; the shades are made from a lattice of bronze, set with small pieces of favrile (iridescent) glass. They are marked on an applied bronze pad. £10,000+

LALIQUE

All types of glass made by the most famous glass designer of the Art Deco period, René Lalique, are highly collectable. His prolific output included car mascots, clocks, lighting, jewellery, furniture and figurines. Lalique's distinctive wares were also much imitated so before buying something which you think could be by Lalique ask yourself the following questions…

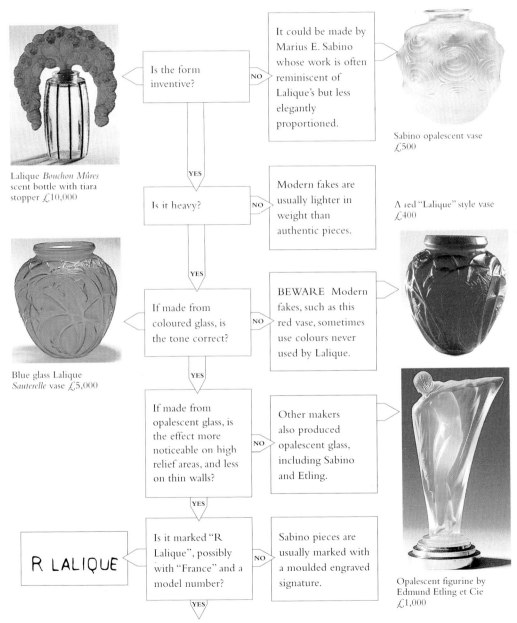

Lalique *Bouchon Mûres* scent bottle with tiara stopper £10,000

Blue glass Lalique *Sauterelle* vase £5,000

Is the form inventive?

NO — It could be made by Marius E. Sabino whose work is often reminiscent of Lalique's but less elegantly proportioned.

Sabino opalescent vase £500

YES

Is it heavy?

NO — Modern fakes are usually lighter in weight than authentic pieces.

A red "Lalique" style vase £400

YES

If made from coloured glass, is the tone correct?

NO — BEWARE Modern fakes, such as this red vase, sometimes use colours never used by Lalique.

YES

If made from opalescent glass, is the effect more noticeable on high relief areas, and less on thin walls?

NO — Other makers also produced opalescent glass, including Sabino and Etling.

YES

Is it marked "R Lalique", possibly with "France" and a model number?

NO — Sabino pieces are usually marked with a moulded engraved signature.

R LALIQUE

Opalescent figurine by Edmund Etling et Cie £1,000

YES

IF ALL THE ANSWERS ARE "YES" THEN YOU PROBABLY DO HAVE A HIGHLY DESIRABLE PIECE OF LALIQUE.

CERAMICS

Whether you prefer the subtle sensuality of the Art Nouveau potters, or the uncluttered modern approach of the Art Deco era, the pottery of the late 19th and early 20th centuries provides something to suit almost every taste. If you are an inexperienced collector interested in ceramics this could be an ideal choice of subject to begin with: there is a wide variety of designers and styles available; most pottery and porcelain is marked by the manufacturer; wares by the most famous potters are usually well documented;

and many pieces are still refreshingly inexpensive.

During the Art Nouveau period the surfaces of plates and vases were covered with floral and organic shapes, or the languid, scantily clad maidens, synonymous with the style of the movement. In stark contrast, the clean bright geometric motifs and dramatic avant-garde shapes which evolved in the Art Deco pottery of the 20s and 30s evoke equally effectively the optimistic and forward-looking spirit of their age.

◀ WILLIAM MOORCROFT
If you see a piece of pottery decorated with raised lines, which look as if they've been applied with an icing nozzle, the chances are it was made by William Moorcroft, at the famous Macintyre Pottery in Staffordshire. This "Iris" vase illustrates the distinctive technique, known as "tube-line" which was made with hand-applied fine lines of slip. £1,200

▶ DOULTON & CO
This factory produced such a wide variety of wares that many buyers collect nothing else! You'll have to pay more if a piece of Doulton was made by a famous designer. This vase was decorated by the prominent designer Mark V. Marshall, and would be worth over £5,000; a piece by a less prestigious designer might only be worth 10% of that price.

▲ ROYAL COPENHAGEN
The serpentine movement of this group, and the soft pastel shades with which it's decorated, identify this as a typical piece of Royal Copenhagen porcelain. The group, known as "The Rock and the Wave", is so popular that it's still reproduced today. Dating can be tricky but different marks were used and these can give a clue as to when the piece was made. £700–900

1894–1900   1894–1922   from 1905

CLARICE CLIFF

The most famous British Art Deco potter, Clarice Cliff, produced such a plethora of diverse shapes and designs that whole sales are now devoted entirely to her wares. Value is largely determined by the rarity of the design. Small objects, or anything in the "Crocus" pattern are usually the most affordable.

Although produced in large quantities, all genuine Clarice Cliff was hand-painted and you should be able to see brush strokes in the coloured enamels.

FUTURISTIC SHAPES

Exemplified by this unusual c.1935 teapot with its bizarrely curving lid, dramatic futuristic shapes are a keynote of Clarice Cliff's adventurous pottery.
£300–500

Condition is of paramount importance to value and restoration can be difficult to spot. Check spouts and handles for signs of chipping and run a finger around rims and bases to see if they're intact.

Most pieces are marked with a printed mark and a facsimile signature.

Decoration is often outlined in black.

The warm yellow "honey glaze" gives the background an ivory colour seen on many Clarice Cliff wares.

FAKES

Many reproductions and fakes of pieces by Clarice Cliff have appeared in the last decade. They can usually be distinguished by their inferior colour and design. Some fakes have photographically copied marks which usually have a fuzzy appearance. This jug looks washed out compared with the vibrant colours of the teapot, and the handle is too thin.

DESIRABLE DESIGNS

- Age of Jazz figures
- Wall masks
- *Inspiration* design pieces (now extremely rare)
- *Circus* series – designed by Dame Laura Knight
- Graham Sutherland designs
- Frank Brangwyn circular plaques.

SCULPTURE

Sculpture, which had hitherto been a rather expensive artistic medium, enjoyed an upsurge of popularity during the early 20th century, as new technology enabled founders to produce smaller scale models of monumental pieces. Inexpensive scaled-down figures epitomizing the Art Nouveau and Deco styles became widely available. One recurring subject is the female form; Art Nouveau sculpture shows women in dreamy poses, or draped across functional objects such as lamps. Sculpture from the Art Deco era is more stylized and reflects the dizzy Jazz Age, depicting elegant ladies dancing, playing golf and smoking.

◀ GUSTAV GURSCHNER
Form, function and decoration are typically intermingled in this bizarre c.1900 bronze nautilus shell lamb by Bavarian sculptor Gustav Gurschner. Similar fluid shapes were favoured by French sculptors; English pieces are usually less stylized. £3,000

▶ FERDINAND PREISS
The most valuable Art Deco sculptures are usually those made from "chryselephatine" – a combination of bronze and ivory. This one dates from the 1930s and was made by Ferdinand Preiss, one of the most famous sculptors of such figures. £4,000

▲ DEMÈTRE CHIPARUS
The bases of Art Deco sculptures are often integral to the composition and can provide a clue to the identity of the maker. The architectural quality of the base of this figure is typical of Chiparus. £9,000

BEWARE

Many less valuable Art Deco figures were made from patinated bronze – a bronze spelter (zinc alloy) base – combined with ivorene (simulated ivory usually made from plastic). To identify spelter scratch the metal underneath – a yellow colour means the piece is made from bronze; a silvery tone indicates spelter and means that the piece is far less valuable.

SCULPTURE CARE

The patination of a bronze is fundamental to its appeal. **Never** polish a bronze or you will seriously reduce its value.

POSTERS

The growth of the Art Nouveau movement coincided with the development of several increasingly versatile lithographic printing techniques. Prominent artists such as Jules Chéret (the father of the modern poster), Alphonse Mucha, and Adolphe J. M. Cassandre exploited the new media with unrivalled originality. Advertising posters were produced in prolific quantities and nowadays these are keenly collected. The designer, aesthetic appeal and condition of a poster all influence value.

PRINTING TECHNIQUES

ENGRAVING – copperplate incised with design, inked and printed.

ETCHING – copperplate coated with wax into which design is scratched, inked and printed.

LITHOGRAPH – design drawn on stone and fixed; different colour areas are treated with ink-resistant chemical, the stone is inked and printed.

PHOTOGRAVURE – image photographed, negative applied to a metal plate which is etched or engraved.

▼ ALPHONSE MUCHA
Mucha's posters usually combine a romanticized female figure with elaborate decorative details such as flora and drapery. £3,000

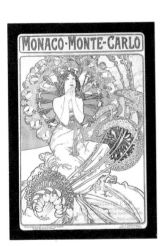

IS IT OLD?

Art Nouveau and Art Deco posters have been much reproduced in recent years; reproductions are identifiable by:

● thicker, usually glossy, modern paper

● colour printing made up from tiny dots you can see with a magnifying glass – lithographs have flat areas of colour.

● a list of known fakes is available; contact the International Vintage Posters Dealers Association.

▲ JULES CHÉRET
Many original Art Nouveau posters were printed on cheap paper and have suffered from foxing, creasing, tearing, fading or staining. Avoid those that are badly damaged or glued onto a backboard. This Chéret poster is in unusually good condition. £900

▲ J. M. CASSANDRE
Art Deco style posters usually have simple but striking designs and focus on a single dominant image, with strong emphasis on lettering. This poster for the liner *Normandie* is the most valuable of the posters by the most famous poster designer of the period, the French artist Adolphe J. M. Cassandre. £6,000

Although many are too delicate to be used for their original purposes, you can often treat old textiles as you would a picture and hang them on your walls – and this is one reason why in recent years textiles have enjoyed a huge increase in popularity.

Because of their inherent fragility, age and condition are fundamental to the value of all antique textiles. Among the earliest and most valuable English needlework textiles are raised work pictures made in the 17th century. These embroidered pictures were padded to give a three-dimensional effect and often contain amazing inconsistencies of scale – figures may be dwarfed by gigantic insects, huge flowers loom over tiny houses – but this is all part of their naïve charm.

In America settlers made a wide variety of textiles using skills brought from Europe; crewelwork and canvas work from the colonies drew on European styles but enjoyed greater and more lasting popularity in the New World.

Textiles produced in the 19th century and early 20th century tend to be widely available and far less expensive. Those made in the Middle East, China, Japan and India are often especially colourful. European tapestries of this period often imitate earlier styles, but with a greater number of brighter colours. If a whole tapestry is beyond your budget you could buy a small fragment or a chair cover and make a cushion from it. There is also an abundance of samplers, shawls and lace from which to choose. These may vary in price from as little as £50 up to several thousand.

EMBROIDERY

Throughout the centuries sewing was an important pastime for ladies and children. Some multi-patterned embroideries served as a visual recipe book of different stitches. In general, the finer the stitching and the brighter the colours the more desirable the piece will be. Silk embroideries are usually more valuable than those sewn in wool. Because 19th-century textiles are relatively abundant, it's best to avoid badly damaged pieces, unless they're particularly unusual.

▲ **RAISED WORK**
Raised work (also called stumpwork) is a style of embroidery which incorporates distinctive areas of raised decoration, formed by padding certain areas of the design. Even though this c.1660 picture has had some restoration done to the ivory silk background, it would still be worth £2,000–5,000.

SAMPLER CARE
As with any textile, samplers are vulnerable to fading, spotting and discoloration and should be hung away from strong sunlight and damp.

If you're storing them in a drawer, roll, rather than fold, the pieces to prevent damage from pressure and creasing. Also make sure they're well protected from moths – use plenty of mothballs.

▼ SUSANIS

According to local legends, embroidered Susanis (the word means stitch or needle in Persian), such as this one from Bokhara, were laboriously stitched by young girls before they were married. They were then used as a covering for the bridal bed and ripped in half when the bride lost her virginity! £1,000–3,000

▲ BERLIN WOOLWORK

Berlin woolwork pictures, such as this, were made in large numbers in the mid-19th century. Subjects can vary enormously including everything from famous paintings to the royal family. This one shows a scene from a Sir Walter Scott novel and is worth about £200–500. Pictures of birds and dogs are always popular and can cost £600–1,000.

► SAMPLERS

Early samplers were conceived as reference sheets showing various stitches and patterns, or as practice pieces. This sampler is worked in brightly coloured silks; typically it contains the name of the person who made it – Mary Read – and the date – 1838. £500–800

WHAT TO LOOK FOR

- Desirable subjects such as: houses, figures, alphabets, animals, birds, insects and flowers. Place names may also increase local interest and value.
- Samplers worked with wool rather than silk.
- Reasonable condition – avoid 19th-century samplers if they're badly damaged or have holes. Those after 1850 tend to be less sought after.

WOVEN TEXTILES

In draughty 17th- and 18th-century interiors, tapestry hangings provided an essential source of warmth. It was only as wallpaper became popular, and houses were warmer, that tapestries dwindled in popularity. Nowadays, although no longer essential, tapestries have once again become collectable as fashionable home decorations. Not all are prohibitively expensive; you can find small snippets of flowery Aubusson, or finely woven Beauvais

◀ TAPESTRY
This 19th-century Beauvais tapestry is so finely woven that you could easily mistake it for an oil painting – a sign that it's of the highest quality. The elaborate border is copied from picture frames of the period and the design is based on a painting by the 18th-century artist François Boucher. £5,000–8,000

◀ TAPESTRY CUSHIONS
Tapestry cushions are often fragments of a larger piece; this one uses 17th-century tapestry which was probably once part of the border of a large panel. Like most cushions of this type, it's mounted on fabric of a much later date. £400–600

LOOK FOR:
- rich, dark colours, especially red, orange, turquoise and gold
- tightly woven, heavy, rich, soft woollen cloth enriched with silk
- lots of individual colours (more colours means more complex weaving)
- complex designs inspired by Indian motifs
- large size – 107 x 57in/ 272 x 145cm is average, some measure over 150 x 76in/381 x 192cm.

▶ PAISLEY SHAWLS
Paisley shawls like this originally became popular because the voluminous crinoline skirts which were fashionable in the mid-19th century made it impossible for ladies to wear coats! Named after the town of Paisley in Scotland, they copied Kashmiri shawls but were mass-produced. Similar shawls were made in Edinburgh, Norwich and France. £300–400

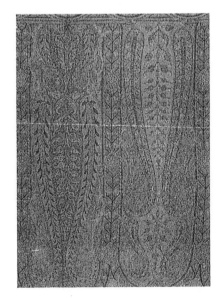

tapestry for quite modest sums. Look out for door hangings (*portières*) and seat covers, or fragments of large tapestries, as these are often surprisingly inexpensive.

If the grandeur of a tapestry is too overpowering from your taste you might find the homely charm of an antique quilt or the delicacy of antique lace more appealing. The majority of quilts on the market date from the 19th and early 20th century and have become popular with collectors in Europe and America, where many of the finest were made. Some American examples bear the name of the maker and are considered folk art.

Most lace seen today dates from the latter half of the 19th century. Handmade lace has an appealing irregularity in its appearance, and early pieces, especially those dating from the 17th and 18th centuries, are particularly sought after by collectors.

▶ **LOOKING AFTER LACE**

- Early lace, such as this 18th-century flounce, was usually made from linen, a robust fibre, so pieces can be framed and hung on a wall. £2,500
- Never display lace by pinning it – rust stains are extremely difficult to remove.
- Store lace between sheets of acid-free tissue paper.

▼ **DATING A QUILT**

Newspaper or scrap paper templates were often used to stiffen the fabric patches in old quilts such as this American one. You might find laundry lists, letters, or news stories – and these can indicate the date and maker of the quilt. £1,000–3,000

Dolls are one of the most enduring types of toy. They have been played with and treasured by children both rich and poor from the earliest times to the present day. Most dolls are categorized by collectors according to the medium of the head (which is often different from that of the body). Among the most valuable dolls are carved wooden examples made in Britain in the 18th century and French dolls made from bisque during the 19th century; both types can fetch several thousand pounds at auction. But you don't have to spend a fortune to build up an interesting collection of dolls. Composition (a substance similar to papier mâché), wax over composition and fabric dolls are far less expensive.

Clothes may add to the value of any doll. Some had extremely elaborate wardrobes and those in their original costumes command a premium. Outfits and hairstyles which reflect the fashions at the time of production are particularly collectable. However, don't ignore badly dressed or even naked dolls. If your doll hasn't got a thing to wear, one way of boosting her value is to buy her a new outfit!

Teddy bears are a much newer type of toy and a relatively recent addition to the collector's market. The jointed bear was only invented at the turn of the 20th century, although soft toy animals did appear slightly earlier. The most sought-after bears are those made by Steiff, the premier maker of German bears. English bears from the 1930s and later tend to be more affordable, although equally appealing.

DOLL TYPES

During the 19th and 20th centuries many new doll-making techniques were developed. Media as varied as papier mâché, Parian, rag, celluloid, wax, plastic and vinyl were all experimented with and used to make dolls. Because the range of dolls available is so extensive, some enthusiasts choose to focus their collections on dolls made from one particular material. The table opposite highlights four different categories of doll; each has its own unique features which can help you identify similar pieces. By no means are all the dolls featured very old or priceless – as you will discover, even your old Barbie or Sindy can be collectable!

Bisque dolls are the largest group of collector's dolls and are covered on the following two pages.

HEAD TYPES
Dolls are classified according to their head types; these illustrations show some of the most common types:

Shoulder head

Swivel head

Open head

Solid domed head

POURED WAX
A Madame Montinari
poured wax doll
£400–2,000

WAX OVER COMPOSITION
A Pumpkin head doll
£100–300

FABRIC
A Lenci pressed felt
doll £1,800–2,000

VINYL
A pair of c.1960s
Barbies £100–400

IDENTIFYING FEATURES

- hollow wax head and shoulders modelled in one piece
- stiff muslin or fabric body
- closed mouth
- inserted eyes and hair
- wax arms and legs

- large hollow moulded head made from papier mâché dipped in wax and painted
- pupilless eyes
- card, cloth or papier mâché body
- turned wooden legs and arms

- moulded fabric head and stuffed fabric body
- painted or stitched facial features
- hair made from wood, cotton or mohair or painted on

- hollow soft vinyl head
- rooted hair
- jointed limbs
- painted or inserted eyes
- registered trademark on head or body

WHAT TO LOOK FOR

- dolls by famous makers, especially Pierotti, Montinari and John Edwards
- softly modelled features
- glass eyes
- well-defined fingers and toes

- good condition – these dolls aren't rare so damage is not acceptable
- real hair or moulded bonnets – rare but desirable
- original, colourful, elaborate clothes

- dolls by famous makers such as Kathe Kruse, Lenci, Steiff
- expressive features, sideways glancing eyes feature on Lenci
- good condition – felt dolls are vulnerable to damage by moths
- elaborate clothes with original labels

- Barbies with holes in the feet – these are the earliest
- Barbies with titian or brunette hair
- dolls from the 60s with designer-inspired wardrobes
- dolls with original packaging
- black Sindys

BISQUE DOLLS

Bisque dolls, whose heads are made from unglazed, tinted porcelain, are among the most elaborate and valuable of all collector's dolls. The first examples were produced by German makers in the 1850s, but the market was soon dominated by the French. The finest French bisques, made by leading makers such as Jumeau, Bru, Gaultier and Steiner, were expensive status symbols even when first made, and remained very much the province of pampered children from the most affluent homes. The earliest French bisques resembled fashionable ladies and came equipped with wardrobes of elaborate clothes, based on fashion plates of the day and are called fashion dolls. Later in the 19th century, the firm of Jumeau began making dolls with child-like features, large eyes and chubby bodies known

as *bébés* – these soon became enormously popular, and although German manufacturers followed suit and produced their own child dolls they could never quite match the quality of the French *bébé*. German manufacturers eventually recovered the lion's share of the market in the early 20th century, when they introduced realistic "character" dolls, which had smiling crying, laughing and even frowning faces.

The price of bisque dolls ranges from thousands of pounds to a few hundred and is dependent on the maker, condition and quality, and on details such as the rarity of the mould number (the number on the back of the head which showed which mould was used) as well as the type of mouth (closed is best), eyes and body.

▼ GAULTIER
FASHION DOLL
Fashion dolls can be dated by the shape of their bodies, which were made to fit the costumes of the day. This François Gaultier doll has a narrow waist and broad hips and shoulders well suited to her bustle dress – which was fashionable c.1870. £1,500–2,000

◀ JUMEAU DOLL
The *crème de la crème* of collector's dolls, Jumeaus, such as this *bébé*, are worth as much as £2,000–5,000. You can recognize a Jumeau by its pale-coloured bisque and large, glass eyes, usually blue. Early Jumeaus had numbers but no marks; later ones may have a red tick on their head.

Many bisque dolls have composition limbs and bodies which are prone to damage. Slight wear is acceptable and you should only repaint as a last resort.

GERMAN CHARACTER DOLLS

This bisque-headed doll was made by Ernst Heubach c.1914. It has an expressive face typical of German character dolls. She is of medium quality and would therefore be worth £200–500.

The value is reduced because the doll has a replacement wig – original wigs are always preferable.

OTHER MARKS TO LOOK FOR

S 15 H
939
Simon & Halbig
(active c.1869–1930)

⋮⋮⋮⋮⋮ HEU: BACH
Gerbruder Heubach
(active 1820–1945)

Made in Germany
Armand Marseille.
Armand Marseille
(active 1885–1930)

J.D.K.
Made in 13. Germany
Kestner & Co
(active 1816–1930)

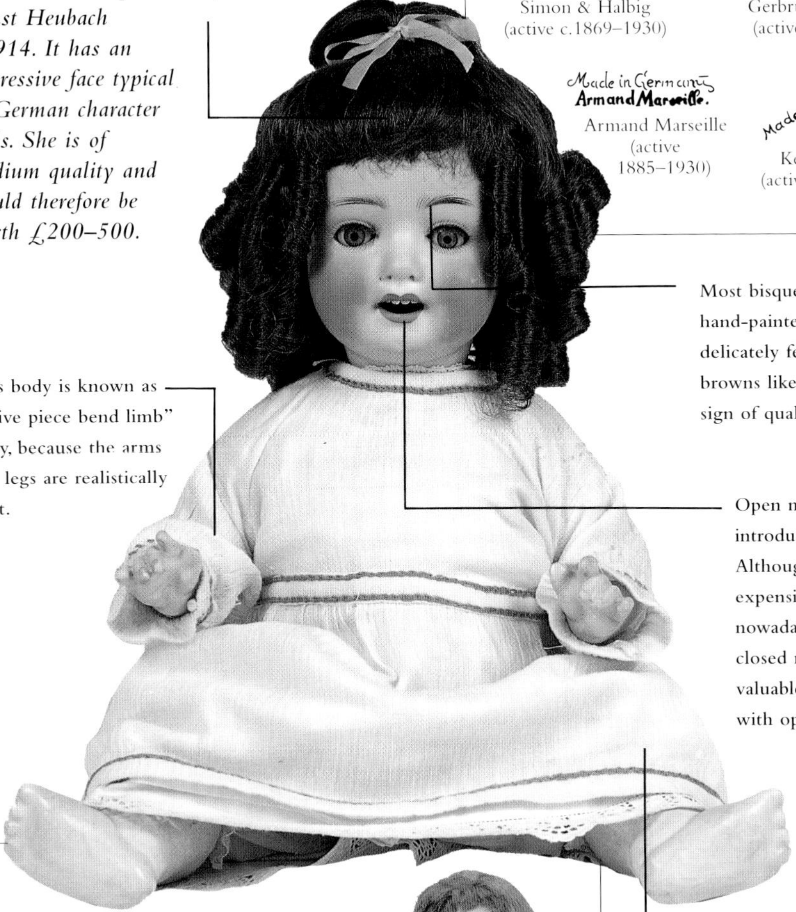

Most bisque dolls have hand-painted eyebrows – delicately featured browns like this are a sign of quality.

This body is known as a "five piece bend limb" body, because the arms and legs are realistically bent.

Open mouths were introduced in c.1900. Although more expensive at the time, nowadays dolls with closed moths are more valuable than those with open ones.

GOOGLIE DOLLS

Some character dolls have very distinctive features and expressions. Dolls such as this, with roguish expressions, large round eyes and impish smiles, known as "Googlies", were inspired by the drawings of American illustrator Grace Debbie. They are among the most sought after types of character dolls. This one would be worth £2,000+.

This doll is wearing her original clothes which add to her value. If you need to replace your doll's clothes you can sometimes find old baby clothes to fit larger dolls, or use old fabric to make replacements. Always try to match new clothes to the doll's date.

TEDDY BEARS

Teddy bears have enjoyed a huge increase in popularity in recent years. The earliest bears were made by the Steiff company in Germany at the beginning of the 20th century. This well-known company was founded by Margaret Steiff who was crippled by polio and confined to a wheelchair as a child. With their pointed snouts, long arms and feet and humped backs, early Steiff bears look much more like real bears than most teddies of today, and are the most valuable of all collector's bears.

Bears are called "teddies" thanks to the American Ideal Toy Company. The company's founder, Morris Michtom, was inspired by a newspaper cartoon which showed President Theodore Roosevelt sparing the life of a grizzly bear. The cartoon was so popular that bears became adopted as the President's mascot, and Michtom reputedly wrote to ask his permission to call the bears he was making "Teddy". The President agreed and bears have been known as "Teddy" ever since.

As bears became more and more popular they were produced by increasing numbers of toy companies on both sides of the Atlantic. During World War I, and in the years that followed, British bear manufacturers expanded to fill the void left after German imports were banned. Prominent companies such as Chad Valley, Merrythought, Dean's Rag Book, Chiltern and J. K. Farnell enjoyed considerable success with their high-quality products.

Few bears were made during World War II, but after the war production resumed once more, although the appearance of bears subtly changed, becoming less realistic and more like the bears of today. Children's books and cartoons featuring bears also affected the market prompting reproductions of well-loved characters like Winnie-the-Pooh, Paddington, Sooty and Rupert Bear.

The most valuable bears for collectors are early examples, in good condition, made by famous makers. In general, Steiff bears remain the most valuable of because of their unique historical appeal and exceptionally high-quality workmanship.

BRITISH MAKERS

Several prominent British manufacturers of teddy bears prospered from c.1915 onwards. Most British bears were originally marked on fabric labels stitched to the foot:

◀ CHAD VALLEY
Chad bears date from the 1920s. Early bears were made of luxuriant mohair, usually gold coloured, with soft kapok stuffed limbs. £200–500

▶ MERRYTHOUGHT
Bears were made from the 1930s; this one has large round ears and joined claws which are typical of this maker. £300–900

▼ J. K. FARNELL & CO.
Farnell supplied teddy bears to Harrods during the 1920s. Winnie-the-Pooh was reputedly made by this company. The angled ears and large amber glass eyes of this c.1918 bear are typical of this maker. £1,500–3,000

STEIFF BEARS

This c.1908 bear is a good example of the most commonly seen type of Steiff bear. The humped back is typical of early Steiffs, as are the close-set eyes and round, widely spaced, ears. Later bears can be recognized by their less prominent humps.
£1,000–5,000

The long curved limbs and large oval felt paws with narrow wrists and ankles are characteristic of Steiff bears.

The earliest bears had black shoebutton eyes; glass eyes were only used after World War I. The eyes were attached by wires which can become loose; old bears should therefore not be left within reach of young children.

◀ MARKS

Steiff bears were marked in the ear with a distinctive button. Early buttons had an elephant logo or were plain. Later buttons had the word "Steiff" written on them.

BEAR CARE

- Holes can be mended without reducing value but use similar fabric for patches.
- Dirty bears need specialist cleaning; untreated dirt makes the fabric rot.
- Put new additions in a plastic bag with mothballs over night to kill any infestation.

Paw pads are usually made from felt and are especially prone to wear; this bear has replacement pads, which will affect its value.

Most bears are made from beige or gold mohair plush. Unusual colours are more desirable. Steiff also made bears using red, apricot and white mohair, and even a few, sought-after, black bears.

AMERICAN BEARS

American bears, like this, were often unmarked but have distinctive wide barrel-shaped bodies, narrow arms and legs and small feet. Some have humps like German bears. £250+

The appeal of collecting old and antique toys and games seems to lie largely in the sense of nostalgia for earlier technologies, lifestyles – and a childhood past – which they evoke.

If you are thinking of beginning a collection of toys it is important to remember that there is a huge range of varieties and prices from which to choose. Many collectors specialize in one particular area, such as clockwork toys, robots or cars, or in a particular maker. You need to be sure of your area of interest before visiting the larger auction houses because many sell different types of toy – such as soldiers, model cars or trains – in specialist sales.

Prices for toys depend on the maker, the rarity of the model and the condition. Although chips and dents are virtually inevitable and therefore acceptable, a toy in mint condition or with its original packaging is what every serious collector longs for. Repainting will nearly always reduce the value of a collector's toy so only repaint items in your collection as a last resort.

Toys made by well-known firms are always sought after, and minor damage is acceptable if the toy is made by a premium firm such as Bing, Märklin or Lehmann.

Viewing sales and visiting specialist dealers is the best way of getting to know which models are the most desirable. But once you have got a good feel for prices, you don't have to buy from an upmarket auction house or dealer. Because many collectable toys are not very old it's always worth scouring the local junk shop or jumble sale for bargains!

WOOD, LEAD & DIE-CAST TOYS

Less sophisticated than toys made from other substances, carved wooden toys have an appealing naivety. Wooden toys were produced in quantity by German makers during the 18th and 19th centuries and some very collectable wooden toys were also made in America by the Schoenhut Co.

Lead became popular as a medium for various types of soldiers and other toys during the late 19th century. In Germany, France and Britain high-quality solid and hollow-cast lead soldiers were produced by firms such as Lucotte, Heyde and William Britain and today these are among the most valuable of all toy soldiers.

Die-cast toys were also made by hollow casting and were first produced in France in c.1910. In Britain, Dinky Toys, part of the Meccano Co., dominated the market for die-cast toys from the 1930s–60s and rare Dinky advertisement vans or unusual series are well worth looking for. In the 1950s Mettoy's Corgi range began to grow, dominating the market by the 1960s and 70s.

DIE-CAST TOYS

Complete sets of die-cast toys are always desirable, especially when they come with the original packaging. Although this c.1937 box is battered it still adds a third to the value of the set of aeroplanes. £600–800

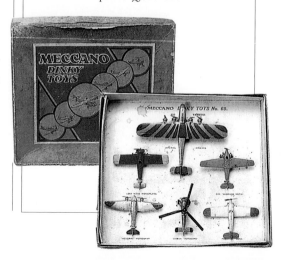

► WOODEN TOYS

Noah's Ark was a popular subject for German wooden toy-carvers. Value depends on size, quality and the number of animals. They sell very well, with prices going up to £6,000 in some cases. This 19th-century one is large (27in/69cm wide), fairly elaborate and contains over 200 animals, so it would be worth £2,000–3,000; smaller, less elaborate arks cost from £200.

▼ VALUE

Many 20th-century wooden toys are still affordably priced. This 1930s apple filled with skittles is worth about £20–25.

▼ TOY SOLDIERS

British toy soldiers are among the most sought-after collectors' soldiers. Many were made using the hollow-casting method. This particular set is very rare, because it is a special order paint finish of Indian Lancers, and includes a European officer. £2,000–3,000

TINPLATE, TRAINS & CELLULOID

Horse-drawn carriages, boats, submarines, cars and even airships are just some of the plethora of tinplate toys made in the late 19th and early 20th centuries which reflect contemporary developments in transport. German toy companies led the field in the manufacture of tinplate toys and those made by well-known firms such as Bing, Märklin and Lehmann are famed for their accuracy and quality. Trains were one of the most important forms of transport from the mid-19th century and not surprisingly trains provided toy-makers with a fertile source of inspiration and have since become one of the most sought-after type of collectable toy. The earliest 1830s toy trains were designed to be pulled along the floor

► **BING**
This c.1906 Bing rear-entry Tonneau with a clockwork mechanism is especially desirable because the high-quality hand-enamelled paintwork is in near perfect condition.
£6,000–8,000

◄ **MÄRKLIN**
Märklin toys, such as this spirit-fired torpedo boat, can be identified by their distinctive maker's mark, which in this case is stamped on the boat's rudder.
£5,500–6,500

▲ **TRAINS**
The most valuable toys, made between 1895 and 1914, are now well outside the price range of the average schoolboy. Märklin were the first company to use a numerical gauge system to identify the different sizes available. This Gauge III engine, made c.1909, is in the second largest size and would be worth £20,000+

or steam powered, but by the 1850s–60s clockwork versions appeared. Eventually c.1890/1900 electric trains – the dream of every schoolboy ever since – began to be produced in substantial numbers.

With the beginning of the space race and the advent of science-fiction films like *The Forbidden Planet*, tinplate robots and space toys became popular. Rare examples of these early robot toys can make £10,000–20,000.

Celluloid toys were made from the late 19th century until the substance was made obsolete with the advent of plastics in the 20th century. These days celluloid toys are keenly collected although they are generally less expensive than tinplate toys of a similar date.

DISNEY TOYS

The earliest toys representing Disney characters were produced by German toy manufacturers such as Distler, who was probably responsible for this 1930s clockwork Mickey Mouse barrel organ toy. This thin, rather gloomy-looking Mickey is the most valuable. Even though he's lost his tail, Minnie has been repainted, and there are signs of rusting, the piece would still be worth over £2,500.

WHAT TO LOOK FOR

- Mickey and Minnie on a motorcyle, by Tipp & Co – a boxed version recently sold for a record £51,000.
- Mickey the Musical Mouse, by Nifty
- Mickey the Drummer, by Nifty
- Donald Ducks with long bills.

◀ LICENSING
The box of this celluloid Mickey riding Pluto, produced in Japan for the Western market, shows that it was made under special licence and is therefore more desirable than an unauthorized version.
£2,000–3,000

CELLULOID

Toys made from celluloid are highly flammable and prone to denting and cracking. The substance is almost impossible to restore satisfactorily, so avoid damaged celluloid toys.

Rock & Pop

Memorabilia associated with the popular music industry of the 20th century is one of the newest, most exciting and often accessibly priced collecting areas – although it does have its high prices too – such as the $2.3 million paid for John Lennon's Rolls-Royce in 1985.

Almost any object in some way connected with a well-known star can be collectable, so even tickets, posters and other printed ephemera made for concerts and tours are saleable. The most sought-after pieces are those closely linked with the stars themselves. Collectors pay especially high prices for the musical instruments with which a star is associated; electric guitars can fetch many thousands of pounds if they were played at a memorable concert. The Fender Stratocaster, played by Jimi Hendrix at Woodstock in 1969, was sold in 1990 for £198,000.

Clothes are another popular collecting area. The most valuable garments are those recognizably linked with the image of their owner. Perhaps they were photographed wearing them, or used them at an important concert, or in a video. Elton John's wacky platform shoes, Madonna's gold leather Jean-Paul Gaultier corset and Michael Jackson's rhinestone-studded glove have all received huge media attention and have attracted prices to match whenever they've come under the hammer. But not all collectable clothes are prohibitively expensive – prices for a roadie's jacket, or a souvenir T-shirt sporting the name and logo of a tour or album start at less than £100.

THE 50s & 60s

The golden era of rock 'n' roll is not surprisingly the focus for many collectors' attentions. Memorabilia from this period is relatively scarce compared with that of the following decades, so even printed concert programmes and magazines, which were made in their thousands, and once cost only a few shillings, are keenly collected. The most desirable memorabilia relates to the big names of the period whose popularity endures today. Among the most popular are Elvis Presley, Buddy Holly, Bill Haley and Bob Dylan – to name but a few.

▲ **BUDDY HOLLY**
Buddy Holly still has a keen following and memorabilia relating to his career attracts high prices. This signed souvenir programme from 1958 marks his group's only tour in Britain. £600–800

▲ **JIM MORRISON**
Jim Morrison, the lead singer of the Doors, has always been collectable but his popularity enjoyed an upsurge after the release of Oliver Stone's film charting his life. These working lyrics for the song *The Celebration of the Lizard* provide a revealing glimpse into Morrison's creative processes and are worth £5,000+.

BEATLES MEMORABILIA

The Beatles have a unique place in the history of pop music: no previous group had enjoyed such enormous and lasting success and they pioneered the vibrant new pop music which epitomized the sounds of the 1960s. Just as they dominated the charts, so they are clearly still 'No 1' to collectors of pop memorabilia, a position unchallenged since regular auctions of associated material began in the early 1980s. In fact almost any object associated with the group is of interest to collectors.

▲ BEATLES DOLLS
The wide range of Beatles merchandise made during the 1960s and 70s reflects the group's phenomenal popularity. Among the diverse Beatles objects which come up for sale are furnishings, jewellery, clothing, games, books, wigs and even confectionary. These Beatles dolls, dressed in Sgt. Pepper's Lonely Hearts Club Band costumes are worth £100–200.

▶ LENNON DRAWINGS
This hand-drawn Christmas card (above) was given to Cynthia Powell by John Lennon in 1958 and encloses a revealing eight-page letter to Cynthia, whom he married five years later. Drawings by John Lennon, who also wrote and illustrated two books, are among the most desirable Beatles memorabilia and can fetch very high prices. £10,000+

▶ RINGO DRUM SET
Although this drum set is only a toy it would still attract collectors because it is rare to find one in near-perfect condition; this one comes complete with sticks, stand, original box and instructions. £250–400

WHAT TO LOOK FOR
- handwritten lyrics to famous songs
- autographed and handwritten letters
- autographed photographs – often faked, so beware
- artwork for record sleeves
- animation cells from *Yellow Submarine*.

THE 70s

The 70s marked the heyday of rock star rebels like Led Zeppelin, David Bowie, Marc Bolan, Bruce Springsteen, Iggy Pop, The Ramones and The Sex Pistols. These artists had a new approach to rock music, based around live performances and album sales, which was to have a profound influence on musicians of the following generations.

As supplies of 1960s memorabilia diminish, it is likely that collectors will turn increasingly to the 70s and that memorabilia from this decade will become increasingly desirable.

▼ PETE TOWNSHEND
The fact that this guitar has been smashed to bits paradoxically adds to its value because it highlights its original owner's "bad boy" image. It was sold accompanied by a letter which details the guitar's history: *"...I broke it in 1973 in a rage of frustration in my studio ..."* £4,000–5,000

▲ THE ISLE OF WIGHT FESTIVAL
Posters relating to important concerts are among the more affordable pieces of rock and pop memorabilia. The pop festivals held in the Isle of Wight in 1969 and 1970 were key events and attracted audiences of over a quarter of a million. This colourful promotional poster, advertising the 1970 concert, is worth £60–100.

◀ ELTON JOHN
Elton John is one star who has pushed the possibilities of stage costume to its limits. Extraordinary glasses and eccentric hats, brightly coloured suits and flamboyant shoes such as these became his trademarks and are keenly collected. £400–800 (a pair)

THE 80s & 90s

The advent of the pop video and the growing importance of television in the music industry was largely responsible for the increased emphasis stars of the 1980s and 90s have attached to their appearance and image. As concerts and tours became increasingly sophisticated, the star's visual impact became as important as the music. Costumes, often made by leading fashion designers, are an obvious way of establishing the star's persona. Unsurprisingly then, outfits of increasingly extravagant design have become the symbol of some of the most famous celebrities of the past two decades.

▶ **PRINCE**

The clothes of the Artist Formerly Known As Prince are specially made for him and, because his colourful, swashbuckling outfits are fundamental to his on-stage image, those that come up for sale are very desirable. This suit made from turquoise and blue silk was sold with a letter of authentication stating where it was made and confirming that it was worn at the 1988 Grammy Awards by the artist. £5,000+

TOP FIVE COLLECTABLE STARS

- **Michael Jackson** leading light so almost anything is desirable
- **Madonna** changes her image for each tour so anything directly connected with one of her "looks" will be very desirable
- **Prince** Neo-romantic clothes always sought after
- **Elton John** shoes, glasses, hats – the more zany the higher the price
- **Queen** anything connected with Freddie Mercury

PRESENTATION DISCS

Among the most valuable awards presented to the star are the "gold" and "platinum" discs celebrating record sales. In the United States gold discs are given for over 500,000 albums, or 1 million singles sold; platinum discs are given for over 1 million albums or 2 million singles sold. This U.K. silver presentation disc for Madonna's *You Can Dance* is worth £300–400.

▲ **MICHAEL JACKSON**

Michael Jackson was often photographed wearing this rhinestone-studded glove which was perhaps the most instantly recognizable piece of rock and pop clothing of the decade. The glove was sold in 1991 for £16,500; a record for any piece of Michael Jackson costume!

Whether because of their historical interest, high-quality craftsmanship, or because they are such potent reminders of the heroics of the past, the relics of war have long fascinated collectors. The terms "Arms and Militaria" cover a suprisingly wide range of objects and include armour, firearms, edged weapons, medals, badges, uniforms, and even prints and cigarette cards.

Armour has been made, in one form or another, from the dawn of civilization to the 19th century but most pieces commonly seen on the market today date from the 16th century onwards. Full sets of armour are rare and extremely valuable, the majority are incomplete and if you're a novice collector you must learn to recognize the numerous "marriages" between pieces from different periods. So long as you realize the set is a composite and this fact is allowed for in the price, marriages are acceptable.

Antique firearms are often the most accessibly priced items in this field. A 19th-century flintlock pistol could cost £150 or less; 18th-century examples are priced from about £300. Arms and militaria tend to be collected by people with a deep interest in the subject, rather than speculators and investors, and as a result prices for all categories of militaria tend to show steady sustained growth rather than the wild fluctuations caused by changing fashions. Before you start buying, remember to check if a special licence is necessary. In most countries you don't need a licence to collect antique firearms, but you do if you intend firing them.

EDGED WEAPONS & FIREARMS

Edged weapons, which include swords, sabres, dirks and bayonets, come up for sale frequently and, depending on the type of weapon you choose, it is possible to build up a collection for relatively little outlay. Most antique firearms fall into one of two categories: flintlocks, which use a flint to make a spark and ignite the charge; or percussion guns, in which a metal cap containing a small explosive charge is ignited by the stroke of the hammer. Even though most antique weapons are never used, the "feel" of a firearm is one of the most important factors to take into account when buying. Firearms should be well balanced when you handle them. Pieces which feel top-heavy and uncomfortable in the firing position are less desirable.

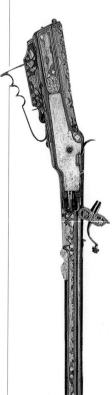

◄ LONG ARMS
Unusual early weapons always command a premium. This German wheel-lock sporting rifle, dated 1666, has several quality features which make it particularly desirable:
- high-quality engraving on the lock plate
- maker's mark
- elaborately inlaid stock decorated with stag horn, silver wire and mother-of-pearl.
£3,000–5,000

SWORD CARE
- wipe blades clean after handling
- wax blades after cleaning
- clean rust spots by rubbing them with a copper coin.

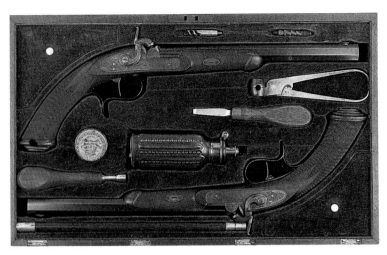

◄ DUELLING PISTOLS

In cased sets of pistols always check that all the pieces belong together and have not been added. This pair of American percussion duelling pistols comes with a range of accessories including balls and Eley caps. £2,000–3,000

◄ SWORDS AND DIRKS

The less than perfect condition and evidence of honest wear you can see on this set of mid-19th-century Scottish regimental swords are a good sign that the set is authentic. It is also unusual to find such an set in its own case. £3,500–5,500

- The small dagger in the centre is a Scottish dirk; these were carried by Scottish Highlanders.

BEWARE

- Fake engraving is sometimes added to swords to increase their value – be suspicious of harsh bright edges, and expect there to be signs of ageing, such as dirt and grease between the lines.
- When fake engraving is added to a piece which already has some decoration it will often be of a different depth from the original and the background colour will be different.

▼ DECORATION

The decoration on a sword usually reflects the status of its original owner and always adds to value. The blued and inlaid Napoleonic sabre (top) once belonged to a high-ranking cavalry officer. The 1831 British general officer's sword (below) is less ornate, reflecting the owner's lower rank. top £800–1,200 below £300–400.

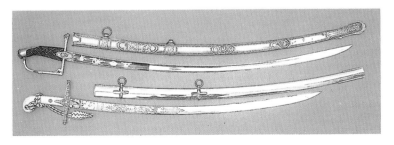

ARMOUR

Antique armour of all periods is highly collectable; swashbuckling armour from the English Civil War (1642–49) is in fact still fought over, but nowadays by collectors! Among the most sought-after items of this period are "lobster-tailed" cavalry helmets, pikeman's pots (simple helmets), breastplates, backplates and gauntlets. Because complete suits of original armour so rarely come up for sale, even good 19th-century reproductions are highly collectable and valuable. Much good-quality armour of this period was made in Germany, France and Spain.

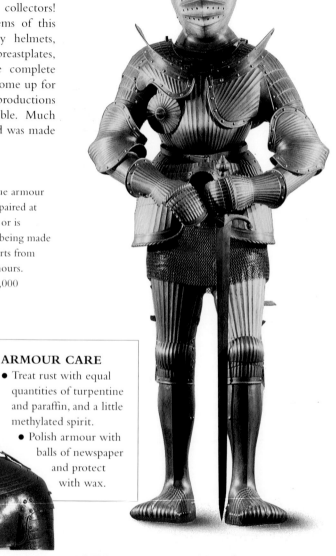

▼ CONDITION
This three-quarter armour dates from c.1640 and was made for a cuirassier (horse-man). It is in unusually fine condition and even has its original buckles.

Most antique armour has been repaired at some stage, or is composite, being made up using parts from various armours.
£8,000–12,000

ARMOUR CARE
● Treat rust with equal quantities of turpentine and paraffin, and a little methylated spirit.
  ● Polish armour with balls of newspaper and protect with wax.

WHAT TO LOOK FOR
● armourer's marks – add to value
● small dents in the breast plate – made from a pistol ball fired to test the armour's strength – a good sign of age
● funerary helmets – worn at funerals.

▲ REPRODUCTION ARMOUR
Although 19th-century armour was intended for decorative purposes, much of it was very well made. The quality of this 16th century-style fluted

Maximilian armour, made c.1820 (possibly by Wincklemeyer of Vienna), is reflected in the thickness of the metal used. A good-quality suit will weigh 58–60lb/26–27kg.
£8,000–10,000

MISCELLANEOUS MILITARIA

The wide range of other collectable military antiques provides would-be collectors with huge scope. You may decide to concentrate on a particular regiment, a type of object, or on a period of military history. Complete early uniforms may be hard to find, but headdresses, badges, fastenings, medals, powder flasks, postcards and prints are readily available and can form fascinating and highly decorative collections.

▶ BADGES

Whether made from metal or fabric badges are increasingly popular with collectors. Officer's headdress badges are larger than most others and particularly sought after. British regimental badges such as these early 19th-century examples are identifiable because they invariably include a crown in the design. £300–400 (each)

▲ SHAKOS

Shakos, the cylindrical helmets, with peaks and often plumes, were popular during the 19th century. The elaborateness of their decoration can affect value. This Austro-Hungarian shako is in reasonable condition and is decorated with ornate gold trimming. It is therefore worth around £300–500.

BEWARE

- Expect badges to show evidence of their age – those in perfect condition should make you suspicious.
- Fake badges usually weigh less than genuine ones and feel waxy.

▶ MEDALS

Before buying a medal check the soldier's and regiment's history to make sure he was entitled to it. This rare group of medals, awarded to a colonel in the Indian Army, is officially engraved with his name. £2,500–3,000

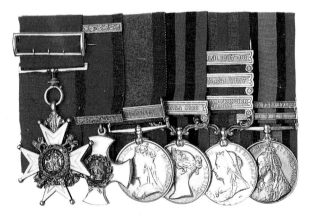

SCIENTIFIC INSTRUMENTS

However tempting it is to imagine some famous scientist of the past making a dramatic discovery with your microscope, sadly this is usually a long way from the truth. Most early scientific instruments were made either for amateur scientists, who regarded them as objects of beauty, or for professionals like surveyors, navigators, architects and even teachers, for whom these were everyday tools of their trade.

You don't have to be knowledgeable about the history of science to appreciate the obvious skill with which scientific instruments were made. At one end of the spectrum are the machine-made precision tools produced during the 19th century, some of which can be bought for little over £100 (even though

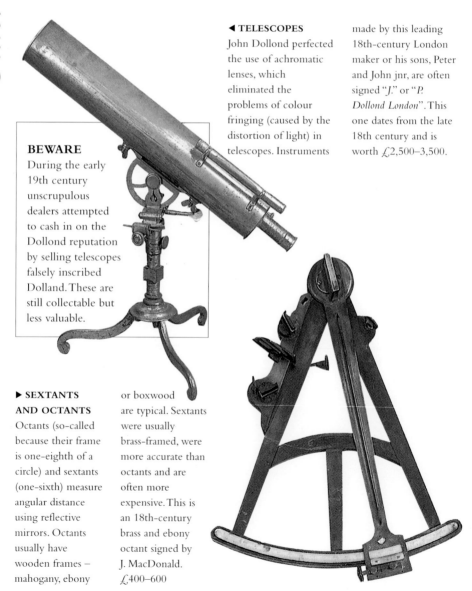

◀ TELESCOPES
John Dollond perfected the use of achromatic lenses, which eliminated the problems of colour fringing (caused by the distortion of light) in telescopes. Instruments made by this leading 18th-century London maker or his sons, Peter and John jnr, are often signed "*J.*" or "*P. Dollond London*". This one dates from the late 18th century and is worth £2,500–3,500.

BEWARE
During the early 19th century unscrupulous dealers attempted to cash in on the Dollond reputation by selling telescopes falsely inscribed Dolland. These are still collectable but less valuable.

▶ SEXTANTS AND OCTANTS
Octants (so-called because their frame is one-eighth of a circle) and sextants (one-sixth) measure angular distance using reflective mirrors. Octants usually have wooden frames – mahogany, ebony or boxwood are typical. Sextants were usually brass-framed, were more accurate than octants and are often more expensive. This is an 18th-century brass and ebony octant signed by J. MacDonald. £400–600

they may originally have cost as much as a small house!); at the other there are the rare, expensive examples of 18th-century hand-crafted objects which are always in demand and important Renaissance instruments which have come to be regarded as works of art in their own right and also command very high prices. Many instruments are also ornately decorated and incorporate materials such as brass, silver, ivory and ebony. The dating of a piece can present inexperienced collectors with problems, as the same design was often repeated over long periods. Some instruments were marked by their maker, and this usually helps with identification and dating, but also will usually increase the price. Fakes and reproductions of early instruments exist, so if in doubt always consult an expert.

NEVER... attempt to polish an old scientific instrument of any type without checking with an expert first. If you do so you may seriously damage its patina, and reduce its value dramatically.

▲ GLOBES
Terrestrial pocket globes like this reflect advances in mapping and circumnavigation of the world and often had cases lined with celestial globes – maps of the stars. This one was made by J. Smith in 1815.
£2,000–3,000

▼ MICROSCOPES
This Culpeper-type microscope dates from c.1730 and is one of the most desirable types of early microscope. £5,000–8,000. Microscopes from the 19th century are easier to find. Quality makers to look out for are: Powell & Lealand, W. & S. Jones, James Powell Swift, Smith & Beck, Nachet & Sons, Carl Zeiss and Secretan.

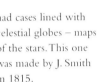

◀ SUNDIALS
Before watches became widely accessible and reliable, sundials were often used to check the time. There are two main types of dial: the pedestal dial, most commonly used in the garden, and the pocket dial, designed to be used at any latitude. This 18th-century octagonal pocket dial has an elaborately decorated brass plate and a folding gnomon (the part that casts the shadow). £300–400

CAMERAS & PHOTOGRAPHS

Although old cameras seem worlds apart from the high-tech models of today, many are still in working order and are bought to use. The earliest commercially manufactured cameras were produced from c.1841 and used the daguerreotype process, developed in France by L.J.M. Daguerre in 1837. However, each daguerreotype image was unique and it was not until Henry Fox Talbot's invention of the calotype that multicopies could be produced from a single exposure. Among the most intriguing of cameras are the novelty, detective and spy cameras which began to be produced as the photographic process became more refined towards the end of the century.

Unlike many other collectables, a camera's age is not necessarily reflected in its value – the rarity and quality of a particular model are often far more important than when it was made. Japanese cameras, which have enjoyed an upsurge in popularity recently, were mass-produced in the aftermath of World War II. Their quality became widely appreciated as a result of photojournalists covering the Korean War who recognized the superior quality of Japanese lenses. Today, rare and limited edition models by companies such as Nikon or Canon can fetch very high prices.

▶ **DAGUERREOTYPES**
Daguerreotypes look like mirrors – the image is formed on silvered metal, usually protected behind sealed glass. Despite their relative rarity you can still find portrait groups such as this for £60–100. An interesting view or a known sitter adds to value, which can be £1,000 or more.

◀ **PHOTOGRAPH ALBUMS**
The value of early photo albums is largely determined by the subject matter of the photos and the quality of the album. This one is made from leather and mother-of-pearl. Some were made of ivory, silver, gold or mauchline ware – wood covered with tartan-printed paper. £150–200

WHAT TO LOOK FOR

- milestone cameras which incorporate unusual technical innovations
- early handmade brass and mahogany cameras
- unusual spy cameras
- rare models by Ernst Leitz (Leica) and Zeiss
- limited edition post-World War II Japanese cameras.

► DETECTIVE AND SPY CAMERAS

Cameras in the form of books, watches, rings and packets of cigarettes may have been made more as curiosities than for any real espionage or skulduggery, but are nonetheless highly popular with today's collectors – and can fetch very high prices. This c.1895 camera looks just like a pocket watch when closed and measures only 1¼in/ 4cm in diameter. Made in America by John C.

Hegelein, it's one of only three examples known at present. £15,000–20,000.

▲ WOODEN, BRASS AND MAHOGANY CAMERAS

Although prices for wooden cameras start from around £200, early mahogany and brass-bound cameras are always sought after, but this 1890 Cyclographe is especially rare because it is the first panoramic camera produced by the prominent French maker V. Damoizeau. A clockwork mechanism rotated the camera around the platform and wound on the film automatically. £8,000–12,000

► JAPANESE CAMERAS

The quality and condition of post-war cameras has important effects on their price. This Nikon S3M is one of only 195 models made in the series, comes with an S72 motor and is in near-mint condition. It would be worth about £25,000–35,000. A similar used model would cost £15,000.

FILM MEMORABILIA

Although there is nothing new about the magnetic allure of the silver screen, film memorabilia is one of the most recent and exciting arrivals on the collecting scene. All the glamour of the movies, from the nostalgic old films of Hollywood's golden age to the high-tech special effects films of the 1980s and 90s, are reflected in the objects which fall into this colourful collecting category.

The major types of collectable film memorabilia are costumes, props, autographs, posters and photographs; but almost anything associated with a particular film or star can be collectable. Props associated with the key stars of cult movies tend to attract the highest prices. If a particular object immediately conjures up an important star you're on to a winner – but you will probably have to pay for it! If you can't afford the thousands neccessary to buy objects such as Charlie Chaplin's bowler hat and cane, or Harrison Ford's whip, you can still join in the fun by collecting the more affordable types of film memorabilia available. Posters, photographs, autographs and publicity stills are often priced at less than £100.

▶ PHOTOGRAPHS

This portrait photograph of Marlene Dietrich dates from c.1935, but even recently reproduced photos are desirable, because to many collectors a classic image of the star is more important than the age of the photograph. £300–550

BEWARE

Autographs on photos are often not genuine:
- Many stars allowed their secretaries to sign photographs on their behalf.
- Sometimes the negative of the photograph was signed.
- Some photographs are stamped with the star's signature.

◀ POSTERS

Among the most desirable film posters are those from classic films of the 50s and 60s. *Breakfast at Tiffany's,* for example, met with enormous success when it was released in 1961, and firmly established Audrey Hepburn as a star of the first order. This poster fetched £400. Posters for lesser films can still be found for under £20.

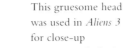

◀ PROPS

This gruesome head was used in *Aliens 3* for close-up sequences of Charles Dance, who played Superintendent Clemens in the 1992 film. Its high value is a reflection of three key points:

- rarity – it was the only one made
- the character was a key one in the film
- The *Alien* films were, and still are, hugely popular. £2,000+

▼ THUNDERBIRDS

The demand for Thunderbirds memorabilia has been fuelled by the various re-runs of the series on TV. Even though this is only a replica of Thunderbird 3, and wasn't used in filming, it's still worth £600–800.

▲ STAR WARS

The best film props are surprisingly well made and sophisticated. Darth Vader's helmet is made from fibreglass and has see-through perspex panels inserted in the cheek and neck areas to give better visibility to the wearer during the fighting sequences of *Star Wars*. £3,000+

▶ CLAPPERBOARDS

Clapperboards are among the least expensive types of film memorabilia. Look for boards which come from popular films, and which are printed with the name of the production and the director. £50+

SPORTING COLLECTABLES

If your attic is filled with mouldering old golf clubs you may be astonished to know that less than a decade ago an antique club fetched £92,400 at auction! While such a staggering price is very much the exception, there are, nonetheless, increasing numbers of sportsmen who bring their passion for field, pitch, or river bank into their homes by collecting objects related to their favoured pastime. Prices have also been boosted by the fashion for traditional décor which has inspired many an interior designer to furnish elegant hallways and studies with the paraphernalia of a time-honoured sport.

In the not too distant past old sporting equipment was usually relegated to the junk shop; nowadays you're more likely to find it in upmarket auction houses, and there are also a number of dealers who specialize in this field.

The most sought-after sporting items relate to the most popular pastimes: hence golf, fishing, football, tennis, cricket, rugby and even skiing memorabilia are keenly collected by enthusiasts. Spectator sports are also popular: for example, horse racing, Formula 1, boxing, the Olympic Games, and in the United States there is, of course, baseball. Collectable items include not only the objects needed to pursue the sport – whether rods, reels, golf clubs, balls or rackets – but also trophies of the sport and ceramic and printed ephemera relating to it.

◀ GOLF
Pre-19th-century golfing collectables are extremely rare, which explains why this late 17th- to early 18th-century club made by a blacksmith reached the world record price of £92,400 when it was sold at auction.

WHAT TO LOOK FOR
- Clubs marked by one of the great makers such as Auchterlonie, Andrew Forgan, Jack Morris or Philp.
- Feathery golf balls – made from hand-stitched leather stuffed with dampened goose down.
- Pottery commemorating golfing events or personalities, especially if made by premier British factories such as Spode and Doulton.

▲ 19TH-CENTURY CLUBS
Early hand-crafted clubs had names rather than numbers. These are drivers and long-nosed spoons of varying sizes. Before c.1850 clubs had long, slender heads, but by the 1880s the head had become shorter with a thicker neck. Value depends on rarity, age, quality and condition. Wood and iron clubs were made until the 1930s and can still be bought for £20–30. These clubs date from c.1885 and range from £1,500 to £3,500.

◀ FISHING

Perhaps as a substitute for "the one that got away", fishing trophies of the late 19th to early 20th century have lured many a collector in recent years. The most desirable fish are those in bow-fronted cases, such as this, which contains a bream caught in 1935. £700–900

▲ FISHING TACKLE

Early reels were finely made from materials such as brass, ivorene (an ivory substitute) and ebonite (simulated ebony); examples with maker's marks are particularly desirable. Among the names to look out for are Hardy Bros of Alnwick, Charles Farlow, S. Allcock and Alfred Illingworth. These reels all date from the late 19th and early 20th centuries and are worth between £150 (top right) and £2,000 (bottom right).

CONDITION

Reels in mint condition are rare, but those with damaged or replaced parts, or which have their owner's name scratched on them (unless he is famous) are best avoided.

▼ TENNIS

Even if he or she never won a match with it, a famous owner can transform a racket into a collector's item. When the racket Fred Perry used to beat Jack Crawford at Wimbledon in 1934 was auctioned, it sold for £23,000. This Wilson racket is autographed by Jimmy Connors, who used it in the 1979–81 US Open, and comes with a letter of authenticity. £1,500–2,000

BOXES

Decorative boxes come in a huge range of shapes, sizes and prices; some of the most exquisite ones were produced during the 18th century to contain snuff, patches or tobacco. The highest-quality boxes were often made from gold or silver, perhaps decorated with precious stones, but others were made from less expensive metals. Enamelled and porcelain boxes were also popular, some of the most attractive being made in the shape of a bird or animal. Boxes have long been fashionable items to collect and small 18th-century boxes can easily cost £1,000 or more, but you can still find attractive 19th-century versions for much less. Price is usually determined by quality and the type of materials used. In general, boxes made from wood or papier mâché are more widely available and affordable.

▲ LACQUER BOXES
Lids of 19th-century lacquer boxes were often decorated with a copy of a well-known Old Master – erotic subjects were always especially popular. This one shows nymphs bathing, with mischievous voyeurs in the bulrushes. Like many boxes of this type it was made in Germany, and is stamped on the interior "*Stobwasser Fabrik*".
£500–800

▼ ENAMEL BOXES
Bilston (Staffordshire), Birmingham and Battersea led the field in producing English enamel boxes during the 18th century. Chipping will reduce value; this late 18th-century box is damaged around the base and is worth £150–200; a similar case in better condition might well cost twice as much.

▲ TORTOISESHELL BOXES
Tortoiseshell, moulded by heat and pressure, was often used for making small boxes during the 18th and 19th centuries. This 19th-century cigar case is decorated with stellar *piqué* (an inlay of gold or silver).
£200–300

◀ TUNBRIDGE WARE
Tunbridge decoration was mostly made, as the name suggests, in the Tunbridge Wells area of Kent. This fiddly technique involved making pictures from long strands of differently coloured woods which were glued together, and sliced transversally into thin sheets. Value depends on the fineness of the decoration; this one is of average quality.
£400–500

VINTAGE FOUNTAIN PENS

Condition is a prime factor in the value of old pens, as they can be expensive to restore, so check carefully for signs of excessive wear. Avoid pens with replacement parts, which have often been forced or glued to the body. Pens in excellent condition are worth four or five times as much as worn ones. Specially designed large and oversized pens are also well worth looking out for.

> **PREMIER PENS**
>
> Quality pens (before 1945) by these makers are especially desirable:
> - Parker (before 1930)
> - Montblanc
> - Wahl-Eversharp
> - Mabie Todd (Swan)
> - Waterman
> - Dunhill-Namiki
> - Sheaffer

1 Pens marked as a calendar with dates and the seven days of the week were only made by Waterman. This was made in 1936 from 9ct gold. £800–1,000

2 The crescent on the side of this c.1916 gold-plated Conklin was a new design patented by this US maker in 1899 to improve the way the pen was filled. £300–500

3 This c.1905 silver Swan eyedropper is especially valuable because of its high-quality scroll and lozenge decoration. £800–1,200

4 It probably took as long as 2 weeks to decorate this c.1935 Dunhill-Namiki pen with such high-quality lacquer decoration. £2,000–3,000

5 The Lily pattern decorating this pen is one of the rarest designs used by Swan

during the early years of the 20th century. £1,500–2,000

6 This Montblanc pen, made c.1924, is of a fairly standard design, but is still worth £2,000–3,000, because the case is decorated with gold overlay.

7 Although this gold-plated Conklin

filigree pen made c.1918 is a more common type than No. 2, it's in a larger size and so would still be worth £300–500.

8 There are fakes of this very rare "spider's web" Montblanc Model 1M c.1924, but they are usually suspiciously "new" in appearance. £4,000–7,000

9 This "Smallest pen in the World" was a novelty made by Waterman c.1910–15; £1,000–1.500. Red versions are much rarer. £5,000–7,000

- Waterman also produced a massive No. 20 safety pen – reputedly used in America for hiding whisky during the Prohibition!

TRIBAL ART

The strong images and primitive shapes which characterize tribal art have enjoyed a huge increase in popularity in recent years. However, because prices have risen steeply and the demand for genuinely old pieces has greatly outstripped supply, there has also been a huge increase in fake pieces on the market. The many fakes produced in Africa and the Far East for the tourist market can be very hard to identify, so if you're an inexperienced collector, buy from a reputable source who can guarantee the age of any piece purporting to be old.

Provenance is fundamental to the value of tribal art. The most desirable pieces are those which have at some time been used for their intended domestic, ceremonial or ritual purpose, and were perhaps collected by colonial settlers or missionaries during the 19th or early 20th century.

WHAT TO LOOK FOR

- Clubs from the Pacific Islands – smaller ones were thrown at enemies to knock them over, larger ones for killing them!
- Maori artefacts with provenance – often faked, so beware.
- North American Indian quillwork and beadwork items.
- 19th-century Congo wood figures
- South African snuff containers, pipes, beadwork and carved headrests.

◀ MASKS
Masks are one of the most popular collecting areas of tribal art; many were used in tribal festivities and have symbolic significance. This Sepik mask is particularly valuable because of its provenance: it comes from the collection of Frank Wonder who acquired it on an expedition to New Guinea in the 1920s. £5,000–7,000

◀ CONDITION
Because of the extreme African climate, wooden objects from before the early 20th century are rare. Such pieces often deteriorate, but a worn patina, as seen on this Urhobo male figure, is desirable and adds to value. £3,000–4,000

▶ CALABASHES
The Hawaiian calabash bowl, was a status symbol made from the finest-quality woods, and passed down the generations within a single family. Before the early 19th century they were usually hand-carved; later examples were made on a lathe. Because the elaborate butterfly repairs on this one actually enhance its aesthetic appeal, it's worth £4,000.

ANTIQUITIES

If, like many collectors, you've always assumed that antiquities are prohibitively expensive, you may be surprised to find out that the average auction of antiquities contains many objects priced at hundreds rather than thousands of pounds. Nonetheless, antiquities have long been sought after, and faking in one form or another has existed throughout the centuries. There is also a further complication in the form of the export laws which exist in most countries where antiquities originate. Collectors should always make sure the piece is being sold legally.

BEWARE
- Antiquities are fragile and condition affects value, but some damage is to be expected – be suspicious of anything which seems too perfect.
- Avoid objects with heavy restoration – particularly if it is on the face of a piece of sculpture or a painting.
- Avoid bronzes which have become badly corroded – their detail may have been irreparably damaged.

▲ EGYPTIAN ANTIQUITIES
Antiquities from ancient Egypt are often extremely valuable. However there are exceptions. This simple redware vase dates from 3,500–3,200 BC and is worth about £300. Other inexpensive antiquities include:
- small Egyptian limestone carvings
- Roman terracotta oil lamps
- small examples of Cypriot pottery.

▼ ROMAN GLASS
It might well seem inconceivable that glass from the 2nd century should be no more expensive than that of the 18th century, but in fact this is often the case. This collection of vases illustrates the subtle colours and iridescence which is typical of much Roman glass and are worth between £300–800 each.

REMEMBER
If you have any doubts about the legality or authenticity of a piece, consult museum experts.

◀ GREEK POTTERY
Ancient Greek pottery is often decorated with scenes from classical mythology. This Attic (made in the are a around Athens) black-figure amphora (two-handled urn) dates from c.510–500 BC, and shows a rider flanked by two satyrs, mythical creatures associated with Dionysus, the god of wine. Later Attic vases, where the image colours have been reversed (background black and figures red), are known as red-figure vases. £10,000–15,000

PART 4

FACT FILE

ABOVE
A JULES STEINER BISQUE DOLL C.1890

LEFT RECORDING PRICES AT BERMONDSEY
ANTIQUES MARKET

WHERE TO SEE

There is an abundance of places where you can see and study antiques. Some of the major collections to be found in museums and houses open to the public are listed below.

American Museum in Britain
Claverton Manor,
Bath, Avon
Ceramics, Clocks,
Furniture, Silver

Apsley House
Wellington Museum,
149 Piccadilly,
Hyde Park Corner,
London W1
Ceramics, Militaria

Ashmolean Museum
Beaumont Street,
Oxford
Antiquities, Ceramics,
Clocks, Glass, Silver

Attingham Park
Shrewsbury,
Shropshire
Furniture, Silver

Belton House
Grantham, Lincs
Ceramics, Furniture,
Silver, Textiles

Bethnal Green Museum of Childhood
Cambridge Heath
Road, London, E2
Dolls, Toys

Birmingham City Museum
Chamberlain Square,
Birmingham
Glass

Blenheim Palace
Woodstock, Oxon
Furniture, Silver,
Glass, Ceramics

Blickling Hall
Blickling, Norwich,
Norfolk
Furniture, Textiles

Bristol City Museum and Art Gallery
Queen's Road,
Bristol
Glass

British Museum
Great Russell Street,
Bloomsbury,
London WC1
Antiquities, Ceramics,
Clocks, Glass,
Silver

Burghley House
Stamford, Northants
Furniture

The Burrell Collection
Pollock Country
Park, Glasgow
Antiquities,
Decorative Arts,
Oriental Arts

Castle Museum and Nottingham Art Gallery
Nottingham
Ceramics

Castle Museum
Tower Street, York
Ceramics, Silver,
Sheffield Plate

Cecil Higgins Art Gallery and Museum
Castle Lane, Bedford
Ceramics, Glass

Clandon Park
West Clandon,
Guildford
Ceramics, Furniture,
Textiles

Cutler's Company
Cutler's Hall,
Church Street,
Sheffield
Silver, Sheffield Plate

Derby Museum & Art Gallery
The Strand, Derby
Porcelain

Dyson Perrins Museum
Seven Street,
Worcester
Ceramics

Felbrigg Hall
Norwich, Norfolk
Furniture

Fenton House
Windmill Hill,
Hampstead,
London NW3
Ceramics,
Furniture

Fitzwilliam Museum
Trumptinton Street,
Cambridge
Ceramics,
Clocks, Glass

Geffrye Museum
Kingsland Road,
London E2
Furniture,
Decorative Arts

Glasgow Art Gallery & Museum
Kelvingrove,
Glasgow
Ceramics, Silver

Greyfrairs
Friar Street,
Worcester
Furniture, Textiles

Gunby Hall
Gunby,
Near Spilsby, Lincs
Furniture

Ham House
Richmond, Surrey
Furniture

Hampton Court Palace
Hampton,
Middlesex
Ceramics, Furniture,
Rugs, Textiles

Harewood House
Leeds,
West Yorkshire
Furniture

Ickworth
The Rotunda,
Horringer,
Bury St Edmunds
Furniture, Silver

Imperial War Museum
Lambeth Road,
London SE1
Armour, Arms

Jewel House
Tower of London,
London EC3
Silver, Metalware

Knole
Sevenoaks,
Kent
Carpets, Ceramics,
Furniture,
Textiles

Laing Art Gallery
and Museum
New Bridge Street,
Newcastle
Ceramics, Glass

Lady Lever
Art Gallery
Port Sunlight,
Merseyside
Furniture

Longleat House
Warminster,
Wilts
Ceramics, Furniture

Manchester City
Art Gallery
Mosley Street,
Manchester
Glass

Montacute House
Montacute,
Somerset
(early April–end Sept)
Furniture, Textiles

National Maritime
Museum
Romney Road,
Greenwich,
London SE10
Navigational
and Scientific
Instruments

National Museum
of Ireland
Kildare Street and
Marrion Street,
Dublin
Glass, Silver

National Museum
of Scotland
Chambers Street,
Edinburgh
Ceramics, Decorative Arts,
Silver

Petworth House
Petworth,
Sussex
Furniture, Sculpture

Pilkington Glass
Museum
Pilkington Bros. Ltd.,
Prescot Road,
St Helens,
Merseyside
Glass

Osterley Park
Isleworth,
Middlesex
Ceramics, Furniture

Polesden Lacy
Dorking, Surrey
Ceramics, Furniture,
Photographs, Silver

Royal Pavilion
Brighton,
East Sussex
Ceramics, Furniture,
Glass, Rugs, Textiles

Rufford Old Hall
Rufford,
Ormskirk,
Lancs
Armour, Arms,
Furniture, Textiles

The Science
Museum
Exhibition Road,
London SW7
Barometers, Scientific
Instruments

Sheffield City
Museum
Weston Park,
Sheffield
Sheffield Plate

Shugborough
Milford,
Near Stafford,
Staffordshire
Ceramics,
Furniture, Silver

Standen
East Grinstead,
Sussex
Art Nouveau
Ceramics, Furniture,
Textiles

Potteries Museum
and Art Gallery
Bethesda Street,
Hanley,
Stoke-on-Trent
Ceramics

Syon House
Brentford,
Middlesex
Clocks

Tatton Park
Knutsford, Cheshire
Ceramics, Furniture,
Glass, Silver

Temple
Newsam House
Leeds
Ceramics,
Furniture, Silver

Victoria and
Albert Museum
Cromwell Road,
London SW1
Art Nouveau,
Ceramics, Clocks,
Furniture, Glass,
Rugs and Carpets,
Silver, Textiles

Waddesdon Manor
Aylesbury, Bucks
Carpets, Ceramics,
Furniture

Wallace Collection
Hertford House,
Manchester Square,
London W1
Ceramics, Furniture,
Silver

Windsor Castle
Windsor, Berks
Ceramics, Clocks,
Furniture, Rugs

Worcester Porcelain
Museum
Severn Street,
Worcester
Ceramics

WHERE TO BUY

MAJOR AUCTION HOUSES

Bearnes
Rainbow,
Avenue Road,
Torquay,
Devon
Tel 01392 207000

Bonhams
Montpelier Street,
London SW7
Tel 020 7393 3900

101 New Bond Street,
London W1
Tel 020 7629 6602

65-69 Lots Road,
Chelsea,
London SW10
Tel 020 7393 3900

10 Salem Road,
Bayswater,
London W2
Tel 020 7229 9090

Christie's
8 King Street,
St James's,
London SW1
Tel 020 7839 9060

Lawrences of Crewkerne
South Street,
Crewkerne,
Somerset
Tel 01460 73041

Lots Road Auction Galleries
71-73 Lots Road,
Brompton,
London SW10
Tel 020 7376 6800

Outhwaite & Litherland
Kingsway Galleries,
Fontenoy Street,
Liverpool
Tel 0151 236 6561

Rosebery's Fine Art
74-76 Knights Hill,
London SE27
Tel 020 8761 2522

Sotheby's
34-35 New Bond Street,
London W1
Tel 020 7293 5000

ANTIQUES MARKETS

Alfie's Antiques Market
13-25 Church Street,
London W1
Tel 020 7723 6066
(Tuesday–Saturday)

Antiquarius
King's Road,
London SW3
Tel 020 7351 5353
(Monday–Saturday)

Bath Antiques Market
Guinea Lane,
Lansdown Road,
Bath,
Avon
Tel 020 7351 5353
(Wednesdays)

Bermondsey Market
Bermondsey Street,
London SE1
Tel 020 7351 5353
(Friday from 5 a.m.)

Camden Passage
Islington,
London N1
Tel 020 7 359 0190
(Tuesday–Saturday)

Chenil Galleries
King's Road,
Chelsea,
London SW3
Tel 020 7351 5829
(Monday–Saturday)

Cloisters Antiques Fairs
St Andrews Hall,
Norwich,
Norfolk
Tel 01603 628477
(Wednesdays)

Gray's Antique Market
Davies Street,
London W1
Tel 020 7629 7034
(Monday–Friday)

Great Western Antique Centre
Bartlett Street,
Bath,
Avon
Tel 01225 424243

Portobello Road Antiques Market
Portobello Road,
London W11
(Saturdays)

Preston Antique Centre
New Hall Lane,
Preston,
Lancs
Tel 01772 794498
(Monday–Sunday)

Taunton Silver Street Antiques
27-29 Silver Street,
Taunton,
Somerset
Tel 01823 289327
(Mondays)

The Antique Centre
56 Garstang Road,
Preston,
Lancs
Tel 01772 882078
(Monday–Sunday)

The Lanes
Brighton,
East Sussex
(Monday–Saturday)

Woburn Abbey Antiques Centre
Woburn Abbey,
Woburn,
Beds
Tel 01525 290350
(Monday–Sunday)

DEALERS' ASSOCIATIONS

British Antique Dealers' Association (BADA)
20 Rutland Gate,
London SW7
Tel 020 7589 4128

London and Provincial Antique Dealers' Association (LAPADA)
535 Kings Road,
London SW10
Tel 020 7823 3511

GLOSSARY

Acanthus Decorative leaf motif used to adorn a wide variety of objects.

Acid cutting A method of decorating glass where objects were coated with an acid-resistant substance, such as wax; a design was scratched on the wax with a steel point and fixed by dipping the object in acid.

Air twist stem On drinking glasses and other glassware, a stem decorated with spiral filaments of hollow glass.

Albarello (-i) A tin-glazed drug jar with a narrow waist.

Ambrotype A photograph made by exposing a glass plate treated with light-sensitive wet collodion. The negative was made positive by backing with black paper or paint.

Appliqué In textiles, applying small patches of fabric to a base fabric to make a design.

Arita An important centre for Japanese porcelain production, and a term used to describe one distinctive type of Japanese porcelain made in the area.

Armorial An engraved design showing a crest or coat-of-arms.

Arts & Crafts A late 19th-century artistic movement led by William Morris which advocated a return to medieval standards of craftsmanship and simplicity of design.

Automata A term covering a wide variety of mechanical toys with moving parts, popular during the 18th and 19th centuries.

Baluster Vase-shaped form with a bulbous base, narrow waist and slightly flared neck. Commonly used on silverware, ceramics and stems of drinking glasses.

Ball-and-claw A furniture foot in the shape of an animal's paw grasping on ball. Used on cabriole legs.

Basaltes Unglazed black stoneware, developed by Wedgwood.

Bergère French-style armchair with wood frame and upholstered sides.

Berlin Woolwork Amateur embroidery using coloured wools on a canvas grid.

Biscuit Unglazed porcelain, fired only once.

Blue-dash charger A delftware dish decorated with a border of blue brush strokes.

Blueing A decorative heat treatment applied to metal weapons which also protects from rust.

Bone china Porcelain made by the addition of large quantities of bone ash.

Bracket clock A type of spring-driven clock, designed to stand on a surface.

Britannia metal An alloy of tin antimony and copper, used during the 19th century as a substitute for pewter.

Cabriole leg A furniture leg in the shape of an elongated S.

Cameo glass Wares made by combining two or more layers of differently coloured glass, carved to make a design in relief.

Carriage clock A small portable clock with a carrying handle.

Case furniture Furniture intended as a receptacle, such as a chest of drawers.

Chasing A method of decorating silver and other metals by creating a raised pattern using a hammer or punch. Also known as embossing.

Chinoiserie Oriental-style fixtures and scenes used to decorate many different types of object.

Creamware Creamy-white earthenware.

Cornice The projecting moulding at the top of tall pieces of furniture.

Credenza A long side-cabinet with glazed or solid doors.

Cross-banding A veneered edge at right-angles to the main veneer.

Cruet A frame for holding casters and bottles containing condiments.

Davenport A small writing desk with a sloped top above a case of drawers.

Delftware Tin-glazed earthenware from England or the Low Countries.

Dial The "face" of a clock, which shows the time.

Distressed A term used to describe an object that has been artificially aged.

Drum table A circular-topped table with a frieze containing drawers and supported by a central pedestal.

Ebonized Stained black in imitation of ebony.

Étui A small case for scissors and other small implements.

Faïence Tin-glazed earthenware from France.

Façon de Venise Glassware imitating Venetian styles.

Flatback Ceramic portrait figures with flat, undecorated backs, designed to stand against a wall or on a mantelpiece.

Flatware Any flat or shallow tableware, such as plates or cutlery.

Gesso A plaster-like substance used as a substitute for carved wood, or as a base for painted or gilded decoration.

Hallmark The marks stamped on silver or gold objects when passed at assay (the test for quality).

Hard-paste porcelain Porcelain made using the ancient Chinese combination of kaolin and petuntse.

Imari Japanese porcelain with opulent decoration inspired by brocade designs, exported through the port of Imari.

Intaglio Incised gemstone or any incised decoration; the opposite of carving in relief.

Istoriato Narrative scenes painted on Italian *maiolica*.

Jacobite glass Wine glasses engraved with symbols of the Jacobites (supporters of Charles Edward Stuart's claim to the throne).

Japanning European imitation of Oriental lacquer.

Jasperware A hard fine-grained stoneware decorated with high relief medallions, developed by Wedgwood.

Joined Term used to describe furniture made by a joiner.

Kakeimon Sparsely-decorated Japanese porcelain made by the Kakiemon family in the 17th century. The style was much imitated by later potters.

Kaolin A fine white granite clay used in hard-paste porcelain, also known as China clay.

Kashan Rug-making centre in Southern Iran, noted for high quality products.

Kazak Rugs from central Caucaus, usually decorated with distinctive geometric designs.

Kelim A flat woven Persian rug (made with no pile).

Kneehole desk A writing desk with drawers on either side and a central recess for the user's legs.

Ladder back A country chair with a back made from a series of horizontal bars between the two vertical uprights.

Ladik A Turkish prayer rug, usually decorated with a niche and stylized tulip flowers.

Lap joint In silverware, the technique used to join a spoon finial to the stem by cutting each piece in opposing L-shapes.

Lead Crystal Glass containing lead oxide which gives extra weight and brilliance.

Library table A rectangular table with frieze drawers, end supports and a central stretcher.

Linen chest A hybrid coffer/chest of drawers, which may have both drawers and a lift-up top.

Loaded In silverware, a hollow object (often a candlestick) filled with pitch and a metal rod to give weight.

Lock The firing mechanism of a gun.

Long arm A firearm with a long barrel.

Longcase clock A tall clock with a case containing weights and pendulum and hood housing dial and movement.

Lowboy A small dressing table, often with a single frieze drawer flanked by a deeper drawer.

Maiolica Tin-glazed earthenwares from Italy.

Majolica Enamelled stoneware with high relief decoration developed by Minton in the 19th century.

Marquetry Design formed from veneers of differently coloured woods.

Marriage The joining together of two previously unrelated parts to form a whole.

Mihrab A niche with a pointed arch, seen on prayer rugs.

Millefiori Glass made by fusing differently coloured rods of glass which resembles "a thousand flowers"; used especially for paperweights.

Monteith Large silver bowl, with a shallow scalloped rim.

Mortise-and-tenon Joint used in furniture; the mortise is a cavity, into which the shaped tenon fits and is held in place by dowels.

Mother-of-pearl Slices of shell often used for decorative inlay.

Motif A decorative detail, often repeated to form a pattern.

Moulded glass 19th-century glasswares manufactured in large quantities by forcing glass into a mould.

Mystery clock A clock of novel form in which the movement is ingeniously disguised.

Nailsea A factory near Bristol famous for novelty glass objects.

Occasional table Small, easily portable table.

Octant Device made from one-eighth of a circle, used for measuring angular distance.

Opaque twist A white or coloured twist of glass within the stem of a drinking glass.

Ormolu Gilded bronze or brass; term also sometimes loosely used to describe any yellow-coloured metal.

Overglaze A second glaze laid over a first and refired; also known as enamelling.

Pad foot A rounded foot, such as that of an animal, on furniture.

Palmette A stylized palm-leaf motif, often used to decorate Oriental carpets and furniture.

Papier mâché Paper pulp mixed with glue, used to make small objects such as boxes and trays; also applied over a metal frame to make larger pieces of furniture, such as tables and chairs.

Parcel gilt Wood that has been partly gilded.

Parian Fine white biscuit porcelain resembling marble; popular from the mid-19th century.

Parquetry Decorative veneers of wood laid in a geometric pattern.

Pate The crown of a doll's head.

Patina The term used to describe the surface colour and sheen of furniture and silver which is built up from years of use and careful polishing.

Petuntse China stone; a granite used to make hard paste porcelain.

Plate A generic term for gold and silver vessels, not to be confused with Sheffield Plate or plated wares.

Porringer A two-handled dish sometimes with a lid, originally for holding porridge or broth. Made from silver and pewter.

Pressed glass 19th-century glasswares formed by mechanical pressure applied to molten glass in a mould.
see also Moulded glass

Quadrant A quarter circle, marked with degrees of a circle and with a weighted line or pointer, used as a navigational aid.

Quarter-veneered Four pieces of identical veneer, laid opposite each other to create a decorative effect.

Quartetto tables A set of four graduating matching tables, stored inside each other.

Rack The structure, comprising several shelves, at the top of some dressers.

Raised work Type of embroidery which incorporates areas of decoration raised up with padding – also called stumpwork

Refectory table Term used to describe the long rectangular dining tables of the 17th century and later.

Reproduction A piece which is a copy of an early design.

"Right" Dealers' term for something which is genuine and authentic as opposed to "wrong", meaning it is faked, altered or restored.

Sabre A curving sword used mainly by cavalrymen.

Sabre leg An elegant outward curving leg, associated with Regency furniture.

Salt A dish or cellar designed for holding salt.

Sampler Needlework pictures; incorporating different stitches and designs.

Scent bottle A small portable flask, often flattened pear shape.

Sconce A plate or bracket on the wall to which lights or candle-holders could be attached. Also used to describe the wall lights themselves.

Settle A long wooden seat with a back and arms, and possibly a box seat.

Sextant Navigational instruments, formed from one-sixth of a circle.

Sgrafitto Decorative techinque whereby the surface has been scratched or incised to show a contrasting colour beneath; used mainly on ceramics and glass.

Shako A 19th century military cap of conical shape with a peak.

Shiraz Centre of distribution in central Iran for nomadic rugs decorated with simple geometric designs.

Slip Clay mixed with water, often used to decorate pottery.

Snuffer Cone-shaped metal implement used to extinguish candles.

Sterling silver Silver of at least 925 parts per 1000 purity. The minimum standard for English silver.

Stock The wooden part of a firearm to which the metal barrel and firing mechanism are attached.

Tester The wooden canopy over a bed, it may cover only half the bed and be supported by two or four posts; hence full tester or half tester beds.

Train A set of cog

wheels and pinions in a clock movement.

Treen Small wooden domestic objects, sometimes in the shape of fruit.

Tunbridge ware Objects decorated with pictures or designs made from bundles of differently coloured wood cut in sections.

Tureen A large bowl on a foot used for serving soup.

Turned furniture Pieces made by turning on a lathe.

Veneer A thin sheet of wood applied to furniture for decorative effect.

Vesta case A small box used to contain vestas – early matches.

Vinaigrette A small portable container containing a sponge scented with vinegar.

Warp Threads used to make the foundation of a carpet running from one end of the carpet to the other and form the fringes.

Weft Cross-wise threads, which run at right angles to the warp in any woven textiles.

Wet plate camera Earliest form of camera, often made from brass-bound mahogany.

Whatnot Tall stand of four or five display shelves and sometimes a drawer in the base.

Windsor chair Country chair, usually with a saddle seat, hoop back and simple turned legs.

Wine funnel Cone, with a spout and often a matching fish for filtering and decanting wine.

Wing chair Upholstered chair with a high back and wing-like side projections.

X-frame The X-shaped construction of some chairs and stools.

INDEX

Page numbers in **bold**
refer to main entries

A
acid etching 211
adverts 27
Aesthetic Movement
45, 130
agateware 113, 116
albums (photograph) 264
Alcock (Samuel) &
Co. 164
Aller Vale pottery 130
amboyna 40
antique shops **18–21**
antiquities **273**
Apostle spoons 198
applied decoration
(silver) **190–1**
Arita ware 108
arm chairs 44, 45, 54,
55–7, 90
armorials 188, 197
armour 258, **260**
arms & militaria **258–61**
Art Deco 79, 143, 205,
232–9
art galleries **276–7**
Art Nouveau **232–9**
ceramics 158, 159,
190, **236**
furniture 49, 79, **232–3**
glass **234**
posters **239**
sculpture **238**
silver 203, 207
Art Unions 164
Arts & Crafts
movement 45, 189
ash 51
Aubusson rugs 231
auctions 9, **14–17, 278**
autographs 255, 266
automaton clocks **225**

B
Baccarat 217
BADA 18
badges 261
Baldwin, Charley 154
Ball, Edward 160
bamboo 98
Barbie dolls 245
Barlow, Florence 126, 127
Barlow, Hannah 126, 127
Baron, William Leonard
126, 130
Baroque style 44, 189

Baxter, Thomas 156
The Beatles **255**
beds 93
beech 40, 48, 49, 50, 98
Belleek **165**
bentwood chairs 49
Berlin **172–3**
Berlin woolwork 241
Bermondsey market 24
Berry, E. 208
Beswick figures **145**
Billingsley, William 156
Bing toys 250, 252
bisque dolls 244, **246–7**
black basalt ware 128
blue & white ware 106,
107, 108, 122
Bohemia 210, 216
bone china 105, 150
bookcases 76, 78, 85
Bourne, Olive 137
Bow 146
bowls (of glasses) 213
boxes 202, 203, **270**
bracket clocks **220–1**
Brannam, C.H. 130, 131
brass 208, 219, 265
bright-cutting 188,
192, 203
Bristol blue glass 213
bronze 237, 273
Brustolon, Andrea 44
bureau bookcases 84, 85
bureaux **84**
burglary 32
Butler, Frank 127
butlers' chairs 57
button back chairs 55
buying antiques **13–27**

C
cabinets **74, 78–9,** 88,
89, 233
cabriole legs 44, 48, 52–3,
66, 69
calabashes 272
Calka, Maurice 102
cameo glass 210, 216, 233
cameras 264, **265**
candlesticks 117, **199,** 208
Cantagalli 166
Capodimonte 176
car boot sales 13, **25–6**
card-cutting 203
card tables 70–1
care of antiques **36–7**
Carltonware **142**
carpets *see* rugs

carriage clocks **224**
Carter, Stabler &
Adams 137
Carter, Truda 137
carving 42, 44, 45, 46, 92
Cassandre, J. M. 239
cast iron 94–5
casters 57, 60, 67, 68
casters (silver) **196**
Caughley 148, 149
celadon 110, 111
cellarets 82, 83
celluloid toys 253
cellulose figures 144
ceramics **104–85**
architectural 137
Art Deco 143, **237**
Art Nouveau 158, 159,
190, **236**
British **112–65**
care & restoration 37
condition 104
Continental **166–81**
dating 105, 145, 147,
151, 155, 165
decorative techniques
105, 109
displaying 28, 34–5
foreign **182–5**
Japanese **108–9**
materials 104–5
see also earthenware;
majolica; porcelain;
pottery; stoneware
Chad Valley 248
chair backs 47, 48, 50, 51,
52–3, 90
chairs 44, 45, **46–57,** 90,
100–1, 102–3, 232, 233
chaises longues 55, 101
chasing 189, 203
Chelsea 105, 146, 147
Chéret, Jules 239
cherry 40
chestnut 40–1
chests **72–3**
China
porcelain 104, 105, **106–7**
rugs 230
stoneware **110–11**
china *see* porcelain
Chinese dynasties 106
Chinese symbolism 107
chinoiserie 44, 47, 98, 148
Chiparus, Demètre 237
"Chippendale" 11, 44, 45,
46, 47, 52
Chivers, Frederick 160

"chryselephantine" 238
Churchill, Sir Winston 205
cigar/cigarette cases **204–5**
Cizhou ware 110
clapperboards 267
Clichy 217
Cliff, Clarice **237**
clocks **218–25**
care & restoration 37, 221
cases 219, 220, 221
dials 219, 220, 222,
223, 224
escapements 218, 221
finials 221, 223
French 220, 224
hands 219, 220, 223, 224
movement 37, 218,
221, 224
pendulums 37, 218,
221, 223
repeaters 224
signatures 219, 220, 224
striking 221
transporting 37, 221
clockwork toys 252, 253
cloisonné 30, 158, 159, 224
clothes
designer 254
dolls' 244, 246, 247
military 261
rock & pop memorabilia
254, 256, 257
coach tables 68
Coalbrookdale furniture 94
"Coalbrookdale" ware 160
Coalport 151, **160**
coffee pots 136, 143, 172,
177, **192, 193**
coffers 92
Columbo, Joe 103
Commedia dell'Arte
figures 169
commission 15, 17
commodes 93
composition dolls 244, 245
Conklin 271
Connors, Jimmy 269
console tables 66, 67
Cooper, Susie **136**
Cope & Collinson 57
Copeland 164
copper 209
Corgi Toys 250
coromandel 41
country chairs 50–1, 90, 95
Cozzi 176, 177
creamware 113, **120–1,**
123, 129

credenzas 74, **75**
Cressent, Charles 44
cristallo 210
cupboards 76–7
cushions 242
cut glass **214–15**

D
daguerrotypes 264
Daum Frères 234
Davenport **163**
davenports 84, 85
Day, Louis F. 130
Dean, William 152
decanters 37, **213**
Dee, Henry William 207
Delft 105, 166
delft (English) 112
Denmark 102, 103
Derby 146
    see also Royal Crown
    Derby
desks 84, **86–7,** 102
Devlin, Stuart 205
Dewdney, James 130
die-cast toys 250
die-stamping 191, 203
Dietrich, Marlene 266
dining tables **60–3**
Dinky Toys 250
dirks 259
Disney collectables 144,
    145, 253
display cabinets **78–9**
display tables 67, 69
displaying antiques 28,
    34–5
Distler toys 253
Doccia 176, 177
Dolland family 262
dolls **244–7,** 255
Doughty, Freda 155
Doulton & Co. **126–7,**
    138–9, 236 *see also*
    Royal Doulton
Dresden 172, 173
Dresser, Dr. Christopher
    159, 209
dressers 74, **75,** 88
dressing-table sets
    200–1, 203
drinking glasses 210,
    212–13
du Pacquier, Claudius 174
duelling pistols 259
Dunhill-Namiki 271
Dutton, William 223
Dwight, John 116

E
Eames, Charles 100, 101
earthenware 104, 112,
    114–15
East, Edward 220
Eaton, Arthur Charles 127
ebony 41, 221
Eclectic style 65
edged weapons **259**
Edwardian style 49, 98, 190
Egyptian antiquities 273
electroplate 37, 186,
    187, 209
elm 41, 51
embossing 189, 203, 204
embroidery **240–1**
Empire style 45, 181
enamelling boxes 270
    ceramics 105, 109,
        132, 150
    clocks 219, 224
    glass 210–11
    overglaze 105, 109
    silver 189–90, 201, 203,
        204, 206
engine-turning 190
engraving
    clocks 224
    fake 259
    glass 211, 212, 213, 215
    silver 188, 192, 203, 204
    swords 259
ephemera 34, 254, 255,
    264, 266
Etling, Edmund et
    Cie 235
Evans, David 156

F
Fabergé 204
fabric dolls 245
faïence 166
fairs **22–3, 24, 278**
fakes
    antiquities 273
    engraved 259
    furniture 9, 43
    glass 211, 233, 235
    hallmarks 187
    porcelain 109, 147, 157
    pottery 123, 125, 128,
        129, 132, 135, 166, 237
famille rose 106, 107
famille verte 106, 107
Farnell, (J. K.) & Co. 248
feet (glasses) 213
figures
    Parian ware 151, 164

porcelain 146, 149, 153,
    154, 155, 161
porcelain (Continental)
    168–9, 176, 179
porcelain (foreign)
    183, 236
pottery 113, 120, 121,
    123, 127, 131, **138–9,**
    141, 143, **144–5**
    see also sculpture
filigree 203, 271
film memorabilia **266–7**
fire screens 92
firearms **258–9**
Fisher, Alexander 130
fishing collectables 269
Fishley, Edwin Beer 130
flatware **198**
Flaxman, John 128, 129
flintlock pistols 258
Fontaine, Pierre-François 45
forks 198
France
    ceramics 107,
        166, 170, 171, **178–81**
    clocks 220, 224
    dolls 246
    furniture 44–5, 56, 57,
        69, 80, 97
    glass 214, 217
    rugs 231
    toys 250
Frankenthal 168, 169
Fry, Roger 137
furniture **40–103**
    alterations 43, 61, 68, 80,
        81, 82, 84
    Art Deco 79, **233**
    Art Nouveau 49,
        79, **232–3**
    care & restoration 36, 65
    colour 41, 47
    condition 43, 47, 51, 54,
        60, 68–9, 70, 78, 91, 97
    construction 40–1, 42–3,
        46, 55, 70, 73, 86
    Continental 44–5, 56,
        57, 63, 65, 69, 76, 80,
        81, 97
    dating 46, 50, 52–3, 58,
        83, 85
    decorative techniques
        42–3, 44, 45, 46, 64,
        68, 69, 74, 78, 92
    drawers 42, 66, 73
    fakes 9, 43
    feet 42, **52–3,** 72, 73,
        84, 89

garden **94–7**
handles 42, 66, 72, 73, 89
joints 42, 73
kitchen **88–91**
legs 44, 45, 48, **52–3,** 62,
    66, 68, 69, 82
locks 42
proportions 41
reproductions 47,
    58, 62, 81
screws 42
styles 44–5, 48–9, 50–1
upholstered 54–6, 57,
    100, 101, 233
woods 40–1, 62
    see also individual items

G
Gallé, Emile 233, 234
games tables **70,** 71
garden furniture **94–7**
Garrard & Co. 200
Gaultier, François 246
Gaultier, Jean-Paul 254
Georgian style 45, 77, 78,
    86, 87
Germany
    dolls 246, 247
    teddy bears 244, 248, 249
    toys 250, 251, 252–3
gilding
    ceramics 159, 161, 174,
        179, 185
    furniture 43, 68
    glass 211, 212, 213
    silver 191
Gillow 45, 49, 57, 87
giltwood 44, 45, 67, 92
glass **210–17**
    Art Deco **235**
    Art Nouveau **234**
    care & restoration 37
    coloured 210, 213, **216**
    commemoratives 214
    dating 211, 212, 213
    decorative techniques
        210–11, 214–15,
        216, 217
    fakes 211, 233, 235
    Irish 214
    marks 217, 234
    reproductions 217
    Roman 273
    and silver 203
    types 210
glazes (ceramic) 105, 111
globes 263
glossary 279–82

Godwin, E. W. 45
golf collectables 268
googlie dolls 247
Goss china **135**, 150
Gothic style 47, 52, 53
"grandfather" clocks
    222–3
Gregory, Albert 152, 153
Gresley, Cuthbert 152, 153
Gurschner, Gustav 237

H
Hadley, James 154
hallmarks **186–7**
Han dynasty 110
Hancock, Samson 152,153
"Hans Sloane" wares 147
Harradine, Lesley 138
Haywood of Derby 94
heat damage 34, 36
Hegelein, John C. 265
helmets 260, 261, 267
Hendrix, Jimi 10, 254
"Hepplewhite" 44, 46, 48,
    52, 53
Herman Miller 100, 101
Heubach, Ernst 247
Holland, Henry 45
Holly, Buddy 254
Holmes, John 223
Hope, Thomas 45
Hovelskov, Jorgen 103
Howard & Sons 55, 56, 57
Hürten, C.F. 162

I
Imari ware 109, 152
inlay 43, 45, 78
Instone, Bernard 201
insurance 30, **31,** 33
inventories 32, 33
ironstone 122, 133
ivorene 237

J
Jackson, Michael 254, 257
Jacob, Georges 45
Jacobite glasses 212
Jacobs, Carl 103
Jacot, Henri 224
Japan
    cameras 264, 265
    ceramics 30, **108–9**
japanning 67, 68, 84
Japonisme 45
jasper ware 122, 128, 129
John, Elton 254, 256, 257
Jones, George 124

jugs
    metalware 209
    porcelain 146, 165, 171
    pottery 115, 126, 130,
        131, 132,134, 136,
        139, 141, 237
    silver 190, **195**
Jumeau, Pierre 246
Jun ware 110, 111
junk shops 20
Jupe, Robert 62, 63

K
Kakiemon ware 108
kelims 227, 228
Kent, William 45
Kestner & Co. 247
kitchen furniture **88–91**
kitchenware 89
Knibb brothers 220
Knight, Dame Laura 237
"knockers" 21
Knox, Archibald 137

L
lace 243
lacquer 84, 221, 270, 271
ladder back chairs 50, 90
Lalique, René 234, **235**
Lamerie, Paul de 189, 193
lamps 234
LAPADA 18
Le Corbusier 101
Le Pautre, Jean 44
Le Roy & Fils 224
Leach, Bernard 110
lead glass 210
lead glaze 105, 113,
    118–19, 120
lead soldiers 250, 251
Lebedeva, Maria 185
Leeds Pottery 113
Leica cameras 265
Lenci dolls 245
Lennon, John 254, 255
Leroy, Désiré 152
Liberty & Co.189,203, 232
library tables 64, 65
lighting 35
Limehouse 148
Liverpool 149
Lloyd Loom furniture 98,
    99
longcase clocks **222–3**
Longton Hall 148, 149
loving cups 112, 117
Lowestoft 149
lustreware 132, 140, 142

M
MacDonald, J. 262
Mackintosh, Charles
    Rennie 49, 232
Madonna 254, 257
mahogany
    cameras 265
    clock cases 221, 223
    furniture 41, 45, 46, 48,
        49, 60, 62, 68, 69
    maiolica 166, 167
    majolica **124–5**
Makeig-Jones, Daisy 140
Malkin, Samuel 114
Maori artefacts 272
marble 67, 96
markets 22, **23–4, 278**
Märklin toys 252
marks
    armourers' 260
    dolls 247
    glass 217, 234
    metalware 208
    Parian ware 164
    porcelain 146, 147, 149,
        153, 155, 157, 159,
        161, 162, 163
    porcelain (Continental)
        169, 171, 173, 175,
        176, 178, 180
    porcelain (foreign)165,185
    pottery 127, 128, 131,
        133, 136, 137, 138,
        139, 142, 143
    pottery (Continental)
        166, 167
    silver **186–7,** 192, 193,
        194–5, 197, 200, 204,
        207
    teddy bears 249
Marot, Daniel 44
marquetry 43, 45, 64, 69,
    74, 222
"marriages" 41, 43, 61, 75,
    77, 78, 85, 258
Marseille, Armand 247
Marshall, Mark V. 127
Martin, Emma 126
masks 272
Mason's Ironstone 122, 133
matting 189
medals 261
Meissen 104, 105, 168,
    169, 170, 171, 172
Mercury, Freddie 257
Merrythought 248
metalware **208–9**
microscopes 263

Mies van der Rohe,
    Ludwig 233
Ming dynasty 106
Minton 124, 125, 151,
    158–9, 164
mirrors 45, 68, 79, 92, 203
Modernist style 100–3
Montblanc 271
Montinari, Mme 245
Moorcroft, William 236
Morrison, Jim 254
movie memorabilia **266–7**
Mucha, Alphonse 239
Mudge, Thomas 223
mugs 114, 134, 184, **194**
    see also loving cups
Murray, Keith 141
museums **276–7**
musical instruments 10,
    254, 255, 256
mystery clocks **225**

N
Nantgarw **156–7**
needlework rugs 231
Neoclassical style 44, 45,
    48, 64, 129, 177, 188
niello 190, 204
Nikon cameras 265
Nixon, Harry 127
Noah's arks 251
Noke, C. J. 138
North American Indian
    artefacts 272
Nottingham stoneware 117
novelty items 124–5,
    131, 170, 172, 205,
    206–7, 209, 225, 271

O
oak 41, 49, 62
occasional tables 69
octants 262
Oeben, Jean-François 44,45
opaline glass 102
overglaze enamel 105, 109
overlay glass 210
owl jugs 115

P
Pacific Islands artefacts 272
Paisley shawls 242
Panton, Verner 102
paperweights **217**
papier mâché 69, 71
parcel gilding 191
Pardoe, Thomas 156
Parian ware 151, **164**

Parker 271
pâte sur pâte 126, 151, 158
patina 41, 47, 66, 187
pearlware 120, 121, 123
pediments 85, 223
Pembroke tables 64
pens **271**
Percier, Charles 45
percussion pistols 258, 259
Perry, Fred 269
Perry, Son & Co. 209
pewter 208
photographing antiques
  32–3
photographs 34, **264**, 266
piano stools 59
pier tables 66, 68
piercing 191, 196
pine 41, **88–91**
plaques 161, 173
police 32
polish 36, 37
Pollard, William 156
Poole Pottery **137**
porcelain
  care & restoration 37
  Chinese 104, 105, **106–7**
  colours 106–7, 108, 109,
    171, 174, 178
  commemoratives 150,
    152, 161
  condition 153, 165
  Continental 104, 105,
    107, 146, **168–81**
  decorative techniques
    150, 151, 154, 155,
    177, 179
  defined 104
  displaying 28, 35
  English 105, **146–55**
  fakes 109, 147, 157
  figures 146, 149, 153,
    154, 155, 161
  figures (Continental)
    168–9, 176, 179
  figures (foreign) 183, 236
  foreign **182–5**
  hard-paste 104–5
  Irish **165**
  Japanese 30, **108–9**
  jewelled 160
  marks 146, 147, 149,
    153, 155, 157, 159,
    161, 162, 163
  marks (Continental) 169,
    171, 173, 175, 176,
    178,180
  marks (foreign) 165, 185

reproductions 171, 180
soft-paste 105
Welsh **156–7**
Portobello Road 12, 20,
  23, 24
posters **239,** 256, 266
potash glass 210
pottery
  advertising items 137, 142
  blue & white 106,
    107, 108, 122
  care & restoration 37
  colours 110, 111,
    112–13, 116, 118–19,
    129, 132, 167
  commemoratives 120,
    132, **134**
  condition 114–15, 125,
    167, 237
  Continental **166–7**
  decorative techniques
    117,126
  defined 104
  Devon 112, **130–1**
  English **112–13, 122–45**
  fakes 123, 125, 128, 129,
    132, 135, 166, 237
  figures 113, 120, 121,
    123, 127, 131, **138–9,**
    141, 143, **144–5**
  Greek 273
  marks 127, 128, 131, 133,
    136, 137, 138, 139,
    142, 143
  marks (Continental)166,
    167
  reproductions 123, 125,
    132, 167
  souvenir items 131, 135
pouffes 59
Powell, Alfred & Louise 141
Prattware 119, 120
prayer rugs 227, 229
Preiss, Ferdinand 238
presentation discs 257
pressed glass **214–15**
Prince 257
printing techniques 238
props (film) 267
provenance 16, 65, 272,273
Pumpkin head dolls 245

Q
Qing dynasty 106
quartetto tables 67, 69
Queen Anne style 44, 52
Queensware 129
quilts 243

R
Raby, Edward 155
raised work 240
Ramsden & Carr 203
Randall, John 160
Ravenscroft, George 210
Ravilious, Eric 140
receipts 20, 24, 27, 33
Regency style
  clocks 220
  furniture 45, 47, 48, 52,
    53, 55, 62, 98
Reisenburgh, Bernard
  van 44
repoussé 189
reproductions
  armour 260
  furniture 47, 58, 62, 81
  glass 217
  porcelain 171, 180
  pottery 123, 125, 132, 167
restoration 15, 36
Riesener, Jean-Henri 45
rifles 258
Robinson &
  Leadbeater 164
Robinson & Rhodes 113
robots 253
rock & pop memorabilia
  254–7
rock crystal 215
Rockingham 150, 151, **161**
Rococo style 44, 45, 117
rose Pompadour 171
rosewood 41, 45, 48, 49
Royal Copenhagen
  182–3, 236
Royal Crown Derby **152–3**
Royal Doulton 13, 25,139
Royal Worcester **154–5**
ruby glass 216
rugs & carpets **226–31**
  care & restoration 37, 227
  Caucasian **228–9**
  Chinese **230**
  colours 226, 228, 229
  condition 227
  dating 229
  European **231**
  Indian **230**
  Kazak 228
  knots 226
  Ladik 229
  materials 226
  Persian **227**
  Shirvan 229
  Turkish **228–9**
Russian porcelain **184–5**

S
Saarinen, Eero 103
Sabino, Marius E. 235
sabres 259
salt glaze 105, 112,
  113, **116–17**
salvers **197**
samplers 240, 241
Sampson Mordan & Co. 207
satinwood 41, 49, 69
Satsuma ware 108
sauceboats 133, 149,
  162, 195
Schoenhut Co. 250
scientific instruments **262–3**
Scofield, John 199
sculpture 34, 135, **238**
"Secessionist"ware 158,
  159
secretaire bookcases 85
security **32–3**
selling antiques 16–17, 21,
  24, 26, 27
services 121, 122, 133,
  159, 163, 182, 183
Sèvres 69, 170, 171, **178–9**
sextants 262
sgraffito 117
Shaeffer 271
shakos 261
Shang dynasty 110
Sheffield plate 37, 186,
  187, 191, 209
Shelley **143**
"Sheraton" 44, 46, 48, 52,
  53, 64
side tables 66, 89
sideboards **82–3**
signatures 141, 219, 220,
  224, 237
silver **186–207**
  alterations 187, 193
  Art Deco 205
  Art Nouveau 203, 207
  care & restoration 37, 187
  condition 187, 190, 191,
    192, 198, 199, 201
  dating 186–7
  decorative techniques
    187,**188–91,** 203
  and glass 203
  marks **186–7,** 192, 193,
    194–5,197, 200, 204,207
  weight 187
silver gilt 37, 202
Simmance, Eliza 127
Simon & Halbig 247
Simpson, John 114

Simpson, Percy 160
Sindy dolls 245
Skeaping, John 141
skeleton clocks **225**
slipware 112, **114–15**
Smith, George 45
Smith, John Moyr 158
smoke damage 36
snuff boxes 202
soda glass 210
sofa tables 64
sofas 54, 55
Solon, Leon 158
Solon, Marc-Louis 158, 159
Song dynasty 110
Song ware 127
soumacs 228
South African artefacts 272
space age toys 253, 267
spelter 237
Spode 133, 150, 151, **162**
spoons 198
sporting collectables
    206, **268–9**
spy cameras 265
St Louis 217
Stabler, Phoebe 137
Staffordshire pottery 104,
    112–13, 118–19, 122, 123
stately homes **276–7**
Steel, Thomas 161
Steiff 244, 248, 249
stem bowls 111
stems (of glasses) 212, 213
Stinton family 154
stone 96
stone china 133
stoneware 104, **110–11,**
    112, **116–17,** 126
stools 44, **58–9,** 93
stumpwork 240
sundials 263
sunlight 34, 36, 37, 70
Susanis 241
Sutherland, Graham 237
Swan 271
Swansea **156–7**
swords 258, **259**

T
tables 45, **60–71,** 89, 91, 233
Talor, William 114
Tang dynasty 106
tankards 116, 194, 195, 208
Tanqueray, David **196**
tapestry 242–3
tea caddies 117, 188, 196
tea sets 148, 164, 171,

179, 181
tea tables 67, 68
teabowls 111
teapots 113, 116, 118, 120,
    125, 150, **192,** 237
teddy bears 244, **248–9**
telescopes 262
tennis collectables 269
terracotta 131
textiles **240–3**
    care & restoration 34,
        37, 240
    condition 240, 241
    displaying 34, 37
    embroidery **240–1**
    woven **242–3**
Thieme, Carl 173
Thonet, Michael 49
Thonet Frères 101
Tiffany & Co. 207, 234
    tiles 137
tin glaze 105, 112, 166
tinplate toys **252–3**
Tinworth, George 126
toby jugs 119, 139
Toft, Thomas 112, 114
Tompion, Thomas 220
Torquay Terracotta
    Company 130, 131
tortoiseshell 270
Tournai 183
Townshend, Pete 256
toys 10, **250–3,** 267 *see
    also* dolls; teddy bears
trade associations 18
trains (toy) **252**
transfer printing 121, 122,
    134, 150
travelling sets 174, 200
trays **197**
tribal art **272**
Tunbridge ware 270
tureens 124, 133, 146, 157

U
underglaze blue 105, 106,
    108, 109
upholstery 54–6, 57, 100,
    101, 233
urns 82, 122, 129, 151,
    160, 175, 209, 273

V
valuation 9–10, 21, **30–1**
Vauxhall 148, 149
veneers 36, 40, 41, 43, 45,
    62, 64, 74
Venetian glass 210

vesta cases **206–7**
Victorian style
    furniture 45, 47, 48, 52,
        53, 55, 62, 86, 87
    silver 190
Videau, Aymé 189
Vienna 168, **174–5**
vinaigrettes 202

W
Wade figures **144**
Wadsworth, John 158, 159
waldglas 210
walnut 41, 44, 48, 49,
    221, 222
wardrobes **80–1**
washboards 89
washstands 76
Watcombe Terracotta
    Company 130, 131
Waterman 271
wax dolls 245
Wedgwood 113, 121, 122,
    124, 125, **128–9,** 136,
    140–1, 164
Wemyss ware 123
Whieldon ware 113,
    118–19
White, Edward 223
wicker 98
Windsor chairs 47, 50–1,
    52, 53
wine coolers 83
wire furniture 97
Wood, Ralph 119
wooden toys 250, 251
woodworm 43
Worcester 105, 146 *see also*
    Royal Worcester
Wright, John 114

X
X-frames 45, 58, 59, 66, 93

Y
yew 41, 50, 51
Young, James Radley 137
Yue ware 110

Z
Zeiss cameras 265

AKNOWLEDGMENTS

14 CSK; 15 t CSK, b B; 16 B; 17 B; 18 L; 19 AP; 20 Po; 21 Po; 22 NEC; 23 Po; 24 t Po, bl BY, br Po; 30 B; 31 B; 34 DS; 36 WD; 37 SR; 38 SP; 39 CL; 43 OPG; 44 SL x 4; 45 SL x 3; 46 r WB; 47 tl WB, Hum, bl WB, br LB; 48 l SL, c OPG, r OPG; 49 l & r OPG, c SL; 50 t SL, l & r SSx; 51 SL; 54 PJ; 55 c Ren, b WB; 56 t OPG, b SL; 57 t OPG, bl & br SL; 58 OPG x 3; 59 t SL, cr, cl & b OPG; 60 SL; 61 t OPG, ct WB, cb JGM, b Hum; 62 SL x 2; 63 t & c SL, b Pe; 64 SL x 2; 65 SL x 3; 66 OPG x 2; 67 l OPG, r SL; 68 l & r OPG, c SL; 69 l SL, c & r OPG; 70 OPG x 3; 71 t & b OPG, c SL; 72 t SL, b WB; 73 JGM; 74 SL; 75 t SL, b LB; 76 tl & b SL, tr OPG check; 77 OPG; 78 tr SSx, b SL; 79 tr SSx, c & br OPG; 80 SL x 2; 81 t SSX, c SSX, b OPG; 82 B WB; 83 T Wil, c SL, b Hock; 84 bl RDA, r SL; 85 bl LB, r SL; 86 SL x 2; 87 SL x 2; 88 OPG x 2; 89 OPG x 3; 90 OPG x 3; 91 OPG x 2; 92 tl CL, cl Wak; 93 l SL, c WB, b CL; 94 SSx x 2; 95 t D, c SSx, bl SSx 96 SSx; 97 OPG x 4; 98 OPG x 3; 99 t Lloyd Loom, c OPG; 100 OPG; 101 t OPG, c OPG, b B; 102 B x 2; 103 t B, c B, bl OPG, br OPG; 104 S; 105 l CL, r CL; 107 t CL; 108 t SL, bl SL, br CSK; 109 c SL, br SL; 110 l SPLL, r OPG/CH/P; 111 t & c SL, b SPLL; 112 l CNY, c SL, r CNY; 113 l CL, c CL, r CL; 114 l SL, tr CI, br SL; 115 t & b SL; 116 t & b CI; 117 l P, tr, bc & br CI; 118 CI x 2; 119 t OPG/CH/P, b CI; 120 t OPG/CH/P, bl CI, br CI; 121 CI x 3; 122 t CKS; 123 c OPG; 124 l OPG/CH/P, br P; 125 OPG/CH/P x 3; 126 tl Be, tr & b OPG/CH/P; 127 P x 2; 128 l P, b CI; 129 c OPG/SL, b CI; 130 l P, b OPG/CH/P; 131 l Be, tr & br OPG/CH/P; 132 l CI, tr JJM, b CI; 133 l OPG/CH/P, tc P, br CI; 134 tl OPG/CH/P, tr OPG/CH/P, bl OPG/IB, br OPG/B; 135 GCC x 2; 136 t SL, b Be; 137 P x 3; 138 P x 3; 139 OPG/CH/P x 2; 140 l SL, r OPG/CH/P; 141 tl OPG/CH/P, rc B, r RDP; 142 t & bl CSK, br OPG/CH/P; 143 t & c OPG/CH/P, b Be; 144 P x 3; 145 tr RD, b P; 146 t CL, b SL; 147 CL; 148 CI x 2; 149 tl CI, bl SL, r SPLL; 150 t OPG, c LS, b SNY; 151 l SL, c OPG, r Den; 152 t P, b OPG/CH/P; 153 tl P, bl CI, r OPG/CH/P; 154 l & r OPG/CH/P, c P; 155 l & tr OPG/CH/P, br CI; 156 l OPG/CH/P, r P; 157 l P, t OPG/CH/P; 158 P; 159 t CI, l & r OPG/CH/P; 160 tl P, tr Be, b CI; 161 tl P, bl & r CI; 162 tl & r OPG/CH/P, bl CI; 163 t OPG/CH/P, b CI; 164 l OPG/CH/P, r CI; 165 CI x 3; 166 bl SL; 167 SL; 168 l SL, r CL, bc SL; 169 t SL, cr SZ; 170 cl CL, cr SL, b CL; 171 t SL x 2; 172 CI x 2; 173 t SPLL, bl & br CI; 174 CI x 2; 175 tl SPLL, tr & b CI; 176 CI x 2; 177 CI x 3; 178 l CI, r SPLL; 179 bl & r CI, tl SPLL; 180 CI x 2, 181 tl & r CI, bl SPLL; 182 C; 183 t CI, l SL, r Be; 184 CI x 3; 185 CI x 2 188 tl & bl OPG/AJP/FL, tr & br OPG/AJP/CSK; 189 tl, tr, cl, ct & cb OPG/ AJP/CSK, b P; 190 t & c OPG/AJP/FL, cl P, cr, bc & br OPG/AJP/CSK; 192 tl CNY, c CNY, bc CNY; 193 SL x 2; 194 l CL, r CNY; 195 t SL, cl CNY, cr CNY; 196 c SL, bl CNY, cb SL, rb SK; 197 CNY; 198 ct SL, cl SL, b SL; 199 c SL, cr CNY, bl CNY; 200 l OPG/AJP/CSK, r CI; 201 t OPG/TR/T, c OPG/AJP/CSK, b OPG/AJP/FL; 202 c SK x 3, bc OPG; 203 CNY x 3; 204 r OPG/AJP/CSK, t OPG/AJP/W, b photograph © W; 205 t P, cl & cr OPG/AJP/FL, b OPG/ AJP/CSK; 206 tl, c & br OPG/AJP/CSK; tr & bl CI/CSK; 207 t & b OPG/AJP/CSK, cl & cr CI/CSK; 208 l SB, r CL; 209 tl SL, c SB, b CS; 210 CL; 211 cl CL, cr SL; 212 l CL, r SL; 213 SL x 2; 214 CL; 215 tl H&G, cr SL, b SL; 216 SL x 2, bc CL; 217 SL, b x 3 CNY; 220 l SL, ct SO, cr SL; 221 SO; 222 c AW, cr SL; 223 SL; 224 SL x 3; 225 l CL, r SL, br DR; 227 SNY x 3; 228 CL x 2; 229 l CL, r CL, b SL; 230 SL x 2; 231 c SL, b SNY; 232 t CL, b SL; 233 tl CL, tr PS, b CL; 234 l SL, r CNY, rb CNY; 235 B x 5; 236 l SL, r RC, b CL; 237 CL x 2; 238 tr SL, cl SL, cr CL; 239 l CNY, c CL, r CNY; 240 SL; 241 l SL, r PC, b B; 242 l SL x 2, b PS; 243 c CSK, b SNY; 245 l SL, cl CSK, cr LS, r CKS; 246 SL x 2; 247 c SP; b SL; 248 SP x 3; 249 c SP, b DA; 250 CL; 251 r CL, c CL, b MaB; 252 t SL, c CSK, b SL; 253 r SL, c CNY; 254 CSK; 255 CSK x 3; 256 CSK x 2, b SL; 257 CSK x 3; 258 SL; 259 t CNY, c SL, b WAL; 260 SL x 2; 261 r PS, c CL, b PS; 262 CL x 3; 263 CL x 3; 264 OPG; 265 CSK x 3; 266 CSK x 2; 267 CSK x 4; 268 B x 2; 269 t & c SP, b SNY; 270 l, c & r CSK, bl SL; 271 B; 272 br B, tr CL; 273 cl & cr CSK, b SL; 274 BY

KEY

AJP A. J. Photographics; AP Adrian Stemp Antiques, Brighton; AW Anthony Woodburn, Leigh, Kent; B Bonhams; Be Bearnes, Torquay; BY Bermondsey Market, London; CI Christie's Images; CL Christie's London; CNY Christie's New York; CS Christie's Scotland; CSK Christie's South Kensington; D Drummonds of Bramley, Kent; DA Dottie Ayres; Den Richard Dennis, Ilminster; DR Derek Roberts, Tonbridge, Kent; DS Dennis Severs, Folgate Street, London; FL Fay Lucas Gallery, Kensington Church Street, London; G & C Goss & Crested China Ltd; H & G Hope and Glory, Kensington Church Street, London; Hock William Hockley Antiques, Petworth, West Sussex; Hum Humphrey Antiques, Petworth, West Sussex; IB Ian Booth; JGM John G Morris Ltd, Petworth; JJM J & J May/John May; LB Lesley Bragge Antiques, Petworth, West Sussex; MaB Mint and Boxed, London; MJ Malcolm Jennings; NEC British International Antiques Fair, Birmingham; OPG Octopus Publishing Group Ltd; OPG/CH/P Octopus Publishing Group Ltd/Chris Halton/Phillips; P Phillips; Po Portobello Road; PC Phillips, Cardiff; PJ Patrich Jefferson Antiques, London; PS Phillips, London; RC Royal Copenhagen; RD Royal Doulton; RDA Richard Davidson Antiques, Arundel, West Sussex; RDP Richard Dennis Publications; Ren Rendall Antiques, London; SB Sotheby's, Billingshurst; SL Sotheby's, London; SNY Sotheby's, New York; SO Strike One, Balcombe Street, London; SP Sue Pearson Antiques, Brighton; SPLL Sotheby's Picture Library, London; SR Sotheby's Restoration Department; SSx Sotheby's Sussex; SZ Sotheby's Zurich; T Tagore Ltd, Gray's Antique Market, London; TR Tim Ridley; W Wartski Ltd, London; Wak Michael Wakelin and Helen Linfield, Petworth, West Sussex; WAL Wallis & Wallis, Lewes, Sussex; WB William Bedford plc, London; WD West Dean College, West Sussex; Wil T. G. Wilkinson Antiques, Petworth, West Sussex